DATE DUE

Two hundred years ago, Samuel Johnson observed that a society's level of civilization could be gauged by the manner in which it treated its poor. By that measure, the United States today is steadily losing ground. Whereas the number of officially defined poor dwindled steadily from the enactment of the Great Society programs in the mid-1960s, reaching a low of 24.5 million people in 1978, it has since risen to more than 32 million people. Although the economy continues to generate large numbers of new jobs, the basic unemployment rate continues to rise and current projections show little likelihood of unemployment rates consistently below 10 percent until some time after 1984, if then. In the years to come, the creation of an equitable and workable employment policy will be a major agenda item for politicians and policy makers at the state level, as well as for national leaders.

This volume combines essays by David Gordon on the working poor and by Roger Vaughan on inflation and unemployment in the 1980s; both of these studies were originally published by The Council of State Planning Agencies. Michael Barker's introduction, new to this volume, places the concerns of Gordon's and Vaughan's essays in contemporary context.

Books of related interest

Duke Press Policy Studies

Rebuilding America's Infrastructure
An Agenda for the 1980s
Edited by Michael Barker

Financing State and Local Economic Development
Edited by Michael Barker

State Taxation Policy
Edited by Michael Barker

What Role for Government?
Lessons from Policy Research
Edited by Richard J. Zeckhauser *and* Derek Leebaert

Being Governor
The View from the Office
Edited by Thad Beyle *and* Lynn Muchmore

Duke Press Paperbacks

America in Ruins
The Decaying Infrastructure
Pat Choate *and* Susan Walter

Published in cooperation with
The Council of State Planning Agencies

STATE EMPLOYMENT POLICY IN HARD TIMES

Edited by

Michael Barker

Foreword by

Robert N. Wise

Duke Press Policy Studies

Duke University Press   Durham, N.C.   1983

Printed in the United States of America on acid-free paper

Portions of this volume are reprinted with permission by Duke University Press as facsimiles of the original editions. The views and findings contained in this volume are those of the authors, and do not necessarily represent those of the members or staff of The Council of State Planning Agencies or any of its affiliated organizations.

Library of Congress Cataloging in Publication Data
Main entry under title:

State employment policy in hard times.

(Duke Press policy studies)
"Published in cooperation with the Council of State
Planning Agencies."
Bibliography: p.
Includes index.
1. United States—Full employment policies—Addresses,
essays, lectures. 2. United States—Economic policy—
1981-   —Addresses, essays, lectures. I. Barker,
Michael, 1951- .II. Council of State Planning
Agencies. III. Series.
HC106.8.S72   1983   339.5'0973   83-5674
ISBN 0-8223-0538-0

CONTENTS

115188

TABLES AND FIGURES

Part I. Tables

Part II. Tables

vii

Tables in Appendices

Part II. Figures

FOREWORD

President Reagan's proposal to "return to the states" the responsibility for a wide spectrum of domestic policy matters has drawn a decidedly mixed reaction—not only from Congressional committee barons unwilling to relinquish their patronage powers, but also from activist groups and others who see greater state involvement in domestic policy as tantamount to a retreat from the social contract of the American welfare state and as a positive attack on the poor, on minorities, on the quality of the environment, and on the safety of the workplace. Conservative and New Right activists, by contrast, have tended to view the Reagan "New Federalism" proposal as a happy means of minimizing the public sector's meddling with the American economy and of reducing the governmental role in societal and community life—apparently hoping that many states will "localize" their treatment of this or that national malady in a prescription for benign neglect. Somewhere between these two extremes are the majority of state officials, who are desperately eager to control the allocation of federal program dollars but quite unwilling to assume the political risks associated with raising those dollars through local tax sources.

For all these reasons and more, Reagan's New Federalism, in and of itself, seems unlikely to have many far reaching effects on federal-state relations.

Nevertheless, there are a growing number of people who believe that state and local governments have a larger role to play in our public life, and that this role can only grow through a diminished federal presence in certain domestic affairs. They are people who hold with Justice Brandeis the belief that state governments have always provided the nation with a margin for innovation and experiment in its public life.

The studies that are republished in this volume grew out of the efforts of the Council of State Planning Agencies to explore this "margin for innovation." They were the most tangible product of a four-year economic development project directed by Michael Barker, who was then the Council's Director of Policy Studies. He commissioned the studies and shaped the final reports, of which more than thirty-six were issued over the years 1978–81. At the same time, he assembled a small group of economic policy consultants, including many of the authors whose work Duke University Press is now republishing, to provide detailed assistance to state officials on the implementation of the recommendations contained in the Council's published research. Much of the current interest in small *ix* business development, the investment of public pension funds, the decay of the nation's infrastructure, and national industrial policy grew out of the formal and informal work of this select group.

Robert N. Wise
Executive Director
The Council of State Planning Agencies

INTRODUCTION

Michael Barker

For nearly thirty years following World War II, the United States took its economic growth for granted. Capital accumulation and the expansion of private employment took place at an extraordinary rate, with minimal prodding from the public sector. Our national commitment to economic equality, established with the New Deal, led to the slow but steady alleviation of poverty. The distribution of income and wealth came to be viewed by many as a purely technical matter. All that is now changed. Persistent inflation and a declining rate of economic growth have made the distribution of income a volatile political issue for the first time in modern American history, with many economists and political figures arguing that renewed economic growth is possible only by increasing the inequality of income distribution through a combination of reduced social welfare expenditures and lower effective tax rates for the wealthy.

Two hundred years ago, Samuel Johnson observed that a society's level of civilization could be gauged by the manner in which it treated its poor. By that measure, the United States today is steadily losing ground. Whereas the number of officially defined poor dwindled steadily from the enactment of the Great Society Programs in the mid-1960s, reaching a low of 24.5 million people in 1978, it has since risen to more than 32 million people. More than 10 percent of working age Americans are out of work as of early 1983. Construction industry employment exceeds 20 percent. Unemployment among black youth exceeds 80 percent.

Although the economy continues to generate large numbers of new jobs, the basic rate of unemployment continues to rise, from less than 4 percent in the late 1960s, to just under 5 percent following the 1970–71 recession. The lowest rate of joblessness achieved in the aftermath of the 1974–75 recession was approximately 6 percent. The partial recovery achieved after the 1980–81 recession brought unemployment figures not lower than 7 percent. Current projections show little likelihood of unemployment rates below 10 percent until some time after 1984, if then.

The economic policies of recent national administrations of both political parties have reflected the basic belief that economic efficiency can be achieved only at the expense of economic equity. Thus, a higher rate of taxation on the wealthy is thought to reduce their incentive to save and

I thank Roger Vaughan and Michael Kieschnick for contributions to this introduction.

invest and, thereby, to reduce the size of the economic pie available to the nation as a whole. Conservative politicians have traditionally chosen to side with efficiency, arguing that the benefits of growth will inevitably trickle down to the poor. Liberals, on the other hand, have usually been more willing to accept a lower rate of economic growth as the collectively paid price for greater attention to the income and welfare needs of the poor and lower middle class. Yet in the real world—in the world in which we all live and work, produce and consume, save and invest—the trade-off between equity and efficiency is less clear cut. Indeed, one could argue just as easily that a more rapid rate of economic growth is not merely compatible with a more equitable distribution of income, it is in the long run dependent upon it. The two books in this volume attempt to show why.

The U.S. economy is far from static. It is constantly adapting and adjusting to an endless stream of external shocks: new inventions, changing world trade patterns, the depletion of natural resources, demographic change, shifts in consumer demand, revolution and war. Unless the economy accommodates these shocks through adjustment and adaptation —through changes in the methods of production, the skills of the labor force, the pattern of private investment—the economy not only loses efficiency by falling below its optimum level of output, it also imposes a disproportionate share of the costs of this efficiency loss on those at the lower end of the income scale, thus producing a loss of equity.

Most public economic development policies at the state and national levels have aimed at retarding this process of change, rather than helping the economy to make the necessary adjustments. This would be of little concern if the economy was still evolving at a relatively slow rate. But the past decade has seen it wrenched by the most violent forces at work since the mechanization of agriculture and the collapse of the financial industry in the 1920s and 1930s. A major advance in data processing and telecommunications has begun a rapid reshuffling of the type and location of jobs in both old and new regions of the country. The initial success of the OPEC oil cartel has savagely reversed a long-term decline in world energy prices. A dramatic expansion of international trade has confronted many of the nation's largest industries with the unpleasant prospect of continuing low-cost competition from abroad. And, finally, the baby boom generation has come of age, entering both the workforce and the housing markets with a vengeance, creating an undersupply of entry-level positions in the labor market, and diverting a considerable share of available investment from industry to housing.

Public policy makers might have responded to these challenges by devising policies which facilitated the economy's process of economic adjustment, and which attempted to remove structural barriers that impede the shift of resources among businesses, industries, and regions. They might have sought to compensate those individuals who suffer from the process of economic change without impeding the transition process itself. Instead, both state and national policy makers spent the 1970s consumed by three successive crises: the energy crisis, the urban crisis, and the industrial crisis. And for each crisis, their response was much the same: protect those individuals harmed by economic change regardless of the impact of policy on the ability of the economy to make the basic adjustments that a new reality required.

For example, rather than removing the many barriers to the emergence of conservation and alternative energy technologies—such as the costs of independent research and development, antiquated utility regulations, or access to capital—policy makers devised regulations which held consumer energy prices at an artificially low level, thereby increasing the nation's reliance on imported oil and reducing incentives for greater domestic production. Similarly, policy makers chose not to retool basic education programs to meet the growing demands of the service economy on which most large cities now rely for employment growth, but to provide costly and inefficient subsidies to maintain artificially the viability of a relatively small number of urban manufacturing jobs. And, finally, policy makers chose not to develop programs to stimulate industrial research and development, or to encourage computer literacy, or to retrain workers in obsolete industries for jobs in growing sectors of the economy, but rather to provide massive tax breaks, financial subsidies, and extended unemployment insurance benefits to the automobile and steel industries. In short, each new crisis provided an occasion for public policy makers to attempt to turn back the economic clock. And in each case the result was much the same: public policy failed to protect either employers or employees from the effects of structural economic change.

Public policies will always be ineffective so long as they reflect an understanding of the economy that disregards the process of dynamism and change. The U.S. economy is today undergoing a transition that is as rapid and far reaching as any in its history, the result of technological change and evolving patterns of world trade. This transition will dramatically increase the need for trained and educated people to work in jobs and industries the nature of which can only be guessed at today, moving the nation from an economy based on the processing of materials (mining, construction, manufacturing) to one based much more directly on the manufacture and processing of information. Hence, to an extraordinary degree, the nation's economic success in the years ahead will hinge on its ability to retrain workers as their existing skills become obsolete. At a minimum, this will mean that public employment and training programs can no longer be viewed as social programs with only a marginal impact on the nation's growth and development.

President Reagan is groping toward an employment program. In the halcyon days of 1981, he appeared to believe that unemployment was solely the product of excessive taxation and personal laziness. By the end *xiii* of 1982 he was saying that it was the responsibility of each American business to hire an extra employee. Today, he seems to have realized that there is little or no correlation between the skills of the unemployed and the technology-based jobs listed in the want ads of *The Washington Post*. It is this mismatch between the demand for labor and the skills of our people that he would now have our businesses resolve in a very unbusinesslike burst of corporate altruism. However slowly, however deficiently, employment training is entering the Reagan economic lexicon.

Most job training is done by business. In 1983 alone, American businesses will spend nearly $20 billion readying newly hired workers for the specific demands of the individual workplace, and more than $30 billion retraining their existing workers to meet the new demands imposed by technological change. By and large, business will get its money's worth. After all, who is in a better position to define the skills individual workers need to deliver the goods than the business producing them? But business will not train everyone who needs training to be employable. Nor can business be expected to impart certain kinds of skills. Workers idled by plant closings, employees of small firms, welfare recipients, and those lacking basic educational credentials are simply not eligible for the kinds of training business provides. Business would not train these people even if it was given a special tax inducement (a "human capital tax credit") to do so. Businesses are not high schools, teaching mathematics or basic literacy. They are not outplacement centers. They do not have the capacity or the time to impart basic work habits. These can only be the responsibilities of government. But they are responsibilities which the present system of public employment training simply cannot meet.

As the pace of economic change accelerates, as technological innovation displaces old industries, occupations, and skills, the "velocity of labor" is failing to keep pace. This produces extraordinary human suffering, burgeoning demands for public services of all kinds, and a genuine threat to the continuing viability of thousands of our communities. It sets class against class, region against region, and industry against industry—all competing for limited public resources in what has become not a zero, but a negative sum game. So long as we carry such a burden, we will never be able to make the social or economic adjustments necessary to compete in the world economy. Our economy will place increasing demands on the basic skills of its workers—on their ability to read, to write, to reason clearly and independently. And it will demand new skills—not only of new workers, but of existing workers as well. We too often forget that fully 75 percent of the American workforce in the year 2000 is already adult, and already in the labor market. It is not our children who will rescue us from the demands of the new technologies, who will make us a people able to compete with the Japanese. It is we ourselves who will do this.

Those able to afford a proper education and the periodic adjustment of their technical skills will find innumerable rewards in this period of economic transition. Their incomes will rise. Their working conditions will improve. Their leisure time will expand. But those who are unable to make these investments—for lack of family wealth, or personal savings, or current income—face a very different future. Already there is a widening gulf within the labor market between the educated and uneducated, between what labor market economists call, with dry finality, the "primary labor market" and the "secondary labor market." Since 1965 the share of national income earned by the poorest 40 percent of our population has plunged from 12 percent to 9 percent. By creating economic opportunities only for those people able to finance investments in their own human capital, the changing composition of our economy threatens to depress this share still further. Quite apart from denying industry the quantities of skilled labor it will need, this growing inequality of income— and therefore of economic opportunity—will seriously jeopardize our ability to sustain economic growth and social progress.

Further tinkering with the existing bureaucratic structure will solve nothing. As this is written, in early 1983, it is less than a year since Congress enacted, in the face of White House indifference, the Job Training Partnership Act as a replacement for the late and unlamented Comprehensive Employment and Training Act. CETA had become synonymous in the public mind with governmental "waste, fraud, and abuse." Few people were equipped with useful skills; a massive, self-perpetuating bureaucracy was created; and industry—the ostensible beneficiary of the program—shunned its graduates. The new job training act was meant to be a response to these problems. Unfortunately, it is turning out to be little more than a new rhetorical wrapping around the same old program.

As with CETA, JTPA subsidizes training institutions, not individuals in need of training. Funds still flow through familiar channels to politically tenacious but professionally ineffective training institutions. Hapless participants still have little or no choice in where they are trained, in what skills they are trained in, in what companies or industries they are trained for.

As with CETA, JTPA is still subject to the vagaries of the annual budget process. Under CETA, it was never clear from year to year how much money would be provided, nor what it would be provided for. Would it be a public sector jobs program subsidizing the paychecks of local government employees? Would it be an income maintenance program providing stipends to a constantly changing clientele? Would it be a retraining program for displaced workers in older industries? Or a job placement service? Or a remedial education program? One never knew from one year to the next. Transitory fashions in public policy, rather than economic need, set annual priorities.

As with the CETA, JTPA still neglects most of the workforce that needs government assistance in securing appropriate skills. More than 20 *xv* million Americans will experience unemployment at some time during 1983. Forty million Americans will remain mired in dead-end jobs paying poverty-level wages, with few if any opportunities to improve their lot. One in five members of the workforce will remain functionally illiterate and totally unequipped to learn the skills they need to compete in an economy experiencing ever more rapid technological change. But JTPA, at best, will train 300,000. It is yet another federal program that is wholly incommensurate with the problem.

The "new alchemists" who would solve all our economic problems with a spirited burst of high technology also ignore reality. The number of manufacturing jobs in shining new high tech firms will be sufficient to employ only a fraction of the workers laid off in our industrial heartland. While these firms offer glittering prizes to scientists and entrepreneurs, half the jobs they provide are ill-paying and often hazardous. Most will soon move abroad as production techniques become standardized and international competition intensifies.

The challenge of technology is not building the hardware but adapting and using it in millions of enterprises across the nation. Unless employees are capable of using the new equipment which high technologies produce, jobs will remain unfilled, incomes will continue to fall, and the much vaunted high technology industry will wither for lack of developing markets for its products. The missing element in our national economic policy is clearly a program that will allow these changes to proceed equitably and efficiently.

What is needed is a means to allow every American, regardless of income, to make the basic investments in knowledge and education that will allow him to compete fairly for the rewards of economic growth and to contribute to our economic and social life to the fullest of his capacities. While policy makers should shrink from advocating the resurrection of federal agencies now resting comfortably—and safely—in their graves, it may now be the time to create a G.I. Bill for the American Worker. Its namesake, the least bureaucratic and most successful of all our efforts to publicly support education and training, allowed millions of Americans to finance the educations—or to acquire the technical skills—they needed to reenter the civilian labor force after a period of military service. Nothing less should be offered the unwilling conscripts in Reagan's War on Inflation or, for that matter, to anyone drafted into service in the international trade wars or domestic battles of today.

All Americans should be able to borrow sufficient funds to pay for any form of education or skill training available through accredited academic or vocational training institutions. Repayment of this debt could be calculated as a percent of gross income earned after the completion of training. By tying repayment to gross income, individuals whose wealth or current or potential income exceeds a moderate level would have a powerful incentive to use their own resources rather than those of the G.I. Bill. The repayment rate could also be periodically readjusted to assure the continuing solvency of the system. The availability of these loans to individuals would eventually replace the present inefficient and manifestly ineffective patchwork of federal and state support for postsecondary employment training, including the Job Training Partnership Act, Vocational Education, the Work Incentive Program (WIN), and Trade Adjustment Assistance. The resulting savings would allow a significant reduction in current payroll taxes. Educational training institutions, denied the annual tithing of state and federal subsidies, would be forced to compete for students and trainees by offering innovative and competitively priced curricula, and by establishing track records for job placement. The expensive and cumbersome administrative apparatus that now absorbs so large a proportion of our employment training resources could be pared dramatically.

This G.I. Bill would not, of course, be a panacea. But the successful adjustment of our economy requires both private and public investments of an unprecedented scope, and there is no better way to begin than by giving the American worker the opportunity to invest in his own economic potential.

In the labor market, as in the capital market, the process of economic adjustment is continual: resources must move among occupations, industries, and geographic areas. When adjustments go unmade, the swift and sure result is rising unemployment, a shortage of appropriately trained workers in growing industries, and a major fiscal strain in older states and cities. Particularly during periods of rapid economic change, the market does an extremely poor job of allocating resources. Economists refer to these shortcomings in the allocation of resources as instances of market failure.

As with other basic resources, labor is allocated among competing employers through markets. The purpose of these markets is to send signals to market participants to indicate when and where they need to alter their behavior. Thus, an employer who is unable to fill available job slots may be receiving a signal to increase wage offerings. Similarly, a job seeker who fails to find employment of a certain type is receiving a signal to alter his expectations or to look elsewhere. When markets work well, the proper signals are generated and the economy responds rapidly to change. But markets do not always work well. Indeed, the traditional justification for public intervention in the economy has usually been couched in terms of market failure. Examples of the types of structural barriers producing market failure include:

■ *Imperfect information*, e.g., an unemployed worker may not know where there are available job openings.

■ *Transactions costs*, e.g., the cost of relocating to a growing labor market may be prohibitively high for an unemployed or economically disadvantaged worker.

■ *Nonconstant returns to scale*, e.g., an economic activity—such as a   *xvii* nationwide job information system—may be performed most efficiently over a wide geographic area, yet there may be no private company able to capture all the benefits of such an extensive system.

■ *Externalities*, where an activity that generates benefits not directly accruing to those paying for the activity will not be undertaken at an optimal level, e.g., a firm will be unwilling to pay the costs of non-job-specific training for an employee out of fear that the employee will leave the company at the completion of training.

■ *Second best*, where an imperfection in one market produces imperfections in related markets, e.g., the denial of capital access to higher risk businesses will produce a rise in the rate of unemployment in higher risk neighborhoods.

■ *Public intervention*, where governmental activities—such as taxation or regulation—distort the operation of markets.

Although this classification is quite adequate for many purposes, several relevant barriers remain unspecified. One reason for this is the static character of the market failure concept. In a dynamic market economy, there will be a tendency for market imperfections to diminish over time, since entrepreneurs can profit by providing a good or service that fills the gap. But this assumes that an adequate supply of entrepreneurs exists to develop these new products, and that adequate incentives exist to induce these entrepreneurs to bridge market gaps. This assumption is not always met. The second shortcoming of the market failure analysis lies in its implicit suggestion that the best way to foster development is to remove all existing impediments to the normal functioning of a market economy. This not only assumes that all development resources are bought, sold, and produced in private markets, but that these markets are self-organizing and self-perfectable. Rather than reflect further on this quaint, eighteenth-century world view, let us turn to several additional barriers to the efficient creation and use of labor resources.

Lack of information. Inadequate or inaccurate information is a chronic labor market problem, as shown by the many efforts to create job information banks and both public and private job placement services. Labor markets include both the skills market, which operates between workers and employers, and the training market, which operates between workers and those institutions that provide the training. The former market works reasonably well; the latter does not. (For example, an individual employee will seldom know what kind of training will put him in the best competitive position; yet the process of increasing the supply of certain skills can take several years.)

Transactions costs. Advertising, screening, and job-specific training are extremely expensive activities. Transactions costs can be especially high when an employer hires an economically disadvantaged worker. (For one reason, the employer has little or no employment history on which to *xviii* base his hiring decision, and no ready network for gathering it.) This leads employers to hoard labor during recessions and to hire only those who can be screened through the recommendations of current employees and other employers. The combination of imperfect information and transactions costs reduces the ability of the labor market to adjust to structural economic change and produces a tendency to exclude the disadvantaged from job contention.

Legal constraints. Regulations governing the minimum wage, occupational health and safety, and affirmative action requirements may discourage some employers from hiring the unskilled. It may also encourage the substitution of capital for labor in order to reduce costs and the possibility of legal action. On the other hand, the regulatory structure can inadequately define an employer's responsibility. The longer a firm can expect to retain an employee, or the higher the costs of termination, the more likely it is that the firm will provide additional training and come to view the development of the firm's labor force as an integral and important part of doing business. This means that a greater portion of the costs of economic adjustment can be internalized within the business sector.

Taxes. There are many aspects of the tax structure that impede labor market adjustment. Human capital, unlike physical capital, cannot be depreciated, although a computer programmer's skills may become obsolete almost as rapidly as the machine that he operates. Education or training costs that are not related to a worker's current job are not tax deductible. The persistent failure to relate unemployment insurance premiums actuarially to the use of benefits penalizes low turnover firms while subsidizing those with a high rate of employee turnover. Thus, volatile companies tend to adjust labor forces rather than inventories. In addition, the fact that unemployment insurance premiums and Social Security payments are not based on a worker's full salary raises the costs of low-wage relative to high-wage workers.

Uncertainty. Uncertainty is the greatest single impediment to any form of investment, and a major aim of employment and training policy should be to reduce it. From the standpoint of policy, however, it is vital to understand that security is not the opposite of uncertainty. An economic development strategy should not be designed to secure people and firms in their current positions but to enable workers and investors to form rational expectations about the future. Risk is an unavoidable aspect of economic growth and development—indeed, of any evolutionary process. Fluctuating public policies do not necessarily increase or reduce risks, but they do increase uncertainty. And uncertainty deters evolution. Anyone betting on a single throw of the dice faces a certain one in six chance of winning. Uncertainty enters into the equation only if it is possible that the dice are loaded. Although the climate for investment often varies, and the course of future innovation is difficult to predict, the most significant source of uncertainty in the development process is the future course of public economic policy. Will the money supply be expanded? Will new tax credits be available in the future? Will regulations be changed? These and similar considerations discourage rational long-term economic decision making. Why should a dynamic new firm strive to overcome a major competitor if the loser may get federal assistance and the winner be subject to antitrust prosecution? Why should a firm develop a new product if its product liability, or the regulatory environment in which it operates, can suddenly be changed? Why invest in a long-term project if future taxes are uncertain and short-term projects offer immediate tax relief? The greater the degree of certainty in the overall economic environment, the more individual decision makers will be able to assess accurately the risks associated with individual decisions. Better risk assessment leads directly to more efficient decision making. Unfortunately, the erratic nature of public policy often contributes to uncertainty rather than ameliorating it. Workers may, for example, be discouraged from seeking alternative employment or acquiring new skills if they believe that a public bail-out of their firm or industry is forthcoming.

Constraints on mobility. The structure of the transfer payment system has also created barriers to the effective redeployment of labor. Unemployment insurance and trade adjustment assistance benefits have surely prolonged the duration of unemployment for many; individuals are less inclined to seek alternative employment opportunities. Welfare payments, to take another example, are not geographically transferable. In addition, laid-off workers may have large investments in their houses, as well as in their accumulated skills; both forms of investment are largely illiquid. Relocation allowances, reverse annuity mortgages, and other similar programs require far more extensive scrutiny than they have received in the past.

> When orthodoxy fails, the political effects are destabilizing. Washington was weary and frustrated by the erratic policymaking epitomized most dramatically by Jimmy Carter's last year in office when he seemed to change direction every other month (and managed to combine both a recession and double digit inflation). Carter's Council of Economic Advisers, dominated by middle-of-the-road Keynesians, had been wrong every quarter for four years in its prognosis and predictions. If the old expertise was wrong, then perhaps it was time for new experts.
>
> —William Greider, *The Education of David Stockman and Other Americans*, 1982.

Before turning to a discussion of the two texts contained in this volume, some mention must be made of the many changes that have occurred in both state and federal policy since the texts were first published in early 1980. No other area of domestic policy has been singled out for such xx radical reform as the employment and training system. President Reagan and his advisers have argued that a growing economy will obviate the need for expansive employment training programs. Although economically disadvantaged workers suffer disproportionately from high unemployment, low wages, and the absence of negotiable job skills, the administration has argued that here, as elsewhere, government programs have wrought more harm than good, and that what good has been accomplished has come at an unacceptably high cost. Unfortunately for those whose poverty and unemployment has been the motivation for the programs now being gutted, there is little evidence to justify the belief that structural unemployment problems can be reduced by an exclusive reliance on the trickle-down economics advocated by the Reagan administration. It is true, of course, that a "rising economic tide" will usually extend the benefits of new growth, however irregularly, throughout the population; doubters need only recall that the total proportion of households with incomes below the official poverty line declined from almost 22 percent in 1963 to less than 14 percent in 1975—a period in which real per capita earnings grew by more than 30 percent. Some of this change is, of course, attributable to the growth of public transfer payment programs —the War on Poverty—but most of it came from the real per capita income gains of low income workers.

Employers today, however, are usually willing to hire disadvantaged workers only when they are unable to hire more traditional workers. Labor markets must be relatively tight, with unemployment rates far below the double digit rates now prevailing in many parts of the U.S. Yet public policy makers now tolerate these rates, perhaps even favor them, in the belief that lower rates—anything below, say, 7 percent—would restimulate the inflationary spiral. Because inflation is feared more than unemployment by both business leaders and politicians, it is unlikely that labor markets will be allowed to grow tight enough to provide jobs for structurally unemployed workers. Thus, while an increase in aggregate prosperity might do much for the economy as a whole, it seems improbable in the extreme to do much for the disadvantaged worker. Complementary policies, which recognize that investments in people are as instrumental to economic growth and development as investment in buildings and equipment, are badly needed.

The Working Poor: Towards a State Agenda

David M. Gordon's "The Working Poor" provides a highly original analysis of the evolving structure of the U.S. labor market and the changing characteristics of the nation's poverty population. Gordon argues that an increasing share of the country's poor is composed of active workers unable to obtain adequate employment because of changes in the way employment itself is structured in our economy. Put somewhat differently, an increasing pro- *xxi* portion of the nation's "poverty problem" is really an employment problem which arises less from the characteristics of workers themselves than from the way employers define the character of work through the increasingly complex job structures they employ.

Gordon defines adequate employment—a "good job"—in the following way. First, it should provide a regular wage at a level which permits the support of a normal household at or above the lower than moderate standard defined by the Bureau of Labor Statistics. Approximately one-third of U.S. workers are currently without jobs paying even this very moderate wage. Second, it should provide full-time, year-round employment to those who wish it. Currently, one-sixth of U.S. workers are without such employment—some 5 million people; an additional 10 million people are believed to be holding on to part-time low-wage employment in the belief that a search for something better would be unrewarding. Third, a good job should provide decent working conditions and not expose the worker needlessly to occupational diseases and injury. And fourth, a good job should allow individual workers a measure of influence over the pace and composition of work, freedom from employer negligence or mistreatment, and protection from arbitrary dismissal and supervisory abuse.

Applying this view of the labor market to the economy at large, Gordon concludes that the overwhelming majority of "good jobs" are contained in primary industries, that is, in industries where large firms and large unions predominate. Yet these same industries appear to limit the number of good jobs they offer. Gordon offers three reasons. First, it is often more economical to extend the working hours of existing employees than to add new workers. Second, large firms actually prefer to offer poor jobs where they can, that is, jobs which are low paying, impart few skills, and afford little prospect of stability. Generally, the occupants of these jobs tend to be women, Southern rural workers, foreign workers, and illegal aliens—all groups which face various barriers to their ability to transform their work environment through employee organizations. And, third, large firms have a natural interest in limiting the extent of their susceptibility to worker influence, causing them to adopt a growing number of job automation techniques, and to proliferate job titles in order to break down the potential for common sympathies among worker groups.

Small firms present a somewhat different problem. The highly competitive environments in which small firms operate make it difficult for them to finance the types of improvements in job structures or the work environment which would permit higher wages, better working conditions, and adequate job security. Gordon provides the first analysis of job quality which incorporates David Birch's research concerning the prodigious job creation power of small and young firms. Using Birch's data, Gordon concludes that the very same small firms that contribute most to employment growth are unlikely to offer stable employment opportunities over time. This is an important finding for development policy makers, particularly those who believe, as the proponents of enterprise zone legislation do, that a simple increase in the rate of new business formation will magically resolve the problems besetting urban economies, providing jobs to the needy, income to the industrious, revenue to the faithful. Gordon also shows that large firms have been relocating their investments with increasing rapidity from areas where worker organizations are powerful, such as the Northeastern and Midwestern states, to areas where workers are unable to organize effectively, including Mexico, portions of the southern U.S., and Puerto Rico.

The result, in many parts of the country, has been the creation of an economy without a middle. Blue collar jobs in areas with traditions of successful labor organizing have steadily dwindled, leading to chronically high unemployment and lower real wages for working people. To compensate, a growing number of families must now send additional wage earners—wives, teenagers, retired adults living with other family members—out into the workforce, increasing competition for already scarce jobs, and driving real wages down still further.

As an antidote to growing underemployment and joblessness, Gordon proposes a community-based approach to economic development—one which would promote the growth of private not-for-profit organizations to furnish needed goods and services, and provide the type of jobs that profit-oriented businesses seem unable to create. Traditional development initiatives, such as tax incentives, interest subsidies, financial assistance, wage subsidies, procurement concessions, and other, familiar devices, would be redirected to the growing not-for-profit sector of the economy, improving these firms' access to raw materials, adequately trained workers, appropriate technology, and sufficient capital, and allowing policy makers to surmount the trade-off which appears to exist between the number and quality of jobs created by the private economy.

The contemporary importance of Gordon's analysis cannot be overstated. In the three years since the studies in this volume were first published, and perhaps in some measure because of them, small business has come to be seen by many as something of an economic panacea, a key to America's reindustrialization, a vital link in the nation's competitive struggle with its Western trading partners. Conservative politicians extol the virtues of the risk-taking entrepreneur: his capacity to turn new ideas into new products and services, his creation of new wealth, and, not least, his traditional aversion to governmental intervention in the economy. Liberal and progressive politicians, on the other hand, tend to view the small businessman as a bulwark against the unbridled power of large financial and industrial conglomerates, and as a crushing counterpoint to those who argue that the natural evolution of a healthy economic system inevitably requires the consolidation of economic activity and industrial organization into large, nearly sovereign, transnational cor- ***xxiii*** porations. Some portion of this interest in small business is no doubt attributable to the sorry performance of the largest U.S. corporations over the past decade. During that period, the net employment of the Fortune 1000 has grown hardly at all (indeed, in 1982, the aggregate U.S. employment of the Fortune 500 actually declined by 8 percent); by contrast, small, young, and independent firms have proved to be prodigious generators of new jobs, creating nearly half of all new employment over the period. While large firms increasingly demand and receive ever greater tax cuts—ostensibly to aid in capital formation and the renewal of the nation's industrial stock—they use their added profit levels only to accumulate cash hoards, to fund economically unproductive mergers, and to shift a growing share of their production facilities from U.S. locations to overseas tax havens. At the same time, they seize every opportunity to replace labor with capital, men with machines. Now, not content with their considerable gains, an increasing number of large corporations are beginning to support various forms of protectionist legislation designed to insulate them from the effects of foreign competition. Much of the luster attached to small business thus derives less from the character of small business per se, than from a growing reaction to the performance, both political and economic, of larger businesses.

Inflation and Unemployment: Surviving the 1980s

Roger Vaughan's "Inflation and Unemployment" addresses, from the perspective of early 1980, the persistent failure of the federal government to control inflation, and examines the effectiveness of countercyclical public works as a job creation device. Each aspect of the book deserves a separate word of introduction.

Vaughan offers two explanations for the failure of federal policy makers to reduce inflation: first, the assumption that there exists an explicit trade-off between price stability and the rate of unemployment; and, second, the belief that interest rates are a more proper and effective target for monetary policy than the money supply itself.

At the time of its original publication, Vaughan's interpretation of inflation was much more controversial than it may now appear. In Jimmy Carter's Washington, a monetarist interpretation of inflation was viewed by many to entail the implicit embrace of a wide range of other, unrelated social policies, a calculated disregard for the impact of inflation on the poor, a reactionary program at best. It was then fashionable to talk of structural deficiencies in the markets for the necessities: food, housing, energy, and health care. Elaborate policies were proposed to restructure those markets, greatly enlarging the role of government in allocating scarce resources, and, correspondingly, reducing the role of the private businesses. Little came of these proposals, in part because their proponents proved more adept at public relations than economic analysis, and in part because the Carter administration could never make up its mind as to the kind of economic policies it wanted to pursue. In time, of course, it came to be seen as slightly ridiculous to assume that anyone offering a monetarist interpretation of inflation was also a supporter of the economic policies of the Pinochet regime in Chile. But this insight came slowly, and was no doubt further slowed by the almost complete lack of interest and expertise in macroeconomic policy among the progressive economists and liberal lobbying organizations that then held sway in Washington.

This history is important because it goes some distance towards explaining the almost sullen reception that Vaughan's book received among the policy makers of the Carter administration. Because many readers tended to focus only on what Vaughan had to say about inflation, his message regarding the effectiveness of countercyclical public works as a job creation device was ignored by many who would have profited from the analysis. This reaction is still important today, as many members of the Congress and the popular press continue to push for the enactment of yet another version of countercyclical public works to reduce the current rate of unemployment.

Since the publication of Vaughan's study, the debate over the proper conduct of Federal Reserve policy has grown extraordinarily fierce. Both liberal and conservative political figures now find fault with one or more aspects of Fed behavior, leading many to call for greater White House and/or Congressional control over Fed activities.

To put Vaughan's discussion in context, it may be helpful to summarize the background of this debate. Prior to Keynes, all macroeconomic policy was known as the theory of money; the economy was thought to be self-regulating, and monetary policy was believed to affect nothing but the level of prices; public expenditure programs played no deliberate role in regulating overall economic performance and growth. Despite the popular perception of Keynes as the father of discretionary fiscal policy and deficit financing, it must also be remembered that he was the foremost monetary economist of his day, contributing to economic policy the notion that monetary policy could exert a positive impact on the economy quite apart from its influence on the price level. The debate among Keynesians in the United States—an extremely diverse group which includes virtually all mainstream economists—has been of an empirical, rather than a theoretical, nature. In particular, it has focused on an effort to define the precise relationship between interest rates, the money supply, and the real economy. During the 1960s, when fiscally oriented Keynesians ruled macroeconomic policy, the Federal Reserve Board was generally concerned to maintain stable interest rates, and so long as inflation continued at a relatively low level, it was quite successful. During the Nixon years, however, the Fed attempted to control both interest rates and the money supply, and it failed miserably on both fronts. Currently, the Fed is attempting to control the money supply through regulation of the reserves in the U.S. banking system. While this has done much to reduce the rate of inflation, it has also produced (1) the most wildly fluctuating interest rates in the nation's history, and (2) enormous instability in the money supply. This, in turn, has devastated the bond market, which depends on relatively stable interest rates.

The second half of Vaughan's study examines the effectiveness of countercyclical public works as a means of providing employment and building needed public facilities. Vaughan first examines the history of federal activity, and concludes that none of the several countercyclical programs initiated in the postwar period has speeded economic recovery, created substantial numbers of jobs for the unemployed, or failed to inflate construction costs. He then turns to a discussion of what state governments can do on their own to ameliorate the effects of recession.

In today's economy, the impulse of Congressmen to turn to talk of public works, particularly during election years, is understandable: millions of Americans are out of work; the nation's public infrastructure— the roads, bridges, sewer and water systems, highways, ports, and water-ways on which commerce depends—is in serious disrepair. By using federal funds to put the jobless to work repairing these facilities, two separate problems could be addressed through a single program.

Unfortunately for the growing number of individuals in both political parties who believe that every national problem lends itself to some simple solution, the reality suggests a very different picture. The rehabilitation of an aging bridge, to take an obvious example, cannot be accomplished by distributing overalls and paint buckets to those in line for unemployment benefits. To understand why, it is helpful to examine the experience of the Local Public Works program (LPW), passed into law in August 1976 over President Ford's veto. LPW provided $6 billion to state and local governments to pay for the construction of needed public facilities. At that time, the economy was already one full year into a healthy recovery. The immediate effect of LPW was a sudden, dramatic slump in state/local spending for public works, for the moment it appeared that LPW would pass, state and local officials chose to defer the vast majority of their scheduled projects in the hope that Washington, rather than local taxpayers, would pick up the costs of construction. Funds were allocated among jurisdictions according to a formula which attempted to take into account such factors as the local unemployment rate, population loss, and other measures of economic and fiscal distress. Each area, however, was expected to get something. Because projects had to be started quickly, the tendency for federal dollars to simply displace state and local spending on already scheduled projects was made more pronounced. In addition, a large number of projects of questionable merit or need were funded: tennis courts and golf courses are obvious examples. Those projects which were truly meritorious were virtually all projects that state and local governments had previously planned, and would have been built anyway, albeit at their own expense. By the time that state and local officials had completed the elaborate application procedures associated with the disbursement of federal funds, the 1974 recession was long passed. In many areas, it was difficult to find idle construction firms able to bid on LPW contracts. Local supply shortages also delayed progress in many communities, as did lawsuits disputing the allocation procedures used to distribute funds among areas. By the end of 1979—four years after the beginning of economic recovery—millions of dollars remained unspent.

What few jobs were created by the LPW program did little to help the unemployed. Few advocates of countercyclical public works appear to understand that construction jobs are typically of extremely short duration, as various crafts are phased in and out of use in accordance with an extremely tight construction schedule. Most LPW jobs lasted less than one month, scarcely time for LPW workers to acquire hope and sustenance, let along negotiable job skills. More importantly, few of those rendered jobless by the 1974 recession were even eligible to apply for LPW employment: carpentry, the operation of heavy equipment, plumbing and electrical work are not the kind of skills facilely acquired in the course of a brief site orientation. Attempts to provide meaningful training became entangled in interdepartmental red tape: by the time regulations were issued for training programs, most LPW projects were completed.

The Local Public Works program did not fail because of bureaucratic mismanagement or careless bill drafting. It failed because the concept of countercyclical public works is irremediably flawed. The federal government cannot hire people quickly. Grants to state and local governments usually replace local with federal dollars. And the construction sector is no place to create jobs for the unemployed. While it is possible to recreate the Works Progress Administration of the Roosevelt administration and to fund projects that would employ labor intensive construction techniques, such an effort would be sure to provide graduates with work skills that are virtually useless in today's economy. Those who grow misty-eyed at the memory of the WPA, and indignant at the neglect of such an obvious solution as the use of unemployed workers as ditch diggers on needed public projects, should be introduced to the backhoe, which has rendered ditch diggers as obsolete as blacksmiths and lamplighters. While we surely need to increase public spending on public works, doing it effectively requires the commitment of tax resources over the long term, not the quick fix of a one-shot federal program. And while we do need to provide the unemployed with a productive alternative to standing in line for unemployment benefits, it would be far more sensible to provide them with funds that would enable them to acquire useful education and training—in effect, the sort of G.I. Bill discussed earlier in this intro- *xxvii* duction—than to create highly specialized and largely obsolete jobs in the construction industry. When the economy ultimately recovers, industry would find its labor force better equipped to meet the skill demands of the coming decades, and workers themselves would find it easier to move from declining to growing industries.

Vaughan then turns to a discussion of alternatives to federal counter-cyclical spending, proposing the creation of a network of state-level economic stabilization funds. Each fund would be used to finance three types of projects: public works, public employment and training, and intrastate fiscal assistance. Each program would function automatically, subject to legislative review, with funds released when local economic indicators passed some predetermined threshold. Because each program would address a discrete countercyclical objective, each would employ a different economic indicator. Individual funds would be capitalized through an unspecified mixture of state, local, and federal contributions.

Stabilization funds would offer state governments several advantages. First, they would require little or no increase in state or local spending. Instead, spending would simply be retimed and redistributed over the course of the business cycle. Public works expenditures would be concentrated in times of slack demand for construction activity. The high level of transfer payment expenditures that a recessionary period requires would be paid for, in effect, during boom years, when the fund was accruing, rather than disbursing, funds. State expenditures would reflect average revenues over the course of the business cycle rather than the current system of year-to-year financing. Second, a stabilization fund would help to maintain the integrity of appropriations during recessions. All too often, in both Washington and state capitals alike, recessions produce revenue shortfalls which require the curtailment of programs for which the legislature has already appropriated funds. Stabilization funds would eliminate the need for such draconian procedures. Third, stabilization funds would reduce the ever-present temptation to expand programs during high revenue years beyond the level that can be sustained over the course of the business cycle. Surging revenues during periods of rapid economic growth, when demands for social services are at a relatively low level, often encourge the expansion of existing programs beyond what can be sustained under tighter fiscal restraints. State surpluses, on the other hand, frequently lead to pressures to reduce taxes for political gain. A stabilization fund would eliminate the appearance of false surpluses, and avoid stresses our political system has proved particularly unable to contain. And, fourth, a stabilization fund would encourage a more rational approach to state-level budgeting. By blunting the fiscal impact of recessions and retiming capital expenditures, overall public spending might actually be reduced.

Vaughan's proposal is unusually detailed, and requires little comment. *xxviii* The only state which currently operates a stabilization fund is Michigan, which created the fund at the instigation of the state's business community in the aftermath of the 1974 recession. Contributions and withdrawals are triggered by changes in the state's rate of personal income growth. Between the commencement of operations in September 1977 and the end of 1979, when Michigan's economy slumped into a deep recession from which it is yet to emerge, the fund accumulated about $275 million. That money was subsequently used to partially offset a massive budget deficit, and to forestall service reductions in a variety of areas. Had additional money been available in the fund, the state would have undertaken public works projects as well.

Since the first publication of Vaughan's study, the question of potential federal assistance to states in capitalizing such funds has been drowned in a sea of red ink. The federal grant-in-aid system, on which virtually all states rely for funding for innovative economic development programs, has been decimated through recent budget actions, many of which were supported by the states themselves. As suggested earlier, the recent proposal to revive a federal role in countercyclical construction is less a serious policy proposal than a political gambit made by one party against the other. The only basis for hope for progress on Vaughan's proposal lies in the possibility that the growing concern over the state of the nation's public facilities, the subject of another volume in this series, will lead policy makers to consider an alternative to the pork barrel spending practices which now dominate national policy.

Part I

THE WORKING POOR
TOWARDS A STATE AGENDA

David M. Gordon

INTRODUCTION

"We have to tell a state considering additional restrictions on business: 'The next plant doesn't go up here if that bill passes.'"

—a corporate executive at a recent management conference (quoted in Silk and Vogel, 1976: 66).

State governments are currently facing a wide variety of serious employment problems. Wages are low and many state residents are unable to make ends meet. At least in some regions, jobs are scarce and unemployment rates are high. Occupational health-and-safety problems are attracting increasing attention and, in many respects, getting worse. And management/labor relations have been seriously strained in many areas over union prerogatives and right-to-work initiatives.

These problems are confronting State governments with particular urgency, in part, because other levels of government within the federal system will not or cannot place priority on employment problems. At the federal level, both the recent Republican administration and the current Democratic administration have explicitly sacrificed employment programs for the sake of anti-inflationary policies. At the local level, the fragmentation of metropolitan governments has meant that city administrations cannot easily mobilize either the revenues or the political leverage to confront employment problems in their areas. State governments are left with a critical public responsibility for employment problems and their potential moderation.*

Many State governments have adopted a common approach to this responsibility, often identified as an "economic development strategy." The approach begins with essential reliance on private business for solutions to current employment problems, hoping to support business efforts through some combination of public programs—such as tax relief, development subsidies, and supportive training programs. There is every indication that this approach is spreading, that it represents much more than a temporary reflex reaction to the first signs of the "tax revolt" and "Proposition 13 fever." According to

---

*Throughout this essay I have adopted the convention of capitalizing the word "State" in order to clarify my continuing reference to the problems and policies of State governmental units within the federal system.

a comprehensive 50 state survey by the *New York Times* in the summer of 1979, "farmers, manufacturers and other business interests around the country have been granted state tax relief on a scale unknown in recent years . . . " (Herbers, 1979). This relief has not been an inadvertent by-product of the citizens' revolt against taxes, the *Times* survey concludes:

> The relief extended to business interests stemmed in part from the emphasis that is being placed on private economic development, both by government officials and other leaders throughout the country . . . [In addition to middle class taxpayers] the state actions were . . . intended to benefit . . . commercial interests that have long maintained powerful lobbies in state capitals and have capitalized on middle class protest.

Many State government officials justify this approach to economic development on either or both of two grounds—(1) that tax relief and business subsidies will actually help generate jobs and reduce employment problems; and (2) that there are no other alternatives to public support for private business in the employment area.

This essay disputes that policy orientation. It argues that State government relief and subsidies for private business will not reduce and may even intensify many State employment problems. It also argues that other approaches, centered around public support for and management of non-profit, locally controlled community economic development programs, are possible and hold much greater promise for moderation and eventual solution of current employment problems. It argues, in short, that a careful analysis of State employment problems suggests the need for a dramatic re-orientation of State government policies toward economic development.

This argument is developed in four steps:

■ Chapter 1 reviews the character and magnitude of employment problems in the United States. Its major conclusion is that recent public discussion has largely misperceived the nature of those problems. The economy does not simply need *more* jobs, no matter what working and living conditions they provide. *The economy needs more "good jobs,"** and that requirement should frame discussions of State employment policies.

---

*Throughout this essay I continually refer to "good jobs" with quotation marks in order to indicate that the phrase requires definition and that the notion of "good jobs" is not a concept about which there is common agreement. Chapter 1 provides a provisional definition of "good jobs" and Chapter 2 a more rigorous one.

■ Chapter 2 reviews explanations of current employment problems, focusing particularly on why the economy does not generate enough "good jobs." The discussion compares two quite different answers to that question: (a) the mainstream economic analysis which has shaped and helps justify the current strategy of tax-and-subsidy support for private business; and (b) an alternative structural analysis which, in my view, both provides a better explanation of the sources of current problems and helps reveal the reasons for the inadequacy of more traditional analysis.

■ Chapter 3 discusses the implications of that analysis for policy approaches to current employment problems, focusing on how State governments could, in general, help generate more "good jobs" in the economy. The chapter argues that the distinction between the mainstream and alternative analyses discussed in Chapter 2 translates into a distinction between what can be called "traditional" and "community" approaches to the solution of current employment problems. The "traditional" approach builds upon a faith that support of private business will *also* improve the working and living conditions of the vast majority of State residents. The "community" approach, drawing on an alternative economic analysis, suggests that there may actually be a conflict between support for private business and concern for the welfare of most State workers and residents.

■ Chapter 4 applies that discussion of general policy approaches to a review of specific policy tools which State governments currently apply or which are potentially available for the State government policy arsenal. Using earlier arguments about the sources of employment problems, the chapter distinguishes between "promising" and "unpromising" uses of policy instruments. If State governments want to help promote a much larger supply of "good jobs," the chapter suggests, they will need to consider a wide variety of new policy directions in their employment and development programs.

The arguments advanced in these chapters directly challenge the conventional wisdom. I have no illusions that these kinds of policy changes can happen immediately or that they would come easily if suggested. Viewed in that perspective, this essay seeks nothing more than a discussion based on common sense. I think that current employment policy is based on misperceptions of the problems and a misguided analysis of their sources. Policies based on that analysis are likely, if anything, to make our problems worse. It seems to make much more sense to move in promising (though difficult) directions than to pursue policies which are more likely to intensify than to solve the problems they are supposed to address.   *5*

1

CURRENT EMPLOYMENT PROBLEMS: NOT ENOUGH "GOOD JOBS"

State residents confront a wide variety of serious employment problems in the United States. The mix of problems varies among states and regions. Despite the multi-dimensional and regionally varied character of current employment problems, however, a common thread runs through all of the most important problems throughout the country: The U.S. economy needs millions more "good jobs."

This chapter develops that argument in two sections. The first section reviews the current character and magnitude of the four main employment problems confronting State residents: *poverty, unemployment and underemployment, indecent working conditions,* and *inadequate job control.* The second section argues that all of those problems flow from a common source—not enough "good jobs." The section provides both a definition of "good jobs" and a summary of the implications of this view of employment problems for the objectives of State economic development policy.

THE MAJOR DIMENSIONS OF STATE EMPLOYMENT PROBLEMS

This section argues that the four main dimensions of employment problems require urgent attention, are not going away (and, in several cases, clearly getting worse), and are not confined to any specific region in the country.

Poverty

Since the belated discovery of the poor in the early 1960s, the federal government has encouraged the public to consider poverty as a residual and dis-solving problem. The government and most economists have defined poverty as a marginal problem which economic growth was gradually eliminating. Many if not most State governments have followed suit.

In fact, as even government studies admit, official federal poverty standards are inadequate.[1] The official Social Security Administration (SSA) poverty level income builds upon the estimated costs of a minimal necessary food basket. But as the original studies formulating that budget standard noted, the food standard was based upon prospective diets for people seeking to survive in bomb shelters during civil emergencies, a nutritional diet designed only for "temporary and emergency use." No one ever intended that diet as the basis for regular subsistence; according to nutritional studies, health problems would soon result if people tried to subsist at that dietary level for more than a few months, let alone many years.

And still, the federal government persists in considering households as poor *only if* their incomes are too low to afford food consumption at this "temporary or emergency" level. Judging by these standards, the government and many experts have noted the virtual disappearance of poverty in the United States. Federal data suggest that the percent of the U.S. population living in "poor" households has declined from 22.1 percent in 1960 to only 11.8 percent in 1977. By 1977, "only" 25 million Americans lived in poverty.

If this official federal poverty standard seems inadequate, are there other definitions of poverty which might more effectively reflect the real dimensions of poverty in the country and among States?

Many economists have suggested applying another federal budget standard as a more adequate and realistic "poverty" standard—the "lower-than-moderate" budget standard developed and updated by the U.S. Bureau of Labor Statistics. Although higher than the SSA Standard, it provides a spare existence. For instance, each adult in the family is allowed two beers a week in the food budget. The entertainment budget permits each adult five movies a year. Families earning incomes lower than this standard, as many economists have argued, have trouble sustaining their families at minimal levels of nutritional health and well-being. The federal government does not directly tabulate the number of households who remain poor by this definition. The author has elsewhere estimated that roughly *30 percent* of Americans live in households which, by this more meaningful standard, should be considered "poor" (Gordon, 1977: Ch. 4). With nearly a third of Americans falling below this budget standard, it is difficult to consider poverty a "marginal" problem.

Is poverty a regional or national problem? Historically, because wages have always been lower in the South, the incidence of poverty has been higher in the Sunbelt than in the Northeastern States. In 1960, for example, poverty (measured by the SSA standard) was twice as high in the South as in the West, North, or North Central regions of the United States.

Another historic pattern, particularly since World War Two, has also been that poor Southerners tended to migrate to the North in large numbers, providing a safety valve to Southern poverty and, at least eventually, increasing Northern burdens for welfare expenditures and social services. Even after the net flow of total migration shifted back from North to South during the 1960s, it appeared that the net flow of *poor* migration was continuing to move northward—that, as a Census observer recently put it, the South "was continuing to contribute, on an annual basis, to poverty levels elsewhere" (Long, 1978).

But this historic pattern has now shifted. Since 1970, there has been a net *in*-migration of poor people to the South (and the net in-migration of poor people to the West has continued). As economic opportunities have expanded in the Sunbelt, poor people have been staying in the South rather than searching for steady income elsewhere. The incidence of poverty in the South has continued to decline, but much more slowly. Recent data indicate that the Sunbelt and the Frostbelt will become more and more similar along this dimension. (See Pack, 1978.)

It is important to note, finally, that poverty by either standard is *not* principally a problem of those who cannot work—the elderly or disabled or single parents without access to day care facilities. In the early 1970s, even according to the SSA poverty standard, a majority of all poor people lived in households where the head worked at least some weeks during the year; a quarter of the poor lived in households where the head worked year-round (Plotnick and Skidmore, 1975). Measuring by the BLS "lower-than-moderate" budget standard, the heads of nearly a third of poor households in 1975 worked *full-time and year-round.* Only about one-fifth of the poor (as measured by the BLS standard) lived in households where the head did not work at all (Gordon, 1977).

In short, millions of U.S. households earn too little to support themselves at a minimally adequate standard of living and a substantial majority of those households—as high a fraction as four-fifths—remain in poverty despite the fact that the households' heads worked at some time or another during the year.[2] This means that, for most of the poor in the United States, their poverty does not arise because they cannot find work or are incapable of holding a job. Rather, their poverty continues despite the fact that they work repeatedly and often steadily. Correcting their poverty would require, therefore, higher wages on the jobs they hold, not more jobs at prevailing wage levels.[3]

Unemployment and
Underemployment
The second dimension of State employment problems has received the most attention in recent discussions of regional 9

decline and growth. The media seem to suggest that *unemployment* has become an essentially regional problem, concentrated in the "declining" Northeast. But these impressions are somewhat misplaced. They reflect much too partial a view of the problem of "unemployment." When we consider the issue more broadly as an issue of jobs—of "employment" itself—then we begin to see that there are severe problems of unemployment *and* underemployment throughout the country. The main difference between regions lies in the *form* in which these general problems *manifest* themselves.

What is the general problem? In the U.S. economy, most people are not able to support themselves (at adequate incomes) for long unless they can find stable and decent employment. This means that the basic problem of employment, unemployment, and underemployment has a simple definition. People have "employment problems" when they are unable to secure a steady job which pays an adequate wage or salary. Some people experience this "problem" in the form of unsteady employment. Others experience it in the form of inadequate wage or salary. Many experience the problem in both forms. In any case, unemployment rates—as most economists now admit—measure only part of this nexus of problems.

The conventional government definition of unemployment includes only those people without a job *who have looked for a job during the past four weeks*. This means that a wide variety of people with "employment problems" are not counted in the unemployment rates: (1) those who would like to work but have grown discouraged from their search and have stopped looking, (2) those who want full-time work, cannot find it, and have settled for part-time work; (3) those who work full-time but earn inadequate labor incomes; (4) those who might be looking for jobs in the civilian labor market but who, for largely economic reasons, are settled elsewhere—in prisons, for example, or in the armed forces; and (5) those whom the census takers never locate.

As with the problem of poverty, the federal government has consistently failed to compile data which would fully measure this broader conception of what many economists now call "underemployment." Some approximate estimates of the problem have been developed, however, incorporating various definitions of critical concepts like "adequate" wage-and-salary income and "discouraged" workers (Gordon, 1977). In 1975—the most recent year for which complete data were available at the time of calculation—the "official" unemployment rate was 8.5 percent. By the most conservative combination of definitions of "underemployment," a minimum of 16 million people—or 17 percent of the labor force—suffered employment problems. By more liberal definitions—including the spare BLS "lower-than-moderate" budget standard as the basis for "adequate" wage-and-salary income—roughly 35 million workers—or 33.8 percent of the labor force—were "underemployed."

In other words, at a minimum, twice as many workers suffer employment problems as the official unemployment data suggest. More plausibly, something like four times the official unemployment rate experience basic employment problems. By the more inclusive definitions, roughly a third of the labor force is unable to secure a job providing adequate wage-and-salary support.

These figures don't even account for the "steadiness" of those jobs. All employment data, including the expanded figures for under-employment discussed above, measure such problems *at one time*. They do not provide estimates of the number of people, for example, who experience unemployment *at one time or another during a year*. Roughly two and a half times as many people experience *at least one bout of unemployment* during a year as those counted as unemployed at any time during the year. Indeed, so severe are the problems of steady employment in the United States, particularly during the current period, that only two-thirds of all workers are able to work *full-time year-round*.

In short, somewhere from a third to a half of all U.S. workers suffer employment problems of one sort or another. These problems are not simply confined to central city ghettos in declining States.

Nonetheless, there are important differences in the character of those employment problems among States and regions.

In the Northeast, one of the most important problems has been rising relative unemployment rates. Compared to the national average, the official rates of unemployment in the Northeastern States have been increasing steadily since the late 1960s. This has meant that national economic growth has been less and less likely to generate additional employment opportunities for those living in the Frostbelt region.

In the Sunbelt, in contrast, the major problem remains one of low wages. Throughout the Sunbelt region, many jobs pay wages which are far too low to support workers and their households at adequate income levels. Although aggregate per capita income in the Sunbelt has been increasing more rapidly than in the Frostbelt during the recent period of regional shift, it remains true that much of the Sunbelt employment generated during the region's recent prosperity has not afforded employment at decent wages for much of the Sunbelt labor force.

In both regions, despite these differences, the basic problems are similar. Even in the Sunbelt states, unemployment rates are often very

12

high. In 1977, for example, when the national "official" unemployment rate was 7.0 percent, Alabama, Arizona, California, Florida, Mississippi, and South Carolina all had unemployment rates above the national average. Even in the Frostbelt, where average wages have been higher, millions of jobs pay far too little for adequate household support. In 1977, for example, 36 percent of all households in the ten largest Northeast and Midwest central cities earned less than $10,000—the level required for a family of four to achieve the BLS poverty standard.

It is important to emphasize, moreover, that simply expanding a State's employment base does not provide full protection against the problems of unemployment and underemployment. Many jobs typically provide *unsteady* employment, jobs in which workers are particularly likely to suffer dismissal or layoff. Many of the same kinds of jobs also typically provide such low wages that they do not establish a foundation for households' maintaining an adequate standard of living. A large number of studies have recently shown that very high proportions of workers suffering frequent bouts of unemployment and of those earning inadequate wages are concentrated in a group of what we can call "secondary" or "poor jobs." (See below for definitions; see also Edwards, 1979; and Gordon, 1980a, for a summary of recent studies.)*

Does unemployment and underemployment really matter? Isn't it possible for State government officials to remain content with expanding employment and to pay less attention to the quality of the jobs which workers find and hold? Why should State economic policy focus on the third to half of jobs which fail to provide steady employment at decent wages rather than the seven percent of the labor force which is unemployed at any given moment?

Many economists have pointed out that high unemployment rates and unstable employment opportunities impose heavy social service costs on State and local governments—not only through public support of the unemployment compensation system but through higher relative welfare and social service costs. These costs of high unemployment and low wages seem fairly obvious.

There are some more subtle and possibly more important social costs of underemployment. Crime offers one of the most important examples. High and rising crime not only imposes property losses on local residents but also creates an acute sense of public insecurity and

---

*Throughout this essay I refer to "poor jobs" as the opposite of "good jobs" and requiring similar definition. The definition emerges from the definition of "good jobs" later in this chapter and then again in Chapter 2.

social malaise. Crimes are not solely or even primarily committed by marginalized citizens—by roving bands of professional criminals. Recent economic evidence suggests that crime varies directly and closely with two critical economic variables—unemployment and inequality. As unemployment rises, so does crime. And as the gap between the incomes of the wealthy and the relatively poor increases, so do crime rates rise. The largest proportion of those who commit "street crimes" are people who occasionally work in "secondary"jobs, who suffer frequent bouts of unemployment, and whose wages at work are inadequate to support their families (McGahey, 1979).

These direct effects spill over between the generations. Problems of underemployment among parents contribute to feelings of frustration and low expectations among children. Those communities in which underemployment rates are high tend also to be those in which a variety of social problems persist among teenagers into young adulthood. The quality of schooling suffers, which infects future opportunities for children who themselves come from families supported by steady jobs. The consequences of underemployment spread throughout such communities like ripples in a pond (see Gordon, 1975).

The problems of unemployment and underemployment, in short, cannot be marginalized. Millions of U.S. workers are unable to find steady jobs at decent wages. This underemployment creates severe problems not only for those workers directly affected but also for many others in neighboring communities.

Indecent Working   Another dimension of State employment
Conditions   problems has only recently received serious attention. Many jobs expose workers to treacherous hazards, including the risk of fatal accidents or potentially fatal diseases. Since the passage of the Occupational Safety and Health Act of 1970, working people have been complaining more and more frequently about these basic hazards. And their complaints have finally begun to highlight the enormity of the problem.

Conservative government estimates suggest that between 115,000 and 200,000 Americans die each year from an occupationally related accident or disease. At least two million workers suffer occupational accidents every year; some government studies have suggested that so many accidents or diseases go unreported that closer to 20 million U.S. workers suffer some kind of occupationally related accident or disease *each year*. Recent studies have suggested that at least one in four U.S. workers is exposed to working conditions which increase their risks of potentially fatal disease.[4]

Many media reports on occupational health-and-safety problems

have tended to view the sites of this exposure as confined to limited pockets in specific industries—like the mining or the textile industries. Obviously, however, it would be difficult to draw a map of the U.S. in such a way that one out of four workers (exposed to potentially fatal working conditions) were isolated in a few pockets of dangerous industrial areas.

Comprehensive data on the geographic incidence of health-and-safety problems are difficult to muster and interpret. One reasonable index of the geographic distribution of problems can emerge from cancer mortality figures. Most studies conclude that from two-thirds to three-fourths of all cancers are environmentally caused and that large proportions of those cancers result from on-the-job exposure. The variation of cancer mortality among States therefore provides an interesting glimpse at the varying intensity among States of dangerous working conditions on the job.

Data for cancer mortality among States for 1969 reveal a common pattern. States with the traditionally highest concentration of manufacturing industry and population have the highest cancer mortality rates: New Jersey, Rhode Island, New York, and Connecticut, for example, were the four States with the highest rates in that year. This common pattern suggests an obvious implication for the Sunbelt states. As industry shifts to the South and West and as population density also increases, there is a strong likelihood that cancer mortality rates will increase as well. Sunshine may be the best disinfectant, as Justice Brandeis once remarked, but no one has yet shown it to provide a cure for cancer.

Many health-and-safety problems are also concentrated disproportionately in "poor jobs." Industrial accident rates are highest in some industries like mining and construction where the character of the work is especially likely to expose workers to physical hazards. But it turns out that accident rates are *also* highest in industries where high competition and low profit rates mean that firms rely on outmoded technology, cannot afford improvements and maintenance, and must drive their workers unusually rapidly to try to keep up their profits. If we compare accident rates among manufacturing industries in the 1960s and 1970s, for example, we find that accident rates in what economists sometimes call "peripheral" industries average roughly twice as high as those in "core" industries. (See Chapter 2 for definitions.) (Health problems deriving from carcinogenic substances are much more widespread throughout industry.)

Health-and-safety problems are not disappearing, moreover, but have intensified since economic instability began to intensify during the late 1960s. Industrial accident rates increased by 27 percent between 1963 and 1970 after years of decline. During the 1970s, based on new and more comprehensive data collected under the auspices of the Occupational Safety and Health Administration, workdays lost from industrial accidents increased by one-third, on average, between 1971-73 and 1975-77.

Job Control

Many workers also face serious employment problems because they have relatively little control over their working conditions, exposing them to the risks of employer negligence or mistreatment. A variety of employment problems can sometimes flow from this common source: The less influence workers have over the pace and organization of work, the more vulnerable they may be to health-and-safety problems. The less protection workers have against arbitrary dismissal and supervisory abuse, the more difficulties they may have with sudden layoffs and intermittent employment.

These concerns have fueled workers' historic drive to win the right to unionization. During the 1930s, according to most labor historians, workers participating in the drive to form industrial unions were at least as concerned with supervisory abuse—leading to demands for grievance procedures—and arbitrary hiring and promotion—leading to proposals for seniority systems—as they were with more tangible issues like wage rates. (For example, see Bernstein, 1971: p. 774 ff.) These concerns also obviously motivate more recent union support for strong government regulation of health-and-safety hazards.

One measure of trends in workers' influence over their working conditions, therefore, focuses on trends in unionization. The evidence here suggests a very clear tendency. The percentage of the non-agricultural labor force represented by labor unions increased steadily during the 1930s and 1940s. It peaked at roughly 35 percent in the early 1950s and has since fallen to roughly one quarter. In many Western European countries, by contrast, the percentage of the labor force in unions ranges from half to more than two-thirds. While labor union membership is hardly sufficient to provide workers with substantial influence over their jobs, it is nonetheless much more difficult for workers to improve their working conditions *without* the protection and leverage which labor unions help afford. Why has there been such a striking decline in relative union representation?

Business leaders often argue that declining proportions of workers

Photo: Earl Dotter/ALEC

want to join unions because unions fail to serve their interests. Union leaders typically argue that millions of additional workers would join unions if there were not so many obstacles in their paths and if companies opposed unions less insistently.

There is certainly some truth on both sides. Several observations seem to support the union argument. First, the relative decline in union strength coincides historically with the period since the 1947 passage of the Taft-Hartley Act, which dramatically increased firms' ability to resist unionization and reduced the tools with which unions could seek to organize workers. Second, there is plentiful evidence that current legislation does not fully guarantee workers' rights to unionize, since companies can and frequently do delay elections and contract negotiations for years through stalling and legal challenges. Third, recent surveys indicate that roughly a third of workers not currently represented by labor unions would prefer to join and be represented by unions.[5]

Some other observations provide at least partial support to the business argument: Unions have become increasingly likely to lose decertification elections during the 1970s, for example, indicating that significant portions of workers have been willing to express their dissatisfaction with their current union's practices. Second, recent surveys also indicate that large portions of current union members are only moderately satisfied, at best, with their unions' performance.

There is a composite interpretation which probably more accurately reflects recent historical experience than either the business or union arguments. It seems reasonable to conclude that very large portions of U.S. workers want a significant degree of influence over their working conditions *but* that many are not currently satisfied with the manner in which some labor unions help provide such influence *and* that business opposition to union and worker influence, in many quarters, also substantially increases the obstacles to workers' influence (much less union representation and effectiveness). Is there evidence on worker preferences for influence over their working conditions? The same recent surveys indicate that more than 90 percent of U.S. workers want at least "some say" over wage determination, conditions affecting job security, and decisions affecting health-and-safety conditions. It seems reasonable to conclude that the recent relative decline in union strength and the aggressive business promotion of its own interests have *not* been increasing workers' ability to realize these preferences.

It is important to note, finally, that this problem of worker influence is not simply a regional problem, confined to those areas, particularly in the Sunbelt, where workers have traditionally faced the greatest difficulty in organizing unions. It is true that rates of unionization differ substantially between the Frostbelt and the Sunbelt. In 1974, for example, more than 30 percent of the (non-agricultural) labor force was unionized in most of the Northeastern states, while from seven to 17 percent of the labor force in the Sunbelt states was unionized. But it is also reasonably clear that the issue of worker influence over working conditions affects State economic policymakers throughout the country. As firms have tended increasingly both to move away from the Frostbelt areas of the country (both to the Sunbelt and overseas) and as many companies have moved more and more aggressively to combat union influence, workers and State government officials in even the more pro-union states have experienced substantial pressure to grant more privileges and concessions to business in their areas. This has begun to have two important effects. First, even unionized workers are feeling growing pressure to relax their demands for greater job security and safer working conditions. Second, the "demonstration effect" of unions has probably been weakening. While it has historically been true—and most business observers would agree with this observation—that union successes in unionized sectors have pushed non-union employers to improve wages, job security and working conditions in order to try to forestall unionization, it seems likely that the recent decline in union strength and the recent increase in corporate aggressiveness have moderated this pressure on non-union employers—particularly in traditional union areas like the Northeast.

These two effects combine to generate a common result: Almost all workers in the United States want some effective influence over their wages, job security, and working conditions, but recent developments have tended to push that objective further and further from their grasp.

SO WHAT'S A "GOOD JOB"?

All four of these main dimensions of current employment problems reflect a common denominator: *The U.S. economy provides too few "good jobs."* Problems of poverty, underemployment, indecent working conditions, and inadequate job control all reflect this underlying problem.

Simple employment is not enough. As Eli Ginzberg, a noted manpower economist, has concluded (Ginzberg, 1977) "most specialists would agree that the following [job] characteristics are significant: wages, fringe benefits, regularity (or intermittency) of employment, working conditions, job security and opportunities for promotion." As Ginzberg also concludes, "more often than not, . . . favorable elements go together." A "good job" is one which provides, *19* therefore, *adequate wages and fringe benefits, job security and stable employment, decent working conditions, and opportunities for both advancement and control.*

I shall provide estimates of the number of "good" and "poor" jobs in the U.S. economy after I derive a method for more precise definition in Chapter 2. In the meantime, it is important to review and clarify the argument about the importance of "good jobs" for State employment policies.

One of the arguments about the importance of "good jobs" can be stated simply: *Simple job expansion by itself will not guarantee. solution to any of the four main dimensions of State employment problems:*

■ If job expansion creates "poor jobs," poverty is unlikely to moderate significantly, since large numbers of the poor already work in "poor jobs." Indeed, recent estimates indicate that 92 percent of a representative sample of households who had received welfare over a five-year period had household heads who had worked at some time or another during that period (Harrison; 1979). The problem lay in the quality of jobs they held, not in the presence or absence of work itself.
■ If job expansion creates "poor jobs," the real problems of unemployment and underemployment are unlikely to abate more than marginally. Growing numbers of economists agree that many workers move in and out of "poor jobs" with great frequency—suffering layoff, dismissal, or disappointment in their hopes for stable employment with potential advancement. While we might reasonably expect that measured "official" unemployment rates might decline if the aggregate rate of "poor job" expansion increased, it is not at all clear that the numbers of people who experienced unemployment at some time or another during the year would decline or that the rate of *under*employment would be affected to any significant degree.
■ If job expansion merely increases the number of "poor jobs," there is a significant likelihood that workers' exposure to unsafe and possibly injurious working conditions would *increase* dramatically. "Poor jobs" are not only much more likely to manifest health-and-safety problems but they are also much more likely to expose workers to the problems of stress and anxiety which flow from intermittent employment and arbitrary supervisory authority (Luft, 1978).
■ Job expansion does not necessarily provide improved opportunities for advancement and job control. If the number of "poor jobs" increases, the problems flowing from inadequate control may increase correspondingly. (See Chapter 2 for elaboration of this point.)

There is another argument about the importance of "good jobs" which reflects the *indirect* consequences of the quality of work: Simple job expansion by itself may do nothing to moderate (and may actually intensify) some of the most serious *social* problems currently plaguing State and local governments:

■ A wide variety of studies have shown that people who receive welfare benefits and commit "street crimes" often work in "poor jobs." Indeed, it appears that welfare and crime incidence increases with the gap between the incomes and working conditions of "good" and "poor" jobs—rather than increasing with higher unemployment by itself. The more that the U.S. labor market confines certain groups of people to "poor jobs" and seems to preclude their entry into "good jobs," the more the economy will reinforce the circulation of many people among the labor market, welfare, and street crime in a kind of continuous flow (Harrison, 1974, 1979).

Photo: Robert Gumpert

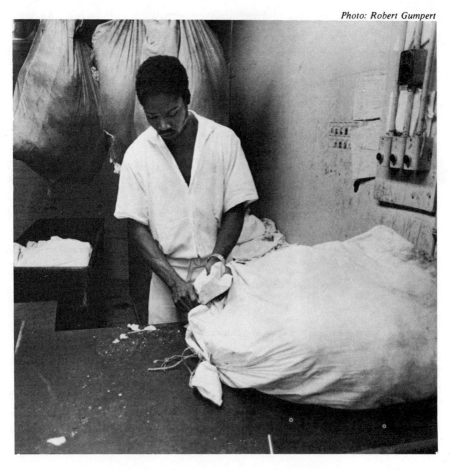

■ These arguments can be extended to even more generalized observations. Many note declining work satisfaction among U.S. workers and a growing cynicism about the country and its prospects. If job expansion does not provide growing proportions of the labor force with "good jobs," then we must certainly accept the possibility that labor market developments will do nothing to counter these trends toward dissatisfaction and cynicism. Charles Wilson used to argue that "what is good for General Motors is good for the country." One might suggest a more plausible maxim: "What is good for people's jobs is good for the country." The more that people can enjoy decent wages, job security, decent working conditions, and job control, the more likely they will be to contribute positively to the country's political economic welfare. The greater the numbers of people who are confined to "poor jobs," the greater the risks to our general welfare and the strength of the social fabric.

The argument of this chapter can be simply summarized. As we review State employment problems, it appears that we must define those problems somewhat more carefully than is common in general public discussion. It appears that *the moderation of State employment problems requires more "good jobs," not simply more jobs of whatever quality and characteristics.* This suggests that we must pose a very specific question for further discussion. Why does the U.S. economy fail to generate enough "good jobs"?

Footnotes to Chapter 1

1. On the inadequacies of the federal poverty definitions, see Levine (1970) and Rainwater (1975).

2. It is important to emphasize once again that almost all the data upon which these kinds of conclusions depend revolve around the federal (SSA) poverty standard. Despite all the inadequacies of that definition, the federal government does not provide data which would permit accurate conclusions about the relationship among welfare, poverty, and employment. Without such data, many of these conclusions remain approximate.

3. For a useful summary of the indications that poverty has not, in fact, been reduced and that it remains a critical and sizable problem, see National Advisory Council on Economic Opportunity (1979).

4. For basic references to data sources and summaries of these magnitudes, with appropriate discussion of the definitions on which they rely, see Ashford (1976) and Berman (1979).

5. These observations on workers' preferences about unions and working conditions all derive from Institute for Social Research (1979).

2
WHY AREN'T THERE ENOUGH "GOOD JOBS"?

Recent discussions of State economic development problems have typically pointed toward strategies of support for private investment and job expansion. These strategies flow not only from business pressure but from an underlying assumption—that market pressures and adequate corporate profit levels will promote the kinds of aggregate and regional growth necessary for the moderation of employment problems. The pervasiveness of the current "economic development strategy" derives in part from the prevalence and uncontested acceptance of these assumptions.

The foundation for these common viewpoints lies in mainstream (or "neoclassical") economic analysis. In order to ask why the economy does not provide enough "good jobs," we must obviously explore mainstream analyses of employment and income. This chapter reviews the predominant mainstream analyses of jobs and wages and compares those views with an alternative "structural" explanation of employment problems. Four main points are developed in the course of this review:

■ Mainstream economic analysis provides an inadequate account of labor market behavior, fundamentally compromising the policy recommendations which depend on it.
■ In particular, it provides a misleading set of answers to our questions about why the economy fails to provide enough "good jobs."
■ An alternative structural perspective appears to provide a much more promising account of labor market mechanisms and the determination of wages and employment.
■ In particular, this structural perspective seems to offer a coherent and consistent explanation of the economy's insufficient supply of "good jobs."

MAINSTREAM ECONOMIC ANALYSIS

Neoclassical economists typically burst with confidence about their explanatory powers. But recent events have tempered that self-confidence.

Many State and local officials have asked some obvious questions, for example, about the causes of rapid regional employment shifts and 23 the relative decline of the Northeast. There are pieces of analysis which might potentially help, according to many mainstream economists, but there is no consistent underlying framework which fits all those pieces together. Two leading regional economists introduced a recent book of essays on *Revitalizing the Northeast* with exactly this kind of warning. Constructing a coherent theory of regional growth and decline, they admitted, "severely taxes present theoretical capacities as well as empirical resources . . . [There] is little we can do but be cognizant of this limitation and make it explicit" (Sternlieb and Hughes, 1978).

If this kind of hesitation is so pervasive, why are so many economists nonetheless confident about the kind of "economic development strategy" which dominates recent public discussions? I would argue that the underlying *tools* of mainstream economics provide the basis for recent policy formulations and that economists' continuing confidence in those basic tools frames their support for specific economic development strategies. In order to reconsider the basis of current policy perspectives, we must briefly reconsider the fundamental analytic perspective of neoclassical economics itself.[1] Two main aspects of that perspective warrant primary attention—its focus on "supply and demand" and its focus on workers' "productivities."

Traditional Supply and Demand Analysis

The starting point for most traditional economic analysis is the classic supply-and-demand framework. This set of ideas begins with some simple premises: In market economies, buyers and sellers adjust their demand and supply until they agree on a common price and quantity for the goods and services involved. Once they agree, an exchange takes place. The logic of the process is supposed to guarantee a stable "equilibrium," or resting place, for the exchange process. If we assume that there are available supplies of resources and prevailing "tastes" or preferences, then we can assume that the economy will keep reproducing the same basic structures of allocation and exchange over time.

This framework, in general, has an obvious implication about the sources of change in market economies. Since a market equilibrium will be continually reproduced with *given* resources and tastes, changes in the basic pattern of allocation must be caused by changes in basic *resources* and/or *tastes:* nothing would change if there weren't changes in what the market began with in the first place. This suggests that important economic changes must be due to significant shifts in the underlying conditions of supply and demand, not in the market processes themselves.

What does all this have to do with analyses of State employment problems or regional decline and growth?

Many analyses of current State economic problems begin with the basic supply and demand framework. They assume that there was some moment in the recent past when State and regional economies were in equilibrium, when buyers and sellers in factor markets and buyers and sellers of final goods and services were content with the terms of their exchange. The accelerating changes in State and regional fortunes, this framework suggests, *must* be the result of some underlying shifts in the conditions affecting the supply and demand of factors of production and goods and services.

The examples of this kind of analysis seem fairly obvious:

■ Many current problems are attributed to basic shifts in people's *preferences about where they live.* Much of the shift to the Sunbelt has been explained by a rapid movement in population for reasons of climatic preference. Once population began to shift, according to this argument, jobs began to follow. Nothing internal to the economy changed at all. The economy simply made accommodations to the change in people's preferences about residential location and older people's growing capacity to satisfy those preferences.

■ Many analyses also place a strong emphasis on *energy constraints.* Particularly since 1973-74, the costs of energy have been increasing rapidly. Climatic conditions tend to create different energy costs by region, and some historic differences in transportation patterns compound these variations in energy costs. Industry has been moving to the Sunbelt in growing numbers, the analysis concludes, because it can no longer afford the relatively higher energy costs of Frostbelt production. Nothing changed in the way the economy works, but changes in the technical conditions of energy resource production and distribution generated significant changes in market outcomes.

■ Business decisions about location also depend heavily on other conditions affecting their supply curves, economists argue, like basic *wage* costs. If industry has been moving to other regions where wages are lower, the supply and demand perspective suggests that it must be happening at least in part because wages have been rising "too rapidly" in the regions from which capital has been fleeing. Nothing about the economy has changed, once again, but some external changes in the power of workers and their unions to increase their wages has unsettled the traditional spatial equilibrium and driven business away.

The character of this supply and demand analysis helps explain why it *appears* to many economists that there is no coherent analysis of the 25 dynamics of regional decline and growth. Within that general analytic framework, *any* change in underlying conditions—no matter how large or small, long-term or temporary—has equal credentials as a source of changes in market equilibria. And none of the changes is necessarily connected to any others. Each of the factors, as the authors quoted above also admit, is seen as a "discrete factor" in isolation from every other factor. The analysis seems more like a patchwork quilt than a structured analytic framework. Nothing matters more or less than anything else.

There are two main theoretical problems with this supply-and-demand framework. First, it assumes that everything can matter, and all changes in any conditions are equally likely to have some important effects in causing serious employment problems. In this sense, the analysis is very *undiscriminating,* failing to distinguish between different kinds of causes or different orders of importance. If something small happens—like small changes in workers' wages—the analysis assumes that those small changes are sufficient to bring about continuing and structurally important changes in economic conditions.

At first blush, this seems to be a plausible assumption. When we investigate its implications more carefully, however, it seems inherently implausible. It suggests that economic resources are organized in a sufficiently flexible manner, that firms can always and automatically make necessary marginal adjustments in resource allocation and production. But the real economic world involves significant structural *rigidities.* Firms can't change to a new location if there is no transportation, no infrastructure, no marketing mechanism, no stable governmental support for their needs, no regular accommodation with workers and labor unions. Just as a bee sting may not phase a hippopotamus, small changes in the costs and markets affecting firm decisions may not have *any* immediate impact simply because they are dwarfed by the more fundamental determinants of business activity. Structural rigidities, in short, may preclude small changes in the business environment from having much influence on basic paths of economic development no matter how "real" or "important" those small changes may seem. (This will have critical implications, as we shall soon see, for analyses of "economic development strategies" like reduced business taxes.)

The second main theoretical problem with the supply-and-demand framework is that it depends on the notion that the market is automatically self-correcting, that problems and inefficiencies in the economy will work themselves out smoothly. In neoclassical economic theory, this notion depends on several critical assumptions: (a) that

economic markets are very competitive (and that firms cannot affect their economic environment); (2) that everyone in the markets has more or less *perfect* and *immediate* information about all alternative exchange possibilities; and (3) that buyers and sellers have more or less equal power to affect market outcomes.

But none of these assumptions makes much sense as a starting-point for analyses of the modern U.S. economy. (1) The largest corporations can clearly exercise significant influence over their environments; few markets are "perfectly competitive." (2) Information is very spotty and imperfect, with some insiders not only getting it more quickly than others but also actively hiding it from their competitors and potential market partners. (3) Market transactions typically involve buyers and sellers of very uneven and unequal power—large firms and small firms, large corporations and individual workers, firms and consumers.

If, indeed, these three assumptions make little sense, we cannot easily assume that the market has generally been in "balance" or "equilibrium" and that important changes have emanated from factors outside of the market framework. It would be just as plausible to assume that the economy was constantly in a state of "imperfection" and change, that large and powerful economic forces and actors, like corporations, are always trying to achieve differential advantage through manipulation of market exchange, and that they are frequently capable of achieving these kinds of results. Their activities **27** and influence, rather than "external" events, might easily explain many of current employment problems.

None of this means that supply-and-demand factors never matter. It suggests, rather, that the supply-and-demand framework builds from such misleading assumptions that we should never assume it is the *only* useful perspective for analyzing economic issues like State employment problems. Indeed, on theoretical grounds alone, its weaknesses suggest that we should place high priority on developing and considering alternative economic analyses. When we look at the most important structural factors affecting economic change, it may turn out that supply-and-demand adjustments are much *less* important than the economic environment and power which establish the boundaries within which market forces have effect.

Productive Efficiency and Workers' Skills   A second important theoretical perspective informs many traditional discussions of State employment problems. This view pays principal attention to the *characteristics* of workers in different regions, States, and cities, building from analyses of the *supply* of labor in different labor markets. It suggests that firms may have trouble producing efficiently in particular areas if there are too few available workers possessing the skills those firms need. If they can't find the right kinds of workers, they may go out of business or move somewhere else.

During the recent rush of proposals for business tax reduction and investment subsidies, this focus on labor supply and workers' skills has received less attention than in earlier years. During the 1960s, however, economists' preoccupation with workers' skills *dominated* local, State, and federal manpower policy. Almost all public policies designed to solve "employment problems" aimed at improving the skills and working attitudes of less-skilled or "disadvantaged" workers. Although that emphasis no longer dominates public policy in this problem area, the analysis which framed the earlier preoccupation with workers' skills still remains as an important backdrop to current discussions of State employment problems. Several examples illustrate its persistence:

■ Many who discuss employment problems in older central cities ascribe some of the problems of present or potential central city employers to the low skills and poor working habits of ghetto workers. This often leads to the suggestion either that minimum wage levels should be lowered or that firms cannot be attracted to those areas in increasing numbers unless they receive heavy skills-training subsidies.

28

■ The skills perspective provides a convenient excuse when discussions turn to the millions of workers, particularly those in older central cities, who have difficulty finding work. If their job problems can be attributed to their low skills, then business can comfortably shift the spotlight of employment discussions *to* the workers and *away* from employers. And if one could reasonably argue that individuals are responsible for making basic decisions about how high a skill level they have attained—which economists of the "human capital" school essentially argue—business can even more comfortably allow "blame" for workers' problems to settle onto the workers' shoulders. "What can you expect?", one hears employers asking. "If they didn't have the sense to stay in school and acquire skills, how can they expect to compete in today's job market?"

Those who place special emphasis on the problems of productive efficiency and workers' skills would all agree that there are only two possible solutions to the problems highlighted by this analytic preoccupation: More money should be invested in subsidy of workers' skills improvement; and workers should receive encouragement—mostly called "motivation"—to improve their skills. Since many also argue that skills are best acquired on the job, the former policy suggestion typically devolves into suggestions for subsidies to employers for on-the-job skills training. And both suggestions provide an easy excuse for fatalism: If there is not enough public money

Photo: Robert Gumpert

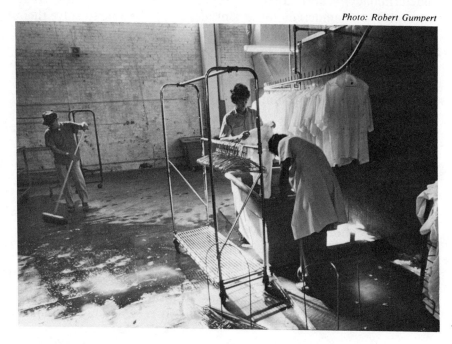

available to support skills programs, or if "disadvantaged" workers simply won't commit themselves to their self-improvement, then there is nothing more we can hope to accomplish. You can lead a horse to water, one hears, but you can't make him drink.

There are two main theoretical problems with the workers' skills perspective.

First, the perspective, as typically applied, encourages a critical theoretical mistake in the way it views workers' productivities. A given worker's productivity is actually a function of *two* kinds of factors— the features of the *job* in which the worker is employed and the worker's own *skill* or productivity characteristics. If a brilliant and dextrous college graduate works in a piece-work garment shop, there are obvious limits to his/her productivity. If an "unskilled" worker with little job experience manages to land an auto assembly job, that worker's "productive contribution" to the firm and the economy may suddenly soar—even though the worker has changed neither skills nor attitudes.

In this context, one cannot establish *a priori* whether workers' employment problems should properly be attributed to their own lack of skills and good working attitudes or to the paucity of available jobs which, no matter how low their initial skills, would permit highly productive use of those skills. The way in which traditional analyses typically discuss workers' skills completely overlooks this theoretical indeterminacy. Those analyses suggest, however implicitly, that unemployed or underemployed workers would be able to solve their labor problems on their own if only they learned more and worked harder. In fact, pending more careful investigation, it would be perfectly consistent with this analytic emphasis on workers' productivities to conclude that there is nothing that "disadvantaged" workers could do "on their own" until the supply of "good jobs" dramatically expanded.

The second theoretical problem relates directly to the first. Most traditional analyses of skills dramatically mis-state the kinds of skills which make workers "productive." There are some jobs in the economy, to be sure, which require considerable education, critical intelligence, and problem-solving capacity. (The author's own research suggests that these jobs comprise, at most, one quarter of all jobs in the economy; see below). Most jobs require nothing of the sort. Workers with virtually no skills and no training can easily learn the necessary tasks. What matters most, in those situations, is workers' relative willingness to work hard at relatively undemanding and boring jobs. That willingness depends, in turn, primarily on the job security and monetary rewards available in return. This argument

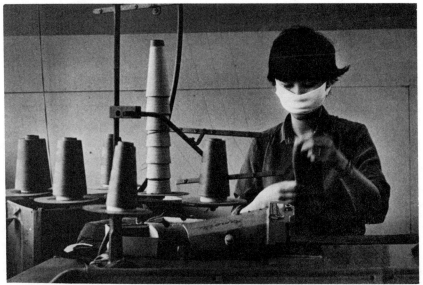

suggests a quite simple theoretical conclusion. In most jobs, workers' success may have nothing to do with the level of their "cognitive" achievement, or IQ, or reading and writing skills, or manual dexterity, or specific vocational skills, or other attributes conventionally associated with workers' "productivity." Their productivity *and* their success may depend, in contrast, on the wages and job security of the *job* which they find through the labor market. Policies which aim primarily at improving workers' skills, viewed from this consideration, might make little or no difference in improving the job opportunities of more "disadvantaged" workers.

There is also a wide variety of *empirical* evidence one can marshal against the traditional arguments about workers' skills. Three examples of such evidence should help convey the weakness of the traditional concern about "disadvantaged" workers' skills.

First, many studies have found that workers with more education and vocational training earn relatively higher incomes *only* in a narrow range of professional and technical jobs. In at least two-thirds of all occupations in the economy, workers' employment success— measured by their wages or annual incomes—bears almost no relationship to their formal "skills" training and is almost completely determined by the characteristics of the industries and jobs in which they work. Even if their schooling experience has helped channel them into the jobs they have, it is only because firms rely on school degrees **31** as "screening" devices, not because there is anything about their formal skills training which prepares them specifically for the jobs they hold or precludes their learning how to do other kinds of work (Gordon, 1972; and Edwards, 1979).

Second, some pioneering empirical work has documented the critical importance for workers' job success of their *attitudes* to their jobs. One study found that workers' "dependability" and "responsiveness to authority" in middle-level bureaucratic jobs was three times more important in explaining their wages and supervisors' rating than the combined influence of their education, cognitive achievement, or previous formal skills training. Those who were content to accept the behavioral demands of the job did relatively well, while those who weren't were penalized by their employers. "Skill levels" mattered much less (Edwards, 1976).

Doesn't that raise the possibility that there are some workers who have such poor work attitudes that they just can't adjust to the world of work? The third piece of empirical evidence places that question in a very special light. During the late 1960s, many corporations instituted special training programs for "disadvantaged" workers. The results of those experiments were striking and uniform: people with poor work experience blossomed in jobs where they were promised security and advancement, while people with comparable backgrounds grew restive in training and motivational programs which did *not* point directly toward jobs with similar promise (Cohn, 1971). The experience suggested, very concretely, that the horses would drink water if they were convinced that it was the real thing.

These considerations suggest that, for most jobs and workers in the U.S. economy, what matters most is the character of the jobs available. If the job provides decent rewards, workers will be able to perform in them with little additional training and encouragement. If the job provides "indecent" rewards, many if not most workers will prove surprisingly immune to inducements for skills advancement and motivational incentives. If skills and motivation don't matter in some jobs, why should workers care about them anyway?

Mainstream Analysis This initial review of mainstream eco-
and the Supply nomic analysis provides enough back-
of "Good Jobs" ground to highlight the neoclassical
answer to the question motivating this
chapter. Although most mainstream economists rarely focus on the question of "good jobs" as such, we can nonetheless infer how they would answer our question, "why aren't there enough good jobs?"[2]

Neoclassical economists would argue, in general, that there is a shortage of "good jobs"—assuming even for a moment that they would accept the arguments of Chapter 1—because of some combination of a *shortage* of skilled workers, suitable technology, or capital funds/profits for investment or higher wages. Each of these possible explanations requires separate attention.

The argument about workers' skills relies on a supply argument. If we define "good jobs" as those which, in particular, pay decent wages and provide adequate job security, then neoclassical economists would argue that employers can only afford to provide "good jobs" if there are workers whose skills and productivity warrant such rewards. It would logically follow, within the neoclassical perspective, that a paucity of "good jobs" must mean—to a very large degree—that there is an insufficient supply of workers with enough skills to justify additional "good jobs."

But there is plenty of evidence which suggests that there has been a growing surplus of workers with very substantial skills and that a corresponding increase in "good jobs" has *not* resulted. Berg (1970) and Freeman (1976) have shown, for example, that the supply of college-educated workers with substantial "general educational" skills has increased steadily since the 1950s, but that the number of jobs utilizing those skills has stagnated. The neoclassical perspective would have suggested that employers should have created jobs which made increasing use of those workers' skills. Nothing of the sort has happened. Similarly, many studies have shown that large numbers of workers in "poor jobs" are very "over-qualified" for those jobs; this surplus supply of relatively skilled labor has not resulted in the creation of more new jobs which would utilize those surplus skills (Gordon, 1972; Edwards, 1979).

There is little convincing evidence, in short, that employers have created more "good jobs" even though there have been increasing supplies of workers with productive skills.

Similar problems confront the second kind of explanation which neoclassical economists would offer for the inadequate supply of "good jobs": that workers' productivity depends not only on their skills but also on the technical support they receive. If workers can work with more machines and coordinate technology, their productivity can increase (even if they have relatively lower skills). If there were more productive technology around, there might be more "good jobs."

The available evidence does not dub this explanation the crown prince of plausibility. Large corporations have been using more and more advanced technology at a continuing rate throughout the postwar period. As we shall see below, however, their use of technology   *33* and automation has generally *reduced* the level of employment, not increased it. Moreover, large corporations have increasingly deployed advanced technology in regions and countries where local conditions permit their paying low wages and avoiding union influence. For the time being, at least, it appears that (a) rapid automation tends to eliminate jobs, not to create them; and (b) large corporations are taking advantage of their current leverage over workers to modernize in areas where workers' chances of securing decent wages and adequate leverage over their working conditions are least promising. This suggests that we cannot easily assume that accelerated business investment in new technologies would contribute to the pool of "good jobs" in the United States to any significant degree.

These arguments help frame the third neoclassical argument—that there would be more "good jobs" if businesses had more funds for investment or higher wages. Let us distinguish between small competitive firms and large corporations. Among small businesses, there is no guarantee that an increase in investment funds available to those firms would necessarily create "good jobs"; it may be that the competitive conditions and insecurities confronting those businesses will preclude their creation of "good job" opportunities no matter how rapidly their profits increased. Among large corporations it seems likely, particularly during the current period, that (a) they have adequate capital funds anway (*Fortune* reported that the 500 largest industrial corporations earned profits in 1978 at the highest rate since the mid-1950s); (b) that they are very likely to apply large portions of their available funds to mergers and acquisitions, not to productive investment; and (c) that whatever productive investments they make, for the reasons adduced in the previous paragraphs, are not necessarily likely to generate more "good jobs."

It seems necessary to conclude, in short, that neoclassical economics provides flawed tools for the analysis of employment problems and does not provide a promising explanation for the lack of "good jobs" in the U.S. economy. Isn't there a better way?

A STRUCTURAL ANALYSIS OF EMPLOYMENT PROBLEMS This section outlines a more promising way of viewing State employment problems. It sketches an alternative structural analysis of the sources of those problems and applies that analysis to the question of the availability of "good jobs."[3] This outline employs three separate building blocks: (1) an analysis of the contours of labor market structure in the U.S. economy; (2) a discussion of the factors influencing regional economic growth and decline; and (3) a brief review of the sources of aggregate economic instability during the 1970s. These three building blocks provide enough material for some relatively clear answers to our questions about the supply of "good jobs"; this synthetic analysis is provided in the fourth part of this section.

Labor Market Structure

A small group of economists (including myself) has recently developed a suggestive analysis of the character and structure of the labor market in the United States.[4] This analysis concludes that there are some major differences among jobs and the labor markets feeding them—among what we call *segments*—which dominate the influence of individual employers' and workers' characteristics. Any analysis of the character of State employment problems, we suggest, must begin from a consideration of the basic structure of the jobs and labor markets within its economy.

What are the segments and where do they come from?

The analysis begins with an appreciation of the fundamental importance of the largest corporations in the economy. The largest 200 industrial corporations control close to two-thirds of all industrial assets. The largest financial and service corporations have nearly comparable power in their respective sectors. These large firms have achieved a size and power in the modern U.S. economy which permits long-term planning and considerable flexibility in how they organize their basic productive operations.* These firms differ significantly from the millions of smaller enterprises which survive on narrower margins; count on much less secure futures; therefore plan over much shorter horizons; and ultimately have much less flexibility in how they structure production and organize the jobs of their workers.

The distinction between these two kinds of firms shows up clearly in basic data on corporate profits. Almost all firms in the U.S. economy earned an average rate of profit during the late 1950s and 1960s of a little more than eight percent per year on capital assets. Firms which were very large *and* which operated in industries dominated by a few firms earned average profit rates of 10.8 percent on capital assets. Firm size, by itself, or industry structure, by itself, didn't matter; profit rates in those cases hovered around the eight percent level. Only if a firm was *both* large *and* shared a "concentrated" industrial structure could it achieve a higher profit level (Edwards, 1979).

---

*I shall refer in all the subsequent discussions to "productive" work and "productive" operations when talking about the ba•ic tasks of producing goods and services—the non-supervisory workers who are counted as "production workers" in government data.

We call those powerful firms "core" firms.

During the period from 1900 through the 1930s, after the first wave of mergers from 1898 to 1902 had created a pool of very large firms, giant corporations tried to use their size and power to control workers in a wide variety of ways—breaking strikes with ethnic workers, using complicated job titles and incentive schemes to pit workers against each other, encouraging craft unions to compete with nascent industrial union movements, relying on arbitrary promotional schemes to push workers into competition for foremen's promotional favors. When the industrial union movement crested and finally broke through employer opposition in the Depression, workers focused much of their protest on some of these "arbitrary" uses and abuses of employers' power. They demanded a rationalization of wage and promotional systems. Once employers began to accept the permanent existence of industrial unions (and World War Two enforced the discipline of war-time cooperation on both the corporations and the unions), a much more structured system of production emerged in many industries as the joint product of large corporate flexibility and large union power. Since those structures seemed to moderate workers' opposition and militance, many other employers—particularly those employing white-collar workers—copied these new systems of rationalized wage and fringe payments, promotion by seniority and experience, and advancement over time. Technological change

Photo: Robert Gumpert

conformed to and helped support the crystallization of these new job structures, permitting wage advancements in structured shops and offices, and eliminating jobs of production workers to save on the costs of these increasingly expensive arrangements. We call the jobs which resulted "primary jobs."

Smaller firms—those which we call "peripheral" (in contrast to "core")—could not match the changes in job structures which large employers were institutionalizing. This led to an increasingly sharp *divergence* between the character of jobs in competitive industries and small firms—like the garment industry, food processing, and wood processing in manufacturing and small offices and retail trade in the service sectors—and those in some parts of core-firm production. The small firms continued traditional systems of production, featuring labor-intensive systems, low wages, little room for advancement, and little margin for union victories. We call these kinds of jobs "secondary" jobs.

Large firms did not organize all sectors of their productive operations along the lines of the new internal structures, however, since they were sometimes able to save money and avoid union influence by retaining secondary organizations. In the tobacco industry, for example, the companies' success in beating the infant industrial union of tobacco workers in 1947-1948 permitted a continuation of the relatively lower wages and insecure job systems which had dominated tobacco work since the late 19th century. Though tobacco firms and steel firms have similar industrial characteristics, workers' job privileges and security in the two industries differ substantially as a result of the differential power of workers in those industries. Steel workers enjoy much higher wages and much better security as a result. And their relative power has helped promote an increasingly structured "internal labor market" since the 1930s.

Core firms operate many "primary" production operations, in short, even though they also retain some secondary operations. Peripheral firms find it extremely difficult to duplicate those systems because of their firm and industry characteristics—even when, as in the case of the garment industry—an industrial union represents their workers. The result is a sharp distinction between the characteristics of *primary* jobs and *secondary* jobs.

One other distinction is important for our analysis. In the 19th and early 20th centuries, workers developed technical skills and general productive knowledge through the *craft* system of apprenticeship. During the early 20th century, when corporations sought to free themselves from their dependence on craft workers, they began to construct alternate paths to technical skill and general competence, *37* building private vocational systems and encouraging technical institutes providing engineering skills. This led directly to the proliferation of general technical training through colleges, universities, and vocational institutes.

By the 1950s, these alternate paths to professional and technical skills were firmly rooted in educational institutions outside of the firm; the site of advanced skills training had shifted, in other words, from internal craft systems to colleges and universities. (Among other advantages to large corporations, the public shared the costs of training workers in colleges and universities through their tax dollars.) Increasingly, professional and technical jobs in large corporations (and other voluntary and public organizations) were located in separate parts of the organization, with different job ladders and ports-of-entry, relying on different kinds of skills and offering different kinds of rewards.

Small firms provide few of these jobs. Large organizations provide most of them. This divergence between jobs requiring more *general* skills and those requiring *routine* skills has led, in our view, to an increasingly sharp distinction among primary jobs between what we call "independent primary" jobs, in which workers have some (relative) autonomy and independence in their work; and "subordinate primary" jobs in which workers execute routine tasks strictly according to rule and the commands of their supervisors.

With these distinctions, it is possible to summarize our analysis of the main kinds of work in the U.S. economy. Below are listed these segments along with a brief characterization of the kinds of jobs within them and the labor markets feeding them.

■ *Independent primary* jobs: Technical, professional, managerial, and craft jobs; requiring some general skills and problem-solving abilities; high pay with some job security; rewards to personal characteristics of initiative and general analytic ability. Technical and professional jobs fed by labor markets beginning with the formal education screening process and then reproduced through screening process based both on credentials and work experience. Craft jobs still fed through apprenticeship systems.

■ *Subordinate primary* jobs: Decent pay and substantial job security; low general skill requirements; some skills learned on the job through experience; authority relations and internal job structures very important fulcrum for corporate administration of production process and individuals' personal advancement. Workers get such jobs through personal contacts as much as through formal labor market processes, and advancement comes much more easily through internal promotion than job-shopping in the external labor market.

■ *Secondary* jobs: In small firms or small shops/offices of large firms; low pay; few skills required; no opportunity for advancement; virtually no inducements for workers to remain on the job. Jobs filled through casual and virtually random general labor market shape-ups and advertisement. (Employment offices also feed workers into these jobs.)

What are the relative sizes of these three segments? Using data from the 1970 Census to estimate their relative size, we reach several conclusions. Of all those counted as "economically active" in the 1970 Census, 92 percent were employed and 8 percent were self-employed. Table 1 provides a complete distribution of the 92 percent who were employed among the three main segments identified by the analysis of labor market structure discussed in the preceding paragraphs:

Table 1
The Distribution of Employment, 1970

	Number of Employed Workers (in millions)	Percent of Total Employment
Independent Primary Jobs	22.466	32.5%
Subordinate Primary Jobs	21.144	30.6
Secondary Jobs	25.541	36.9
	69.151	100.0%

SOURCE: Data from *1970 Census of Population.* Definitions and compilation from Gordon (1980a).

What is striking about these figures, at first glance, is the large size of each of the three segments—none is an insignificant or insubstantial fraction of the total labor force—and the continuing size and relative importance of the secondary segment—the largest of the three and accounting for more than a third of the entire labor force.

The full implications of this analysis will be summarized in a following section. For now, four main conclusions seem most important.

First, both blue-collar and white-collar jobs are important in all three segments. Both garment work and the typing pool exemplify secondary work. Both steel work and book-keeping jobs typify subordinate primary jobs. Both electricians and doctors illustrate the **39** independent primary segment. In the data for the 1970 census, all three segments are divided between blue-collar and white-collar jobs in roughly comparable proportions. Table 2 provides these distributions:

Table 2
The Distribution of Factory and Office Employment, 1970[a]

	Blue-Collar Employment		White-Collar Employment	
	Number (in millions)	Percent of Total	Number (in millions)	Percent of Total
Independent Primary Jobs	7.094	29.0%	15.370	35.1%
Subordinate Primary Jobs	6.820	27.8	14.324	32.8
Secondary Jobs	10.584	43.1	14.042	32.1
	24.498	100.0%	43.736	100.0%

a) The total figures exclude those tabulated as agricultural employees and unpaid household employees.

SOURCE: Data from *1970 Census of Population*. Definitions and compilations from Gordon (1980a).

Second, the analysis of segmentation helps clarify some of the important differences between private and public employment. Public jobs are also distributed among the three segments. The difference in the distribution, however, is that more public jobs are independent primary jobs—obviously reflecting the large concentration of teaching and health professionals and technicians in the public sector—and that correspondingly fewer are secondary workers—also partly reflecting community and union pressure for minimally decent pay in lower-level public jobs. See Table 3 for these distributions.

Third, the principal determinants of the existence of these differences among segments lie in the characteristics of *firms* and the *job systems* they employ, not in the characteristics of different workers. Workers in the subordinate primary and secondary segments differ remarkably little in terms of skills, for example; those in the former segment have simply been lucky enough to land jobs providing higher wages and more structured advancement opportunities (Gordon, 1980a).

Fourth, the structures defining jobs within each of the segments are *not* very flexible, *not* easily adjusted to changing labor market conditions or labor supply proportions. The historical processes through which these divergent conditions emerged have meant that firms cannot easily change the ways in which they organize production

Table 3
The Distribution of Public and Private Employment, 1970

	Private-Sector Employment		Public-Sector Employment	
	Number (in millions)	Percent of Total	Number (in millions)	Percent of Total
Independent Primary Jobs	17.885	30.8%	4.581	41.3%
Subordinate Primary Jobs	17.372	29.9	3.772	34.0
Secondary Jobs	22.801	39.3	2.740	24.7
	58.058	100.0%	11.093	100.0%

SOURCE: Data from *1970 Census of Population.* Definitions and compilations from Gordon (1980a).

or hire and promote workers.

Two examples illustrate this general point:

■ One study of welders in a shipbuilding yard found that the firm could have saved money on welders by hiring skilled welders from outside the firm rather than training them through internal apprenticeship systems. The firm would have needed to pay higher wages to welders than it was currently paying, however, because of the higher external wage. The rigidity of its internal wage structure meant that those higher wages to welders would have to be translated into higher wages for every other production worker. The savings on welder training costs they might have realized could not be generalized because of the interdependence between welders' wages and all other wages within the firm (Ryan, 1977).

■ In the computer business, the distinction between the independent primary segment and the subordinate primary segment is illustrated by the difference in job tasks and skill requirements between "systems analysts" and "processing programmers." Over the past 15 years, computer firms have encountered substantial problems whenever they sought to downgrade the tasks of individual systems analysts' jobs because systems analysts have clear and unyieldingly high expectations about the quality of their work. As a result, they have often been forced to restructure the operations of an entire shop completely, changing the organization of work tasks from top to bottom, in order to save money on systems analysts' jobs; their employees' expectations limited their freedom to make small changes and forced them to make major ones. Once the distinction between systems analysis and *41* programming took root in the 1950s and early 1960s, firms were caught in a web of their own creation (Kraft, 1977; Greenbaum, 1979).

Regional Investment and Disinvestment

The preceding analysis has clear implications for the analysis of forces affecting the supply of different kinds of jobs— both "good jobs" and "poor jobs"; these implications will be elaborated in the final section of this chapter. But State policymakers must be concerned not only with the structure of available employment but also with its location. What forces account for the geographic distribution of "good jobs"? In particular, what can we learn about the sources of the recently accelerating shift of employment to the Sunbelt?[5]

Many media accounts treat the flow of jobs to the Sunbelt as a recent phenomenon, beginning in the late 1960s. In fact, the rise of the Sunbelt began during and immediately after World War Two. Studies of manufacturing location during the 1950s and 1960s all noted the most important difference between pre-War and post-War patterns: there had been a sudden shift to the South and Southwest during the 1940s.

What accounted for this shift? One could hardly attribute it to the energy crisis of 1974. There had not yet been a flood of older people to the sunshine. What had changed?

Photo: Earl Dotter/ALEC

I have argued elsewhere that critical changes in the geographic pattern of firm location have flowed historically from corporate efforts to find new ways of gaining more control over their employees and escaping from mounting worker unrest (Gordon, 1978, and 1980b).

One significant moment in this history came at the very end of the 19th century. Firms had been locating in the downtown factory districts of the largest industrial cities like New York, Philadelphia, Chicago, and other new Midwestern cities. During the 1880s and 1890s, workers' protests grew rapidly, spilling into the streets of the central city factory districts. The factories and workers' housing districts were so densely packed that "strike fevers" seemed to spread like contagious diseases. Increasingly, employers began to long for an escape from the central cities in order to avoid these disruptions.

The merger movement of 1898-1902 created firms of sufficient scale and assets to afford such moves. What were then called "industrial satellite suburbs" (such as Gary, Indiana) began springing up on the outskirts of the largest manufacturing cities. For the first time in the history of the United States, manufacturing employment began growing more rapidly in the "rings" of large cities than in the "centers." The decentralization of manufacturing had begun.

One cannot attribute this early dispersal of factories to the early development of the truck, since all transportation economists agree that the truck was not a viable freight substitute for the railroad until the 1920s. Nor can one attribute it to new land-intensive technologies like the assembly line which placed a new premium on less expensive land in the suburbs; there is no evidence that the technologies used in the suburbs were more land-intensive, and there is even some evidence suggesting that the opposite tendency prevailed.

My own argument turns conventional interpretations on their head, and suggests a substantially different view of manufacturing decentralization. Rather than accepting the traditional notion that the truck and new technologies encouraged and permitted the movement of factories out of the central cities, I would argue that employers' initial flight from labor unrest called forth the development of the truck and eventually permitted the development of more land-intensive technologies.

Once the movement to the satellite suburbs began, of course, the general pattern of urban investment and disinvestment began to structure the satellite suburbs into the system. Suburban plants were more modern and often more efficient simply because they were newer. Employment continued to grow rapidly on the outskirts of the largest cities. Central business districts became more and more **43** specialized in office and service functions. Coupled with the end to suburban annexation at the turn of the century, the manufacturing decentralization helped create increasing political fragmentation, with metropolitan areas becoming patchwork quilts of overlapping political jurisdictions. The titles of two noted books about this era in metropolitan development, Robert Woods' *1400 Governments* (1959) and Robert Fogelson's *The Fragmented Metropolis* (1967), evoke this pattern of increasing fragmentation.

The industrial union movement of the 1930s threw a monkey-wrench into that pattern. The unions were forced to develop industrial strategies to overcome the isolation of workers in industrial plants and the divisions which fragmented patterns of industrial locations created. Once the CIO unions succeeded in linking up and uniting these dispersed groups of workers, employers lost a critical advantage they had held and exploited for nearly 40 years. Growing evidence suggests that they made another critical decision—wherever and however possible, they would begin creating the possibility for movement away from the regions where workers had achieved the greatest strength.

World War Two proved to be a turning point. During the War, the federal government helped subsidize billions of dollars of new plant construction and infrastructural development. Much of it was located in the South and Southwest, certainly a far higher proportion than the previous proportions of total industrial capital investment in those areas. After the War, the federal government turned much of that plant and equipment over to private corporations. A sudden and significant shift in the geographic distribution of industrial capital had been achieved. Particularly after the passage of the Taft-Hartley Act in 1947, with its proscription of secondary boycotts and sanction for State right-to-work laws, large corporations had a new leg up on the industrial unions. Increasingly during the post-War years, they were able to plan plants and output expansion with a careful eye to the relative militance of Northern (unionized) workers and the relative quiescence of Southern (non-unionized) workers.

Once again, these initial geographic shifts were frozen into infrastructural steel and concrete. Sunbelt capital and infrastructure, since it was newer, was in many cases more efficient. Disproportionate infrastructural investment was flowing to the Sunbelt. The older capital of the Northwest was not being maintained, both in the central cities and in the suburban factory belts established after the turn of the century.

The impact of this differential pattern of regional investment and disinvestment was not immediately noticed, of course, because continuing post-War prosperity permitted the continued utilization of capital structures and equipment of both *more* and *less* recent vintage. It was only during the late 1960s, when corporate profit margins began to narrow and foreign competition became more threatening, that firms began to shift plant utilization more rapidly. The acceleration of the movement of manufacturing employment to the Sunbelt coincided with the growing uncertainty in the economy around 1968-69. But that accelerated movement would itself have been nearly impossible if it had not built upon and taken advantage of the longer-term construction of an industrial base and infrastructure in the Sunbelt states.

As with the earlier discussion of labor market segmentation, this discussion of regional investment and disinvestment will be more fully applied to a discussion of current State employment problems in a subsequent section. Two important points seem most important as background for that later synthesis.

First, this account places critical emphasis on the importance of private and public *infrastructural* investment as the *foundation* for the growth of manufacturing within and among geographic regions. Significant shifts in the geographic location of manufacturing activity cannot take place without significant changes in the historic pattern of industrial investment and infrastructural facilities. Those decisions do not come through gradual evolution and accretion; rather, they reflect qualitative and purposeful decisions by powerful decision-makers with access to the capital assets necessary to launch new patterns of investment. Neither the decentralization of manufacturing at the turn of the century nor the first construction of Sunbelt capital during and after World War Two occurred by accident or as the product of inadvertent "exogenous" shifts in people's preferences. Nor were these shifts induced by the marginal enticements of State and local tax subsidies and incentives. Rather, these historic shifts in the pattern of capital investment reflected decisive steps by private and public decision-makers to mobilize capital resources in new directions. If one wanted to have some opposite effect on the geographic distribution of economic resources, one would have to mobilize private and public decisions affecting capital resources on a comparable scale.

Second, this account suggests that such shifts are not likely to reflect historically and politically "neutral" decisions, guaranteed to benefit all citizens in equal proportions. I have argued that corporate efforts to flee from workers' growing power have played a critical role in channeling new patterns of capital investment.

In order to make room for a novel and potentially controversial argument, I have undoubtedly simplified the complex of historic   *45* forces which paved the way to new patterns of capital investment. But it remains clear, in my view, that corporate efforts to achieve new leverage in their continuing battles with their employees played a decisive role. As far as their workers were concerned—not to mention the workers' families and surrounding communities—the corporate decision to change venue was hardly benevolent. Those corporate policies arose from corporate decisions to take advantage of their access to capital funds in order to improve their bargaining power with their workers (and their unions). The decline of relative union power during the late 1950s and 1960s, as well as the difficult bargaining position in which industrial unions now find themselves, bears partial witness to the importance of these historic developments.

More Than Just An Impending Recession

A third piece of analysis is necessary to complete the background for an alternative account of the sources of current State employment problems. This piece of analysis builds from a concern with the character of the economic instability which presently plagues the U.S. (and world) economy.[6]

Many conventional economists and public officials continue to talk as if the current dynamic of recession and recovery is "more of the same," susceptible to the same kinds of macro-economic instruments as the business cycles of the 1950s and 1960s. But evidence belies that complacence. There are mounting signs that the kind of macro-economic dynamic currently driving the economies of the advanced countries differs sharply from the pattern of stable growth and continued prosperity in the first two post-War decades.

One piece of evidence is obvious. The "trade-off" between inflation and unemployment has experienced virtually complete transformation. We used to get less inflation with greater unemployment, and vice versa. Now we get more inflation and more unemployment than we have had for years, without anything like the obvious inverse relationship which characterized them during the 1950s and 1960s.

Other indications draw more attention in the business press than in the public media.

First, business investment in real "structures and equipment" has been stagnating since 1976. One can compare the rate of real business investment since the trough of the recession in 1974-75 with investment at comparable points in recoveries during other business cycles in the post-War years. As both *Business Week* and *Fortune* have observed several times in special issues, that comparison shows that the business sector is investing at a far *slower* rate than during any other post-War "recovery." Corporate profits are high and their capital funds are very

47

Photo: Earl Dotter/ALEC

liquid, but they're buying up companies and engaging in commodities and currency speculation rather than building factories and machines.

Second, most business analysts agree that corporate investment is lagging at least partly because of corporate fears about the political and economic climate in their traditional turfs. As a result of threats to their continued privileges, corporations have been moving their capital overseas at an accelerating rate. The symptom is contraction in traditional industrial locations. The evidence lies in the accelerating expansion to the Sunbelt and the extraordinary increases in U.S. corporate overseas investment since the mid-1960s.

Third, the stagnation of investment and the rapid redistribution of investment have contributed to a growing unpredictability and instability in world trade. Traditional trading patterns have been unsettled. The world market seems more and more like a kaleidoscope.

Fourth, this has contributed to precarious monetary instability in the world economy. The value of the dollar has plummeted. Other currencies are fluctuating rapidly. Eurodollar market speculation remains unchecked. Third World debt to the World Bank and other banks remains a critical problem and a potential source of international instability. Most international financial authorities admit that there are no easy answers to these sources of uncertainty.

All of these signs, taken together, suggest an economy which is not behaving "normally" at all and which cannot easily "recover" from these destabilizing dynamics. They point to some increasingly evident signs that the economy's private mechanisms for investment and production are not working as they did during the 1950s and 1960s, that some kind of collective private and public action will be necessary to reverse a dynamic of growing instability.

This should not be surprising if we view the world economy from a historical perspective. There have been successive stages of alternating prosperity and stagnation since the 18th century. It appears that one of the main sources of those alternating cycles has been the effect of concentrated infrastructural and commercial investment after a period of stagnation and before a period of sustained prosperity. Around the turn of the century and again after World War Two, heavy and concentrated investment in the infrastructure—particularly in transportation and communication networks—helped fuel the new waves of prosperity and rapid investment during the succeeding decades. Inevitably, the extra fuel provided by those investment episodes burned itself out and the economy was caught in another ebb of stagnation and increasing economic uncertainty.

The lesson of those earlier episodes seems fairly clear. A new level of

collective organization has been necessary on each occasion to wrest the economy from the dynamic of spreading stagnation. At the turn of the century, corporate mergers and the intervention of the New York banks provided that impetus. During and after World War Two, federal discipline and capital funding helped rescue the economy from the slough of the Depression. If these historic parallels have any meaning for the current period, they suggest that some kind of active and guided intervention will prove necessary to help guide the economy back onto a stable track.

The question raised by those lessons, of course, is *whose intervention in whose interests?* Multinational corporations have been acting in their own interests and have apparently concluded that their own interests are best served by a rapid movement of capital to other countries. It is not at all clear that public policies to deal with State employment problems can rely on multinational corporations—or the largest domestic corporations—to move in directions which will serve any other interests beyond their own. This suggests that State governments cannot easily assume that subsidies and support for private business in their own backyards will either have the kinds of effects they have had in the 1950s and 1960s or exert sufficient influence, on their own, to alter the trajectory of corporate responses to a continuing international economic crisis.

Why Aren't There Enough "Good Jobs" —A Structural Interpretation   Our structural analysis of employment problems has been developed in three stages.

■ The first section argued that the segmentation of jobs has created important inflexibilities in the U.S. labor market. Many jobs do not reward individual workers' initiative or skills and cannot easily be changed. Other jobs—what we call primary jobs—provide opportunities for decent incomes and advancement. Because of the rigidities of job structures in primary segments, however, the basic supply of those jobs, not the skills or attitudes of workers in them, determine their availability. Changes in the basic supply of primary jobs, not changes in the supply characteristics of workers, would be necessary to increase the number of "good jobs."

■ The second section reviewed the history and dynamics of urban and regional growth in the United States. The analysis suggested that structural forces have more influence on regional economic fortunes than quantitative variations in factors like taxes and energy costs. Major shifts in firm location have followed from corporate efforts to evade workers' control. Those evasions have triggered dramatic **49** changes in the flow of capital for modernization and infrastructural investment. Those capital shifts, in turn, have generated changes in the relative "efficiency" of firms in differing regions. One could not influence the relative efficiency of firms in different regions, according to this argument, without first affecting the character of infrastructural capital investments among regions.

■ The third section suggested that the current crisis of growth and investment is itself a structural crisis—whose resolution will eventually require the kinds of massive and coordinated interventions which finally fostered recovery from the Depression of the 1930s. Special breaks, subsidies, and incentives provided to business on an uncoordinated basis will not be enough to stimulate greater economic activity. Instead, direct and coordinated intervention on a substantial scale will probably be required to affect the current climate of economic instability and to provide sufficient encouragement for further investment and growth.

These arguments can be combined, finally, to provide a structural answer to our recurrent question about the supply of "good jobs." The answer in its simplest form is straightforward: *The economy does not provide an adequate supply of "good jobs" because the structure of the modern economy, and particularly its domination by several hundred giant corporations, neither promotes nor permits the generation of "good jobs."*

This simple conclusion can be developed through several separate steps of elaboration.

The Definition of Good Jobs. In Chapter 1, we defined a "good job" as one which provides adequate wages and fringe benefits; job security and stable employment; decent working conditions; and opportunities for both advancement and control. Most influential discussions of "good jobs," like Ginsberg's 1977 article, collapse this definition into a one-dimensional wage criterion, but we have learned that a complex of factors affect the quality of employment; wages are only one reflection of job quality.

Our analysis above suggests that a working definition of "good jobs" should be based on the structural characteristics which permit individual success and advancement. It would seem to make sense, therefore, to define "good jobs" as *primary* jobs and "poor jobs" as *secondary* jobs precisely in order to emphasize the roots of job quality in the economic structures which influence the organization of production.

Are our observations on the separate dimensions of employment problems from Chapter 1 consistent with this equation of "good jobs" with primary jobs and "poor jobs" with secondary jobs?

■ Decent employment income would require, according to most economists, a regular wage which on a full-time basis provides enough for a household to support itself at levels above or equal to the BLS "lower-than-moderate" budget standard. Roughly one-third of U.S. workers are employed in jobs paying less than this wage level (Gordon, 1977). This seems to fit with the estimate in this chapter that roughly one-third of U.S. employees in 1970 held secondary jobs.

■ Employment security essentially requires that workers be able to work full-time, year-round if they choose. Only two-thirds of U.S. employees work full-time, year-round. While more than ten million workers have part-time jobs because they prefer part-time work, there are probably an equivalent number of secondary workers—particularly older ones—who work full-time at their jobs simply because they have learned that job shopping is unlikely to improve their work prospects (Gordon, 1980a; Edwards, 1979). Thus, our association of "poor jobs" which expose workers to actual or potential employment insecurity with secondary jobs also seems consistent with the aggregate data.

■ Indecent working conditions are more difficult to measure because data are not easily available on the "health-and-safety characteristics" of different jobs. A recent study by Luft (1978) found a substantial correlation between those who suffer occupational disease or injury and those who experience poverty for substantial periods of time. These are apparently workers whose fringe benefits or access to insurance is sufficiently limited that they get trapped in the vicious circle of low incomes and poor health. Luft's data seem roughly consistent with the notion that those in secondary jobs bear the greatest risk of real loss of earning capacity from indecent working conditions.

■ Only one-quarter of the U.S. labor force belongs to unions. This obviously does not mean that three-quarters of the labor force work at "poor jobs" providing little job control. Indeed, many large employers have improved working conditions precisely to prevent the spread of unionization. What seems apparent, from the available literature on segmentation, is that (a) *independent primary* workers attain some control over their working conditions because of the importance of their positions and their particular skills—whether or not they belong to unions; (b) that blue-collar workers in the *subordinate primary* segment have been able to take advantage of the room for union influence which the structure of their jobs permits, while white-collar workers (at least in the private sector) have not yet followed that path; while (c) even unionized workers in the secondary sector, like garment workers, are rarely able to translate their union power into full job *51* control or decent working conditions. (See Kerr, 1979, for a detailed analysis of union impact in the primary and secondary segments.) It seems appropriate to conclude that the structure of job segments is at least as important as unionization by itself in establishing the framework within which workers may or may not acquire significant influence over their working and living conditions.

In short, it seems feasible to treat "primary jobs" as "good jobs." In 1970, as we saw above, 63.1 percent of wage-and-salary employees worked in "good jobs." The remaining 36.9 percent of wage-and-salary employees worked in secondary jobs, or what we can call "poor jobs."*

The Barriers to Good Jobs. This definition clearly indicates that we need to pursue the issue of the supply of "good jobs" in two steps: Why can't secondary employers provide "good jobs" instead of "poor" ones? And why don't primary employers provide more "good jobs" than they do?

The segmentation literature provides fairly clear answers to the first question. Many secondary employers are small firms in competitive industries. Their small assets make it difficult for them to finance or afford the kinds of improvements in machinery and job structures which would permit higher wages, greater job security, and better working conditions. Perhaps more important, the continuing competition to which they are exposed tends to keep profit margins very low—holding firms very close to the edge of survival. Their thin profit margins make higher wages and greater employment security problematic, much less the kinds of changes in machinery and job structures which would reproduce primary working conditions over the longer term.[7]

In other words, most secondary employers cannot provide good jobs because their firm and industry structure precludes it. Small firms still exhibit the kinds of working conditions which were nearly universal in the late 19th and early 20th centuries. "Good jobs" are better today because large firms and large unions have combined to create a new kind of firm and job structure which permit "good jobs." Small firms in competitive industries are essentially barred from that kind of qualitative transformation.

---

*The techniques used to categorize workers are somewhat complicated. Gordon (1980a) presents a full description of the method. It essentially relies on an industry-by-occupation analysis of job characteristics, separating between core and peripheral industries on the one hand and between jobs providing room for the application of workers' skills (or on-the-job skill acquisition) and those neither rewarding nor offering skills development on the other. In both cases, the method of categorization relies on the characteristics of jobs—of industries and occupations—and not on the characteristics, like race, sex, age, or schooling, of workers who hold those jobs.

The second question requires a somewhat more extended answer. Three points seem essential.

First, many large firms find it uneconomical to provide more "good jobs" because it costs more to hire new workers than to extend the hours of current employees. Their fixed costs of providing decent wages and working conditions—embodied in fringe benefits, taxes, and insurance payments—have shifted the calculus of employment toward hiring current employees for longer hours rather than hiring new employees for shorter hours. This explains why many manufacturing firms make such heavy use of overtime, and why average hours worked per week in manufacturing have remained constant during the post World War Two period while average hours per week in some other industries, such as retail trade, have continued to fall.

Second, many large firms actually operate many secondary operations when and where they can. Large clerical employers maintain "poor jobs" in their typing pools and office maintenance operations. Some large manufacturing firms, like electrical, tobacco, and some textile manufacturers, offer essentially secondary employment because they have been able to tap groups of workers whose personal characteristics—foreign workers or women—or their geographic location—Southern workers or isolated undocumented workers in large ghettos—have undercut those workers' ability to translate firm and industry characteristics into "good jobs." If and when the unionizing drive against J.P. Stevens succeeds, it will be interesting to observe what kinds of changes in job structure occur and how rapidly those changes take place.

There is a third point which is at once more important and more difficult to state persuasively. Essentially, large employers don't want to provide many good jobs *even when they can.* Large employers have invested billions of dollars since the turn of the century in machines and management techniques which improve their control over their workers (Braverman, 1974; Edwards, 1979). Workers have responded by seeking better working conditions and more reliable and predictable systems of hiring, promotion, and work supervision. To the degree that large firms have been forced to accept this increased worker influence, they have moved to reduce their dependence on such "powerful" workers. Large corporations have continually undercut professional workers' status and control, for example, whenever they could afford such changes (Kraft, 1977; Greenbaum, 1979). And large manufacturers continually substitute machines for workers when the technology and investment funds are available. Wherever possible, in short, large firms tend to limit the number of "primary workers" they hire for any given level of labor demand (through more overtime and fewer new hires), and they tend to reduce their aggregate demand for labor through automation and job reorganization when those steps are consistent with other firm objectives. Large corporations are interested in both efficiency *and* control, in other words, and large firms are likely to display a consistent preference, given the choice, for employing fewer (relatively) powerful workers.

The structural argument emerges: The character of competition and the vulnerability of small firms makes it virtually impossible for many secondary employers to "up-grade" the quality of the jobs they provide. And while large firms at least have the potential for providing "good jobs," the logic and requirements of control in large corporations lead them to minimize the number of "good jobs" they provide at any given level of output and investment. The structure of competition and the power of large corporations, in these respects, place stringent limits on the supply of "good jobs."

Evidence for the Structural Argument. Because this structural argument has emerged relatively recently, few studies have yet marshaled or analyzed the kinds of data which would be necessary to test these structural hypotheses fully. There are some fragmentary pieces of evidence, nonetheless, which provide strong preliminary support for this explanation of the paucity of "good jobs."

It is fairly clear, first of all, that the problem stems from the basic structure of the economy and not from the recent years of stagnation and instability. We can look at the period of rapid economic growth between 1948 and 1968, before "stagflation" emerged. During those years, the adult civilian population (and therefore the potential labor force) grew by 30 million. If we eliminate the growth in total employment which was due either to direct government employment or to the employment-generating effects of government expenditures, it turns out that private-sector-generated employment grew by only 2 million over those 20 years. Even when the economy is growing rapidly, in other words, the tendency for many firms to *reduce* employment nearly outweighs the additional employment created by continuing growth.

Moreover, no matter how we measure the distinction between "good" and "poor jobs," it appears that most of the new jobs created by the private economy over the past decades have been "poor jobs," not "good ones." Ginzberg (1977) reaches striking conclusions by applying his earnings criterion to employment changes between 1950 and 1976. He estimates that private sector employment expanded by 25.3 million between 1950 and 1976 (he does not subtract employment generated by government expenditures). Of those new jobs he estimates that 18.2

million were "poor jobs" and only 7.1 were "good jobs"—a ratio of more than 2.5 "poor jobs" for every one "good job." In contrast, he estimates that of the 9 million increase in government employment, there were two new "good jobs" for every one new "poor job." Of the total increase in employment of 34.3 million over those 26 years, only 7.1 were "good jobs" provided by the private sector—a ratio of barely more than one in five. Based on these data, Ginzberg concludes that "we cannot assume that the private sector will be able to create adequate numbers of new jobs." His conclusions about the likelihood of the private sector's generating adequate numbers of new *"good jobs"* flow even more emphatically.

Neither of these first pieces of evidence draws directly on data about firms. This is a substantial disadvantage, since much of the structural argument hinges on differences among firms and not among industries.

Employment analysts have recently paid considerable attention to a new source of data about firm employment patterns developed and analyzed by David Birch and associates at MIT (1979). Many have taken great solace from the Birch data, because they seem superficially to indicate that the private sector still generates millions of jobs through vibrant and dynamic entrepreneurial initiative. Birch's emphasis on the "vitality and job generating powers" of small and independent firms seems to provide substantial encouragement for advocates of free enterprise and the power of competition.

These superficial readings of the Birch data are misplaced. A closer reading suggests, as Birch himself comes close to admitting, that these detailed data on more than five million firms provide relatively striking confirmation of the structural argument outlined in the preceding pages. All of the following facts come from Birch (1979).

■ There is an enormous amount of gross employment change in the U.S. economy. Each year, there is a net loss of roughly eight percent of total employment as a result of firm "deaths" or employment contractions. This means that we must pay careful attention not only to the forces which create jobs but also to the sources of continuing job loss.

■ A very high proportion of net job creation in the economy is generated by small "independent" firms—firms with 20 or fewer employees which are not owned by larger firms. Over the entire period analyzed between 1969 and 1976, there were 6.8 million net jobs created in the private sector. Of those jobs, 67 percent were generated by firms with 20 or fewer employees and 52 percent by "independent" firms with 20 or fewer employees. By contrast, firms with more than *55*

100 employees accounted for only 18.5 percent of net employment change—even though they account for half of total employment. The table below compares these figures with the distribution of total employment in 1973 (based on Social Security data).

Table 4
Total Employment and Employment Growth

Firm Size[a]	Percent of Total Employment 1973	Percent of Net Employment Growth 1969-1976
0-20	24.3%	66.0%
21-100	25.9	15.5
101-500	24.3	5.2
500 plus	25.5	13.3
	100.0%	100.0%

a) The size categories for the distribution of *total* employment are actually 0-19; 20-99; 100-499; and 500+.

SOURCE: Total Employment—*Nation's Business,* 1978, p. 50; employment growth—Birch, 1979; p. 30.

■ Although small firms generate a large percentage of employment, they do not provide "good jobs." Other data show clearly that small establishments provide a disproportionate number of *secondary* jobs; on this basis, we can presumably assume that most small firms' jobs are "poor jobs."[8] Birch's data make clear, moreover, that the jobs generated by small independent firms also provide very unreliable employment since the firms themselves are extremely vulnerable to bankruptcy or layoffs:

■ Of all firms with 20 or fewer employees, 57.8 percent "died" during the seven years studied. Even though small firms grow, they also collapse with alarming frequency. Those who garner jobs with small firms enter at their own risk.

■ Even those small firms which manage to survive an initial period of incubation are no longer very likely to provide employment growth. Of those firms with 20 or fewer employees which had already survived for more than four years at the beginning of the period, only one-third produced net employment growth over the seven-year period.

■ Of all 1.2 million firms in the sample with 20 or fewer employees, only 82,396, or seven percent, sustained "large" employment growth over the growth years from 1969 through 1974. Many firms had some growth for shorter periods, but virtually none were able to generate sizable gains on a continuing basis.

■ In short, the firms which account for employment growth are very unlikely to provide a steady supply of stable jobs over time—regardless of the wages, working conditions, or job control provided in those jobs—simply because the economic condition of those firms is so precarious. To quote Birch's own conclusion:

> The dynamic, growing firm is the one that is frequently taking gambles, that is as likely as not to suffer severe downturns, and that is tough or wise enough to survive them. Having grown, it is just as likely to decline again in the future. In short, it is a banker's nightmare. [Even the stable firm that] minds its business and repays its loans in fact is offering a false sense of security, and is more likely than not to go out of business leaving the bank holding the bag.

■ While large firms are much more stable—only 23 percent of firms with more than 500 employees 'died" between 1969 and 1976—they do

not generate many jobs. Of firms with more than 500 employees and at least ten years' experience, only 35 percent showed a net increase in employment during the period, while 65 percent either died or contracted their total employment. Firms with more than 500 employees and either branches or subsidiaries—which obviously includes all of the 500 largest corporations in the U.S.—accounted for only ten percent of all net employment increase over the study period.

■ Perhaps more important, large corporations have been rapidly shifting their operations to areas where workers have much more difficulty sustaining influence over their jobs. (As Birch makes clear, these movements are not actual "migrations"—what workers would call "runaways"—but the relative expansion and contraction of branches and subsidiaries.) This effect can be demonstrated with a "shift-share" analysis of Birch's data. (Based on Appendix Table C in Birch, 1979.)

From 1969 to 1976, total employment grew in the Northeast region by only 411,000, in the North Central region by 1.674 million, and in the South and West combined by 4.673 million. What explains the disproportionate share of the Sunbelt in total employment growth? As Birch notes, services grew throughout the nation (and helped save the Northeast). The critical shift in employment took place in manufacturing, where the Northeast and North Central regions lost 710,000 total jobs in just seven years and the Sunbelt gained 335,000. Other job shifts followed from these.

If this was due to a more favorable climate in the Sunbelt for the small independent firms which accounted for so much employment growth, then we would expect that there would be a net "shift" to the Sunbelt of employment growth in small manufacturing firms—with those small independent firms generating many more jobs than one would expect if all regions shared equally in total national employment growth. It turns out, however, that this shift in small firms' growth rates had a relatively small effect. Small independent manufacturing employment grew at moderate rates throughout all four main regions. Over the full seven years, there was a net shift to the Sunbelt of only 88,000 manufacturing jobs in small independent firms.

In contrast, the Northeast and North Central regions suffered much larger shifts of large firm manufacturing away to the Sunbelt. If the Frostbelt regions had suffered merely their expected losses of manufacturing employment over the period, they would have lost 232,000 manufacturing jobs in firms with more than 100 employees with branches of subsidiaries. Instead, they lost a total of 710,000 jobs provided by large multiplant firms. This means that large firms (with 58 more than 100 employees and branches or subsidiaries) *shifted* 478,000 manufacturing jobs to the Sunbelt in just seven years—more than five times the shift attributable to the differential fortunes of small independent firms. As Birch also notes, this differential expansion does not reflect a shift of headquarters to the Sunbelt. In the South, for example, 72 percent of branch employment growth was controlled by firms headquartered in the Northeast or North Central region. Large multiplant firms chose, in other words, to shift their manufacturing investment to areas where they felt more comfortable.

Despite all this specific detail, the main contours of our analysis emerge fairly clearly. Small firms generate many jobs but few of those jobs are either "good jobs" or reliable sources of employment. Large firms provide relatively few jobs and, in addition, have been rapidly reallocating their resources to areas where workers have much more trouble ensuring decent working conditions. Birch's own conclusions confirm our analysis:

> It is no wonder that efforts to stem the tide of job decline have been so frustrating and largely unsuccessful. [On the one hand] the very spirit that gives [small firms] their vitality and job-generating powers is the same spirit that makes them unpromising partners for the development administrator. [On the other hand] the easier strategy of working with larger, 'known' corporations whose behavior is better understood will not be, and has not been, very productive. Few of the net new jobs generated in our economy are generated by this group. Furthermore, the larger corporations, using their financial strength, are the first to redistribute their operations out of declining areas into growing ones . . . There is no clear way out of this quandary.

Many State policymakers may be reluctant to accept these conclusions, but they flow naturally from our analysis. The private sector *cannot* generate an adequate supply of good jobs for two critical reasons: 1) Those firms who *could* provide "good jobs" do not generate much net employment over time and prefer to reduce their relative reliance on workers holding "good jobs." 2) Those firms which tend to provide net increases in employment in the economy are either too small or too unstable to provide "good jobs." As long as large corporations maintain the kind of economic control over basic investment which they currently possess, and as long as intense competition assaults smaller enterprises, the scarcity of "good jobs" seems destined to continue.

Footnotes to Chapter 2

1. For a neoclassical review of mainstream theories of wage and employment determination, see Rees (1979). For further developments of the points I make in criticism of that perspective (on its own terms), see Gordon (1972, Chapter 3).

2. There is remarkably little mainstream discussion of the supply of "good jobs" since few would recognize the legitimacy or the importance of the distinction between "good" and "poor" jobs in the first place. As a result, this inferential discussion of the logic of their analysis depends largely on my own application of the general discussion. For some essentially similar applications of the mainstream perspective to at least one employment problem, see Feldstein (1975).

3. For a general review of some of the principles upon which this kind of structural analysis builds, see Gordon (1972, Chapters 4-5) and Piore (1979).

4. The "segmentation" approach is developed in the following sources: Gordon (1972); Edwards, Reich, and Gordon (1975); Doeringer and Piore (1971); Piore (1975); and Gordon, Edwards, and Reich (1980). For surveys of some of the empirical evidence which supports the segmentation perspective, see Harrison and Sum (1978); Edwards (1979, Chapter 9); and Gordon (1980a).

5. This structural approach to regional development is developed in Alcaly and Mermelstein (1977); Tabb and Sawyers (1978); and Watkins and Perry (1979). For some supporting evidence, see Harrison and Hill (1978) and Watkins and Perry (1979).

6. Many of the basic points upon which this section relies are developed in Piore (1979) and Union for Radical Political Economics (1978).

7. Kieschnick (1979) reports data indicating that small businesses earn relatively high rates of profit in any given year. He presents those data in an effort to criticize the performance and the inefficiencies of larger firms. His argument is not inconsistent with the argument I am making in these sections. If we look at short-term rates of profit, many entrepreneurial firms, no matter how small, earn relatively high rates of profit for a time. Eventually, however, they either over-extend themselves and decline or are bought up by larger companies. Over the longer term, as Edwards (1979) shows and as I summarize the data above, large firms in concentrated industries are the only firms which achieve and sustain above-average rates of profit. As the data from Birch (1979) show—see the discussion in subsequent paragraphs in the text—small firms grow for short spurts and then decline. Their growth is often founded upon the low quality of the jobs they provide and the low wages they pay. Small firms in highly competitive industries, I conclude, cannot sustain much higher quality employment for long without structural changes in the conditions within which they operate.

8. For evidence on the association between small enterprises and secondary jobs, see Bluestone (1978); Bluestone, Murphy, and Stevenson (1973); and Harrison and Sum (1978).

3
TOWARD A "GOOD JOBS" POLICY

Many State policymakers favor a traditional "economic development strategy" not only because they think it will work, but also because they see no clear—and practical—alternative. In this chapter I outline two alternative approaches to the provision of more "good jobs"—what I call the "traditional" and the "community" approaches. I argue further that the "traditional" approach offers little promise of moderating State employment problems, while the "community" approach, however much it flies against the tradition of State economic development policy, holds a strong potential for helping provide more "good jobs" for workers throughout the country.

ALTERNATIVE POLICY APPROACHES This section briefly defines two alternative approaches to State economic development in general and to State employment problems in particular. It links those two approaches with the two main analytic perspectives on the sources of State employment problems discussed in the previous chapter.

The current and prevalent "economic development strategy" applies what can be called a "traditional" approach to economic problems. When something needs to be done, it seeks to develop policy instruments which will make it increasingly profitable for businesses to move in the directions desired by State policymakers. If the State wants more workers hired by businesses, then it will provide something like wage subsidies to firms to encourage them to substitute labor for capital. If it wants to encourage more business activity within its own boundaries, then it will seek to reduce some or all of the relative costs of doing business in that State in order to make the local economic environment more attractive to businesses.

The "traditional" approach relies on the simple assumption that States can accomplish their economic objectives by relying on the profit maximization of private sector firms. It presumes that it is possible to induce firm activities by shifting the relative profitability of different kinds of activities. It seeks *indirectly* to achieve an ultimate objective—moderating State economic or employment problems— **61** through policies which *directly* affect business costs and profits but do *not* directly affect workers' earnings, employment security, working conditions, or job control.[1]

The "traditional" approach assumes that firms will respond to policies which affect their relative costs and profitability in ways which ultimately benefit workers and ultimately lead to the desired employment objectives. This assumption depends on mainstream economic analysis in two important ways.

First, mainstream economic analysis, as we have already seen, assumes that any changes in the environment affecting firm costs will stimulate changes in firm activities. This reflects the presumption of continuous substitution at the margin—that any change will matter— and the assumption of equilibrium—that since firms had *already* made all previous necessary adjustments to changes in their environment, current shifts in their related costs will have clear and predictable

Photo: Earl Dotter/ALEC

effects. If one argued, in contrast, that many changes in the economic environment are not large enough to affect firm decisions and/or that firms are currently preoccupied with much more important adjustments, then the presumptions of the "traditional" approach would not appear to provide promising policy guides.

Second, mainstream analysis asserts that private sector activities based on profit-seeking individual firm decisions will always come closer to achieving desired social outcomes than any other kind of economic practice. The mainstream perspective argues that private businesses always tend toward efficient operations and therefore that everyone is likely to be better off, pending appropriate compensation for externalities and diseconomies, than from other approaches. But if we began to conclude that private profit-seeking business activities were either relatively inefficient or that the policies they executed in pursuit of their own profits actually conflicted with the objectives of others in the relevant communities, then States' *a priori* preferences for the "traditional" approach might also seem misplaced.

A "community" approach to State economic policy can be defined as one which seeks to promote community objectives *directly* through the development of community mechanisms for achieving those objectives without the constraint that profit-making businesses provide the medium for achieving such objectives. A "community" approach would seek to accomplish its objectives by acting directly toward those objectives, not by relying on businesses indirectly to accomplish them for the community. (I deliberately use the term "community," rather than "public" or "government," in order to emphasize the possibility and potential desirability of *private* non-profit mechanisms, rather than exclusively government, much less State or federal, control of such activities.) This approach does not seek opposition against small business as such. Rather, it proposes to pursue policy objectives directly, rather than pursuing them through the support of profits. If people currently operating small businesses could organize their activities in a way which directly supported articulated social objectives, they would benefit from the "community approach." What matters are the outcomes of policies, not the names of the organizations which help pursue them.

What might be the mechanisms through which a "community" approach would be applied? Pending further detail in Chapter 4, we can imagine a wide variety of possible mechanisms: government programs directly controlled by local or State governments; special community-elected boards controlling specific projects; producers or consumers' cooperatives aiming to accomplish specific economic objectives; or legally constituted non-profit community-based cor-   *63*

64

Photo: Robert Gumpert

porations with stipulated objectives. What matters, for the purposes of the ensuing discussion, is that such mechanisms be controlled by those for whom service is intended and that private profit not act as an intervening criterion affecting policy decisions. If the community seeks to profit from a given activity on a shared and equitable basis, then it would function as a "cooperative," with reward on the basis of need or direct contribution to desired program objectives, rather than as a private profit-making enterprise in which financial reward is determined on the basis of the previous distribution of wealth.

A preference for a "community" approach over a "traditional" approach would undoubtedly derive from some combination of two principal assumptions: (a) That "traditional" approaches will actually fail to accomplish the desired objectives; and/or (b) that it would make more sense to adopt policies which move *directly* toward accomplishing a set of objectives without also requiring that some public monies enrich private individuals through direct support of private profit.

The analysis developed in the preceding chapter would tend to support both of those assumptions.

■ Pro-business policies aimed at enlarging the quantity of "good jobs" available in the U.S. economy are likely to fail because the structure of the private economy makes it highly unlikely that private firms can or will provide more "good jobs."

■ Large corporations have sufficient economic dominance in the private economy that, if policymakers rely on them for accomplishing public objectives, those private corporations will exact a relatively high price in the form of substantial public support for their profits.

While the structural analysis developed in the preceding chapter suggests that the "traditional" approach has little promise and that corporations are likely to demand high returns for their cooperation with public objectives, it does not speak directly to the potential promise or effectiveness of "community" approaches themselves. The remainder of this chapter reviews some empirical evidence on the actual failures and ineffectiveness of "traditional" policy approaches in the recent past, and raises some arguments about the potential effectiveness of "community" approaches to improving the quantity of "good jobs."

DO "TRADITIONAL" APPROACHES ACTUALLY FAIL? As most States have pursued an "economic development strategy," embodying the "traditional" approach, for many years, we have ample evidence by which to test its relative effectiveness. I shall review evidence of one major strand of the "traditional" approach in order to provide the basis for further evaluation of the claim that this approach holds little promise.

Almost universally in recent years (as noted in the introduction), States and localities have sought to attract (or retain) businesses through special tax subsidies or breaks for business activity. The underlying assumption in those policies is that a shift toward relatively lower business taxes in a particular jurisdiction will make that location relatively more attractive for firms and that, on average, the rate of growth of business activity in that jurisdiction will increase.

There is no evidence that this strategy works. Indeed, there is substantial evidence that it is destined to fail. All available empirical evidence suggests that jurisdictional tax favors for business are unlikely to have any significant effect on the rate of business activity in that jurisdiction.

Roger Vaughan, in a companion volume in this series (Vaughan, 1979), reviews the issues embodied in state tax policy in some detail. As a result, a brief summary of available evidence is sufficient.

■ "There is little evidence that overall tax levels are too high" (Vaughan, 1979). The average U.S. business pays less than one percent of its total revenues in general business taxes.
■ "Counter to many myths, tax differences can be blamed for very little of the regional shifts in employment and for relatively little of the shifts from central cities to suburbs" (Vaughan, 1979). There are several reasons for this. State and local taxes are offset against federal taxes. Tax rates are low to begin with, so that variations have slight overall effect on business activity. More important, the costs of most other factors affecting business activity swamp the influence of variations in taxes. In short, as Vaughan concludes, "the overwhelming evidence from many studies of industrial location decisions suggests that firms select their region based upon broad criteria . . . Compared with these factors, state and local taxes shrink in importance . . . . The near unanimity of findings from all sources gives some credibility to the basic proposition that tax rates have not been important."

An extended discussion by Harrison and Kanter (1978) provides similar conclusions about the broader range of business incentives

67

which State governments have applied: "Our research indicates that neither conventional economic theory nor . . . empirical evidence provide much support for the popular belief that states can significantly affect industrial expansion, relocation or start-up with the kind of incremental incentives they have been using." But if these incentives have so little effect, why do States keep providing them? Harrison and Kanter suggest that businesses have taken advantage of current economic insecurity by seeking tax advantages which are insignificant in the context of their overall profitability. They quote one lobbyist, perhaps more candid than others, who suggested that while businesses would prefer an absolute reduction in corporate income taxes, "tax incentives will have to do."

There is no empirical basis for believing that significant variations in state tax incentives or corporate tax levels exert much influence on business locational behavior, improve the supply of "good jobs" in a State, or offset the opportunity costs of State revenues foregone. Many policymakers will find this counter-intuitive. Aren't favors to business, leading to reductions in their costs, bound to make at least some difference?

Based on the discussion in the preceding chapter, it should now be reasonably clear why these kinds of "traditional" approaches have so little effect.

There are substantial structural rigidities in the U.S. economy. Historically, major business decisions about regional location have flowed from basic shifts in the factors affecting control over their markets and workforces. Substantial shifts in the quality of infrastructure have followed from those major business shifts. State governments would be able to counter the effects of those structural changes only if they were able to mount policies with comparable structural effects.

Are there some policy options which would have such effects and nonetheless remain consistent with the "traditional" approach?

One set of policies which might eventually influence business locational behavior would involve efforts to affect the *quality of infrastructure* in a given State. Private businesses themselves prefer not to spend money on infrastructural investment simply because they cannot typically monopolize the returns to those investments. So public policies affecting the quality of available infrastructure would require direct government action, not support for business activities.

But even if States did pursue such policies, there is little likelihood that private firms would provide any greater quantities of "good jobs" merely because the quality of the supporting infrastructure had improved. Until one had transformed the competitiveness of some firms' environments, millions of enterprises will be incapable of providing "good jobs." And until one directly affects the way in which large corporations organize production, it is unlikely that a better infrastructure would make them any more liable to increase the number of "good jobs" they make available at any given level of production or investment.

There is one other set of "traditional" policies which States could pursue which might potentially affect business location decisions. In Chapter 2, I argued that critical turning points in the dynamics of urban and regional development in the U.S. have flowed from corporate efforts to escape from areas where workers began to increase their relative strength and ability to affect the quality of their work. A variety of studies have shown, for example, that the lower wages of workers in the South primarily reflect their weaker bargaining position, not their lower skills or the particular composition of industry which has located in the South (see, for instance, Malizia, 1976). This suggests that Frostbelt States might conceivably influence firms' location decisions, over the long run, if they both modernized the infrastructure in the Frostbelt *and* dramatically reduced workers' bargaining power—supporting right-to-work laws, or firms' efforts to decertify collective bargaining units, or business assaults on minimum wage laws, or corporate evasion of the statutory intentions of the National Labor Relations Act. Business attitudes about location in the Northeast and North Central regions might be influenced, in short, if States sided much more openly and consistently with firms against workers and unions. Even here, small changes in policy would not be enough; presumably, unions would have to be pushed back to the quanitative and qualitative levels of power and influence which currently characterize both the Sunbelt and, more dramatically, countries like South Korea and Brazil to which large corporations have recently been attracted.

Were State policymakers to move in this direction, the terms of policy objectives would be altered significantly. It would no longer be true that States were pursuing the policy objectives of increasing the supply of "good jobs." Given the character of recent corporate shifts to the Sunbelt and overseas, this kind of policy approach would mean that States were explicitly seeking to support corporate profits *at the expense of the quality of work available to workers*. It seems impossible to argue, in any rigorous or coherent way, that State policies which attracted businesses because they achieved sufficient reductions in workers' power were actually serving the objectives of increasing the supply of "good jobs" in those States.

This discussion helps clarify, in the end, the specific themes which **69**

Photo: Earl Dotter/ALEC

have recurred throughout this essay. The "traditional" approach to moderating State employment problems cannot work for either or both of two reasons. First, most State policy tools which pursue employment objectives through effects on business profits are incapable of affecting the structural characteristics of the economy which create the scarcity of "good jobs" in the first place—either by permitting peripheral firms to provide good jobs or by convincing large firms to change their employment policies. Second, those few State policies which might actually influence the behavior of large corporations would explicitly attack the quality of work and eventually reduce the supply of "good jobs" available in the economy. The structure of the economy, in short, creates conflicts between the level of business profits and the quantity of "good jobs." The "traditional" approach will either have no effects on firms' employment behavior (and provide marginal subsidies to business profits) or will have dramatic effect on business activity at the direct expense of work quality. Those who retain their concern with the quality of work and the supply of "good jobs," this argument suggests, must begin to consider alternative policy approaches.

CAN "COMMUNITY" APPROACHES ACTUALLY SUCCEED?

A "community" approach to State employment problems would seek to develop, encourage, and support non-profit, community-based mechanisms for providing "good jobs."[2] As the preceding discussion has argued, States would presumably move in these directions precisely because they offered a better chance of increasing the supply of "good jobs" than support of profit-seeking business enterprises would afford.

Can such a "community" approach work? Since there is so little non-profit, community-based enterprise at present, how can we be confident that such organizations could, in fact, overcome some of the structural problems constraining profit-seeking enterprises? How likely is it that a "community" approach could actually help moderate State employment problems by increasing the number of "good jobs" available in the economy?

In order to answer this question we need to return to basics. Any enterprise faces six necessary conditions for the effective provision of a good or service. It must be able to gain access to and effectively combine: (a) raw materials (through an available infrastructure); (b) workers in sufficient quantity with required skills; (c) appropriate production technology; (d) administrative and coordinative capacity; (e) the capital funds necessary to generate and sustain the enterprise; and (f) a demand for its output.

None of these requirements constitutes an intrinsically insuperable obstacle to a "community" approach to State employment problems. Indeed, each could be met through a concerted and coordinated public effort to pursue the "community" approach.

■ *Raw Materials and Infrastructure.* At first blush, there is obviously some grounds for concern about the provisioning of community-based enterprises. Can we assume that such enterprises will be able to gain access to energy, buildings, transportation, and other supplies at relatively "competitive" prices—regardless of the location of the communities in which they are operated? Communities in many older cities in the Frostbelt undoubtedly suffer current disadvantages in many of these respects. But this problem can be turned on its head with some careful analysis of the character of those current disadvantages.

One of the major issues currently facing economic policymakers involves infrastructural investment over the next 25 years. What kind of energy system will be developed? Will the truck continue as the dominant form of freight transport? Will industry continue to rely on electrical power as heavily has it has since 1900? Answers to these kinds   *71* of locational and infrastructural questions have been shaped in the past by an underlying corporate concern with control of employees. If a "community" approach were to acquire a dominant influence over infrastructural policymaking, in contrast, it is certainly possible that major decisions about energy, transit, and building structures themselves could be framed by a concern with the consistency of those new infrastructural investments with evenly distributed community development priorities. If decentralized solar heating helps promote decentralized manufacturing (which in turn helps provide many more "good jobs"), for example, then that becomes one important argument in fàvor of intensive technological support for solar alternatives within the framework of the community approach. If renewal of an urban rail network is both economically feasible and consistent with community-based development priorities, to pick another illustration, then that would constitute an important, relatively independent argument for intensive support for renewal of rail networks. In general, since public subsidy of an investment in infrastructure is going to be taking place over the next 25 years anyway, we stand at a crossroad of critical decisions: does infrastructural investment continue to support the advantages of large corporations and other profit-seeking enterprises, or is it fashioned increasingly out of a concern with the potential for non-profit community-based enterprises? If States (and other levels of government) fail to move in the latter directions now, then it is likely that we shall face the prospect of a private sector which provides even fewer "good jobs" in the year 2000 than it does now.

■ *Workers.* The discussion in Chapter 2 certainly indicates that there are more than enough available workers to provide a supply of labor to community-based enterprises. (Indeed, the excess supply of workers in the current economy is precisely the problem.) Moreover, the discussion in Chapter 2 seems to indicate that there is no intrinsic problem posed by the distribution of skills among workers currently available. It is certainly true that those who presently suffer the worst problems of unemployment and underemployment have relatively fewer skills than those with the best jobs. But it is equally true that the skills required for many primary jobs in the current economy can be easily learned or acquired in a very short period of time. It is also true that many workers generally confined to secondary employment are "over-qualified" for those jobs. Experience with corporate training programs of the late 1960s seems to indicate, finally, that people acquire skills quickly if they fulfill the requirements of a "good job" which is clearly available and more or less guaranteed for the trainee. In these respects, therefore, we can safely assume that community-based enterprises would be able to attract and/or train workers with the skills necessary to perform tasks defined by the "good jobs" created in those enterprises.

■ *Appropriate Production Technology.* There is nothing about advanced technology as such which precludes its use by community-based enterprises or its consistency with "good jobs." Coal-mining is a very dangerous activity in the United States, for example, but that reflects the failure of U.S. mining companies to make adequate use of existing technology, not from the character of the work; the miner's job is a much "better" job in Europe than the U.S. precisely because European mines use more modern and safer technology. This example suggests an obvious conclusion: technologies can support "good job" creation as much as they can undercut it—depending on the policies and priorities which frame the exploration and utilization of technology. Non-profit, community-based enterprises would need access to modern technology, but, as long as we assume that there is nothing about advanced technology which intrinsically constrains the provision of "good jobs," then the only barrier which community-based enterprises would have to overcome would be financial, not technological. Such enterprises would need to be able to afford advanced technology, in short, but would not face "technical" obstacles to their efforts to combine effective and relatively inexpensive production with "good jobs."

■ *Administrative and Coordinative Capacity.* One impression that many policymakers have developed about community-based enterprises is that they lack administrative and coordinative capacity. There is undoubtedly some truth in these generalizations about past experience. But the issue is like those we have already discussed for infrastructure and technology. As long as the federal government and energy companies devote almost no research and development to solar technologies, for example, the available set of solar techniques will undoubtedly seem insubstantial compared to the apparent wizardry behind synthetic fuels. In the same way, the administrative skills of many fledgling community-based enterprises will pale in comparison with the technical competence of large corporations until those community enterprises receive substantial commitments of development and capital funding. Once these enterprises began to acquire a future, there would be substantial reservoirs of people with critical administrative and professional skills who would be prepared to devote energy and effort to non-profit, community-based enterprises. (The only logical ground for doubting their availability would be the tenuous assumption that professional workers would *always* refuse to apply their skills except in situations where they could assume the potential rewards of salaries in the range of $60,000-$100,000 a year. 73

While this is undoubtedly true of many professionals, it is undoubtedly not true of many others.) We can take the availability of these resources for granted once community-based enterprises appear to get public and private commitments of support.

■ *Capital Funds.* Non-profit community-based enterprises would also require access to substantial capital funds in order to be able to develop effective, cost-efficient systems for producing goods and services which people need in ways which maximize their abilities to provide "good jobs" for those who need them. Would State governments have to pour substantial subsidies into the reduction of the net costs of capital acquisition in order to create some space in the sun for small enterprises?

In their detailed study in a companion volume in this series, Litvak and Daniels (1979) argue that while variations in the *cost* of capital are fairly unimportant to the success or viability of business enterprises, simple *access* to capital is critical for such success. They conclude, "the key point, then, is not subsidizing the cost of capital, but ensuring its availability for profitable enterprise."

Where could such capital come from? Would State governments have to put up the money themselves? Would this therefore drain public tax coffers or strain governments' current bonding capacity?

There are vast capital resources in this country whose current allocation is nominally regulated by State (and, to some extent, federal) governments. These funds include public and private pension funds, savings bank deposits, and insurance company assets. In each of these three cases, people have amassed savings which have been placed in the hands of the executors of those savings—trust or fund managers, banks, and insurance companies. The government establishes the regulatory framework under which the managers of those funds must operate. Current government policy allows such managers to allocate those investment funds however they wish to whomever they choose—subject to basic regulations on mismanagement and cost effectiveness. But there is no reason why local and State governments could not choose to stipulate a range of activities which deserve investment priority and a boundary to the geographic area in which such funds might be allocated. Such a precedent has been established recently in some anti-redlining legislation, which requires, in effect, that a stipulated percentage of savings bank deposits (say, 25 percent) be allocated for investment (in home mortgages, for example). These precedents could be applied to pension funds and insurance company assets with exactly the same logic as with savings deposits. The point seems clear: If people amass savings, why shouldn't those savings be channeled in directions which best serve the interests of people in their own communities, not the interests of people somewhere else? And why shouldn't people's local and State governments become involved in establishing criteria for such investment regulation?

Free market advocates typically reply that savers want the highest possible rate of return for their savings, that they would not be prepared to make a sacrifice of potential interest and equity accumulation for the sake of the "community interest." But this assumes that profit-seeking enterprises are always capable of paying a higher rate of return on assets invested than non-profit community-based enterprises. Much of the argument to this point should have raised serious doubts about the tenability of that assumption. Investments in small profit-seeking enterprises, as we can see from the Birch data reviewed at the end of Chapter 2, are bound to seem shaky—as Birch puts it, a "banker's nightmare." Investments in large corporations are more reliable, but large corporations must cover profits and dividends which non-profit, community-based enterprises would not need to cover. It is certainly plausible that community-based enterprises, with appropriate access to capital funding and government backing in the short run, would be able to reduce their costs of business per unit of output to levels at least comparable with those of large private firms and that they would therefore be able to pay comparable rates of return on investment.

Thus, a strong argument can be made for the potential viability of non-profit, community-based enterprises *if* governments provide initial support and backing and *if* governments pursue regulatory policies which seek to channel available capital in directions which make sense from the point of view of the general public. The federal government is considering such intervention on behalf of large private corporations—with possible loan guarantees to companies like Chrysler and billions of dollars of technical development to support projects like synthetic fuels which private companies will eventually control. Why shouldn't State governments consider alternative policies of comparable scope in directions which hold much greater promise of "good job" generation?

■ *Product Demand.* Having proceeded this far, the last step seems easy. If we can assume that non-profit, community-based enterprises would receive sufficient public support to solve the other problems they would face, then they could presumably produce goods and services which people need and would buy. Consumers in this country would clearly buy food if it were of higher quality and/or at lower cost than that currently provided by large food processors and chains. People obviously need decent low-cost housing. People desperately

75

need better, less expensive, and more reliable health care. There is a crying need for conservation projects and reliable low-cost energy. Millions need alternative forms of transportation. And millions need services like education and counseling which would help them pursue their other objectives. If community-based enterprises developed the capacity to produce these kinds of high quality goods and services at relatively low cost, the problems of product demand could easily be solved.

Although the preceding paragraphs suggest that there are no *intrinsic* barriers to the development of viable, non-profit community-based enterprises, two further, much more general issues need to be addressed—one at what economists would call the *micro-economic* level and one at the *macro-economic* level.

Is it actually possible that community-based enterprises could compete with and provide equally cost-effective goods and services as profit-seeking private enterprises? Doesn't the "free market" guarantee efficiency? Three points seem important about the micro-economics of this comparison.

First, all large corporations receive and rely on government support; there is no such thing as a pure "free market" in this respect. Large corporations rely on public subsidies for infrastructure and research and development. They have come to expect bail-outs and guarantees. They demand and receive investment tax credits, accelerated depreciation allowances, and support for product demand. Indeed, it is reasonable to argue that even the largest of private corporations, like General Motors and Ford (much less Chrysler), would not be able to operate as they currently do without having received critical public support and subsidy over the years. Isn't it possible that comparable commitments of public resources and support to community-based enterprises would make more sense?

Second, even with all that support, profit-seeking enterprises are not necessarily "efficient." They spend billions on administrative costs necessary to control world markets which much smaller, community-based enterprises would not need to spend. They spend billions on huge salaries for their chief executive personnel. They spend billions on advertising designed to convince consumers to purchase products of questionable quality. All of these expenditures are built into the costs and therefore the prices of the goods of those corporations. They rarely face the competition of enterprises which do not incur those costs because neither the private nor the public sector has ever devoted resources and capital to the development of such non-profit corporations.

76   Third, community-based enterprises would presumably face some

disciplinary pressures of their own which would constrain potential waste. Theory tells us that product-market competition and investors' thirst for profits keep profit-seeking firms honest. Theory would also suggest that consumers' demand for quality (for their money) and community-based political and investment controls would presumably have equivalent effects on non-profit, community-based enterprises. Just as some profit-seeking firms engage in corrupt and inefficient practices, disproving the perfect reliability of the theory of the "free market," so has it turned out that some "community-based" and private organizations have not behaved perfectly either. In theory, nonetheless, there is every reason to expect that a concerted movement toward the "community" approach would develop continuing pressures on non-profit, community-based enterprises to remain efficient and effective.

In short, one cannot predict, *a priori,* the greater efficiency of profit-seeking over non-profit, community-based enterprises. If that is true at the micro-economic level, then the likelihood that non-profit, community-based enterprises would provide "good jobs" more reliably than their private, profit-seeking counterparts seems, by itself, to establish a sufficient rationale for devoting State government policy toward their creation and support.

What about macro-economics? Doesn't the current priority on fighting inflation rule out expanded public commitment to new kinds of policies and activities?

When we look closely at such concerns, it turns out that exactly the opposite kind of conclusion seems more appropriate: Movement toward policies which would seek "good job" generation through non-profit, community-based enterprises would also make important contributions toward the moderation of some of our principal current macro-economic problems. This is not the place to review the sources of those macro-economic problems at length, but two points seem crucial.

First, productivity has stagnated and unemployment remains high *not* because corporations lack profits and capital funds—since corporate profits have recently soared—but because corporations have been reluctant to invest (at least in this country) because of concern for the basic instability of the political and economic climate in the United States. If State governments began to pursue policies that would help "stabilize" the process of investment and employment growth, then some of the current instability would potentially be reduced. Public support for "good job" generation should also help restimulate private investment and demand.

Second, the development of non-profit, community-based enter- 77 prises would help improve the terms of the trade-off between inflation and unemployment. On the employment side, these enterprises would probably generate more jobs per unit of output and investment than large private, profit-seeking enterprises: I have explored the reasons for this in previous discussion. On the price side, they would probably reduce the rate of inflation associated with any given level of output: If we assumed that consumer demand was at a particular level, and that there was a shift toward production by non-profit, community-based enterprises, then production costs at that given level of output might be lower than under present circumstances because fewer resources would be devoted to relatively unproductive corporate expenses like high executive salaries and expensive advertising.

But this immediately raises a final macro-economic question: If increasing support for non-profit, community-based enterprises generated more good jobs, would this not, by definition, increase average wage levels; therefore increase aggregate labor costs; and, consequently, increase prices through cost mark-up pricing? There are two reasons why the "community" approach would not necessarily have those hypothetical effects on prices.

First, some of the increased wage costs would come out of what *currently* goes toward corporate profits. Second, and perhaps more important, the increasing costs for wages paid to workers with "good jobs" could potentially come out of what now covers the salaries of high-paid executives and professionals. Let us assume that there are now about 750,000 salaried workers who earn more than $75,000 a year. (The government does not release separate data on people earning more than $50,000 a year, but this "guesstimate" is relatively conservative.) Their salaries, by themselves, would be enough to cover the wages of nearly four million workers earning $15,000 a year at full-time, year-round employment—accounting for a huge share of those who currently lose working hours to unemployment during a given year. However hypothetical, these calculations suggest an obvious point: If there were a shift toward production in enterprises devoted to providing "good jobs," and if that movement effectively generated an aggregate shift toward a more equal distribution of labor incomes among wage-and-salary employees, then higher wages for those not now in good jobs would not necessarily add to production costs.

Suppose that there were a dramatic policy shift toward the "community" approach? What would happen to the rest of the economy? Would there be a collapse elsewhere?

There is no doubt that a movement in the directions identified by the "community" approach would involve substantial shifts in the character of economic activity in the United States. But it would not involve any necessary attack on the right of private businesses to operate. Private, profit-making businesses would simply face additional and more stringent competitive pressures. If they wanted access to certain pools of capital, they would have to meet the standards by which that capital was allocated. Meeting those standards, they would be able to go about their businesses.

This does not amount to a policy position which opposes business profits just to oppose business profits. It builds from an argument that other social objectives, like the quest for better jobs, deserve higher priority than profits. Where support for profits and support for "good jobs" conflict, support for profits should take second place. If no conflicts exist between those policy objectives, so much the better.

In conclusion, a "community" approach to the generation of "good jobs" is both plausible and desirable. One important topic remains for further discussion. In Chapter 4, I turn to a brief discussion of the policy instruments which one might apply in moving toward a "community" approach to State employment problems.

Footnotes to Chapter 3

1. There is no slackening in mainstream economists' support for this "traditional" approach. The National Commission for Manpower Policy recently released a special report on "Increasing Job Opportunities in the Private Sector." In the introduction, Eli Ginzberg, who has long argued the importance of greater attention to the problems of "good jobs" and "poor jobs," adopts a simple position about current policy directions: "If the enlarged participation of the private sector in federal training and employment programs is a sound objective—and it is difficult to argue otherwise—then tax as well as a range of other devices that might elicit a positive response from the business community are worth exploring." (National Commission for Manpower Policy, 1978: 5.)

2. This "community" approach has not yet been well-developed in great detail, but similar discussions with somewhat more institutional detail and concrete discussion of proposals are available in Rifkin and Barber (1978); Faux and Lightfoot (1976); Case, Goldberg and Shearer (1976); and Conference on Alternative State and Local Policies (1977).

4
POLICY TOOLS FOR DIFFERENT SEASONS

For policymaking purposes, it is obviously insufficient to leave off our analysis with only a sketch of general approaches to employment policy. In this very brief chapter I highlight the implications of the preceding analysis for specific choices among policy instruments aimed at moderating State employment problems, and attempt to exemplify the basic differences between the "traditional" approach and the "community" approach to "good job" creation. I do this in order to show that the specific choice of policy instrument matters much *less* than the basic approach to "good job" creation which State policymakers pursue: Any given policy instrument offers little promise if applied within the framework of the "traditional" approach to moderating State employment problems; but the very same instruments could be employed with more promise in the context of a "community" approach to "good job" creation.

Because the purpose of this chapter is to illustrate an argument rather than to develop a complete and exhaustive menu of policy options, I have chosen a relatively limited set of examples as a basis for the development of this argument.

Skills Training   Many public agencies continue to promote skills training programs as a solution to employment problems. When skeptics cite evidence of the occasional failures of previous efforts in these directions, skills training proponents respond with innovative twists on the traditional models, arguing that slightly more ingenious programs will have demonstrably more favorable results. This kind of discussion largely misses the most important issue: The promise of skills training depends entirely on the *context* in which the training takes place.

On the one hand, skills training programs aimed at jobs in the private sector are unlikely to have any significant effect on the supply of "good jobs" provided by the private sector. Small firms in competitive industries do not currently provide many jobs requiring substantial skills. Increasing reliance on skilled workers, in the case of these enterprises, would require sufficient market stability and capital funding to permit changes in the character of their production process.

Skills training by itself does not address the basic obstacles to "good job" creation in small competitive firms.

In contrast, large firms can afford to hire skilled workers but prefer, other things equal, to reduce their reliance on skilled workers. As I pointed out in Chapter 2, the internal job structures of large firms are so rigid and inflexible that an increased supply of skilled workers—or a public subsidy of training costs—is highly unlikely to increase their inclination to use more skilled workers or provide more good jobs. (The example of the boatyard's calculus on welding costs discussed in Chapter 2 illustrates this kind of rigidity, even though it refers to a somewhat different kind of specific problem.) To the extent that this is true, then public subsidy of training costs for workers who are eventually hired by large firms has the effect *not* of increasing the number of "good jobs" which those firms provide *but rather* of increasing their profits as a result of the reduction in their internal costs of training. This leads, in the end, to public tax subsidy of corporate profits. If we assume that those tax dollars could otherwise help support programs which would help generate "good jobs," we confront once again the apparent conflict between private profit and the supply of "good jobs."

On the other hand, skills training would make considerable sense if pursued in the context of a "community" approach to "good job" creation. While there is a large supply of workers with skills available

Photo: Robert Gumpert

in the labor market as a whole, there are also many workers whose education and employment experience have not provided them with many productive skills. The corporate experiments of the late 1960s, as Cohn (1971) shows, demonstrated that workers from "disadvantaged" backgrounds could and would acquire skills training rapidly if they were convinced that a "good job" awaited them at the end of the training road. Skills training would enhance the "community" approach to "good job" generation for those who need skills development. The costs of skills training, in the long run, would certainly be outweighed by the reduced costs of unemployment insurance, welfare benefits, and crime prevention to which the current policy failures to reduce unemployment rates now contribute.

Tax Incentives and Investment Subsidies

Tax subsidies and investment incentives, by themselves, are unlikely to affect the supply of good jobs. (See Kieschnick, 1979; and the Advisory Commission on Intergovernmental Relations, 1978, for further discussion on these general points.) Indeed, the wide variety of tax incentives and investment subsidies all have the same intended effect. They hope to reduce the costs of business operations along certain dimensions—such as inducing more investment or attracting business to a particular location. But these policies are unlikely to affect firms' behavior at the margin. Structural changes would be necessary in order either to make possible small firms' provision of "good jobs" or to guarantee that large firms would move toward the provision of more (rather than fewer) "good jobs." Without those structural changes, tax incentives and investment subsidies are unlikely to change the structure of employment which private, profit-seeking firms provide and are likely, instead, to subsidize profits, at any given level of economic activity, at the expense of taxpayers' spendable earnings.

In contrast, the equivalent of such tax subsidies and investment incentives might have dramatic effects in the context of a sustained community approach to "good job" creation. Suppose that State governments began to develop infrastructure and other coordinated policies to develop and support non-profit, community-based enterprises (as opposed to such current support of large corporations). Tax incentives and investment subsidies (at levels more or less equivalent to current "tax expenditures" to large private corporations) might then help provide critical support for new community-based enterprises during those early periods of incubation when they "shake out" their problems and try to develop the size of operations which permits decent economies of scale. The point is that such subsidies would be part of an explicit public effort to use government policy instruments to promote "good job" creation (among other policy objectives), not simply to provide inducements to private profit-seeking corporations to undertake whatever investments they prefer regardless of the impact of those investments on State employment problems.

The Government as Many have sought, through their support
Employer of for policy initiatives like the Humphrey-
Last Report Hawkins Bill or CETA appropriations,
to enlist the government as the "employer of last resort" when those desiring work have not been able to find adequate employment in the private sector. Once again, this policy fails to discriminate between the implications of a "traditional" and a "community" approach to employment problems.

If the government functions as an employer of last resort without undertaking other policies to provide capital and administrative support for the labor activities of the workers it hires under such programs, it virtually condemns those workers to jobs which pay low wages and offer insecure futures. Almost by definition, these government programs seek no other productive resources with which "employees of last resort" can work. This means that they may be able to rake leaves but that they cannot easily produce decent housing for those who need it. This means, in turn, that such workers cannot easily command the kind of pay and employment security which would justify the wages required by our definition of "good jobs." Indeed, the very definition of employment of last resort suggests that workers will be laid off as soon as the government decides that employment conditions in the private sector will accommodate those currently employed in those public jobs. (And the presumption that the public sector should not compete with the private sector, leading to no resource funding to support the productiveness of "employees of last resort," inevitably relegates such employees to relatively inefficient activities.) This approach almost explicitly consigns the "last hired" by the private sector to alternating periods of private and public employment, exposing them to bouts of intermittent unemployment, and denying them the opportunity to develop some of the skills and experience which continuing and stable employment might alterna-tively provide.

In contrast, public employment in the service of a "community" approach to "good job" creation could have important additive effects. Suppose the government hires people to develop plans for community-based enterprises (which would emphasize the provision *83* of "good jobs"). Suppose that these employees got the inside track to jobs in those community-based enterprises once they developed a firm foundation. This would mean that government expenditures on current employment would potentially lead to permanent and adequate employment of those employees in the private, non-profit, community-based sector. This approach would not only increase the chances of permanent employment for those whom the government currently employs but would also promise declining government expenditures on "employment of last resort" over time. The difference between government employment in this context and government employment as a residual in a "traditional" approach is that we could presume, over the long run, an increasing supply of "good jobs" from community-based enterprises, whereas we cannot presume such an increase from private sector economic activity. The critical task, if we hope to turn government employment in these relatively more promising directions, is to link current government employment with a complex of coordinated policies aimed at the longer-term development and support of non-profit, community-based enterprises oriented toward "good job" creation.

Wage Subsidies and Employment Vouchers

Some analysts, like Vaughan (1978), have proposed increasing government concentration on programs providing wage subsidies (or employment vouchers) for firms in order to encourage a shift toward a higher utilization of labor and, ultimately, more employment.

These policies hold little promise if applied within the context of the "traditional" approach to employment problems. For small firms, wage subsidies are unlikely to overcome the obstacles to small firm generation of "good jobs." Small firms in competitive industries cannot solve the problems of infrastructure and capital access, regardless of marginal variations in the relative costs of labor they face. Even if wage subsidy programs induced a partial substitution of labor for capital at the margin, small firms would be unlikely to be able to provide the kind of employment security, decent working conditions and job control which we have also defined as necessary components of "good jobs."

The problems with wage subsidies to large firms are similar to those we earlier discussed for skills training. Because of the inflexibility of job structures, wage subsidies might not necessarily induce the substitution of labor for capital within structured internal labor markets. Nor would they be likely to affect large firms' preferences for relatively fewer "powerful" employees. Instead of inducing firms to provide more "good jobs," wage subsidies might principally have the alternative effect of using tax dollars to reduce firms' wage costs and therefore to increase their profits (with respect to internal wage expenditures). Instead of generating more good jobs, in short, wage subsidy programs would be likely to subsidize profits with public tax dollars.

In contrast, within the context of a sustained "community" approach to State employment problems, monies spent on wage subsidies might help support initial start-up costs for community-based enterprises, promoting the development of those enterprises and eventually permitting, after early incubation, a gradual reduction in their reliance on those wage subsidies. What matters, once again, is the context in which such a policy instrument is applied and the longer-term economic directions which those short-term expenditures help sustain.

Whither the "Community" Approach?

I have briefly provided some examples which indicate that the basic approach which policymakers pursue matters *more* than the specific economic activities which their policy instruments are designed to affect. Whether govern-

ments seek to affect skills training, rates of employment, or relative labor costs, the considerations which argue in favor of the "community" approach in general will also argue in favor of the application of any given policy instrument *within the context of that general policy approach.*

State policymakers should seek to apply all policy instruments currently or potentially at their disposal to full support of the "community" approach. This will require a coordinated and sustained effort to encourage, develop, and support non-profit, community-based enterprises devoted to providing growing numbers of "good jobs." Policies aimed at this direction should necessarily focus on improving these enterprises' access to (a) raw materials and infrastructure; (b) workers with adequate skills; (c) appropriate production technology; (d) adequate administrative and coordinative capacities; (e) sufficient capital funds; and (f) access to suitable demand for the goods and services they might conceivably produce. For further detail on some of the specific directions which such a coordinated policy approach might take during the 1980s, see Litvak and Daniels (1979), Coltman and Metzenbaum (1979), Philip (1978), Kieschnick (1979), and Harrison and Bluestone (1980).

This brings us to a point of conclusion.

I have argued that State governments should make dramatic changes in the direction of their policies aimed at current employment problems. I have suggested in sequence:

■ that the economy needs more "good jobs," not simply more jobs regardless of their quality;
■ that a *structural* analysis of the economy's failure to provide enough "good jobs" provides a much more adequate explanation of that failure than traditional mainstream economic analyses of job and wage determination;
■ that this structural analysis suggests the preferability and plausibility of a "community" approach to moderating State employment problems and argues against the currently prevalent "traditional" approach; and
■ that these differences in basic policy approach matter more than the specific character of particular policy instruments which government policymakers normally consider.

I have tried to develop these arguments with as much attention to logical coherence and empirical evidence as possible. I have made virtually no reference to the obvious political obstacles which would confront a sustained government effort to move in the directions indicated by the "community" approach to employment problems.

Many policymakers feel that the citizenry favors the private sector over the public sector, free enterprise over public enterprise, and corporate initiative over public initiative. But these attitudes are themselves the product of public pronouncements and prevailing policy. Many white U.S. citizens displayed obvious racial prejudice through the 19th and early 20th centuries, for example, but when public policies began to change in the 1940s, 1950s, and early 1960s, public attitudes followed closely behind.

Similar changes seem possible with employment policy. We desperately need to move toward rapid moderation of our current employment problems. The arguments of this essay suggest that this will require something like the "community" approach sketched in the preceding pages. The logic of those arguments indicates that we have no other alternative. The urgency of the problem requires that these arguments be addressed directly and openly. I have little doubt that public opinion will respond.

BIBLIOGRAPHY

Advisory Commission on Intergovernmental Relations, "Regional Growth Study," mimeographed, August 22, 1978.

Alcaly, Roger, and Mermelstein, David. *The Fiscal Crisis of American Cities.* New York: Random House, 1977.

Ashford, Nicholas. *Crisis in the Workplace: Occupational Disease and Injury.* Cambridge, Mass.: MIT, 1976.

Berg, Ivar. *Education and Jobs: The Great Training Robbery.* New York: Praeger, 1970.

Berman, Daniel M. *Death on the Job: Occupational Health and Safety Struggles in the United States.* New York: Monthly Review Press, 1979.

Bernstein, Irving. *The Turbulent Years.* Boston: Houghton-Mifflin, 1971.

Birch, David L. *The Job Generation Process.* Cambridge, Mass.: MIT Program on Neighborhood and Regional Change, 1979.

Bluestone, Barry. "The Determinants of Personal Earnings in the U.S.: Human Capital vs. Stratified Labor Markets," mimeographed, Boston College, 1978.

_____. Murphy, William M., and Stevenson, Mary. *Low Wages and the Working Poor.* Ann Arbor: University of Michigan, 1973.

Braverman, Harry. *Labor and Monopoly Capital.* New York: Monthly Review Press, 1974.

Case, John; Goldberg, Leonard; and Shearer, Derek. "State Business," *Working Papers,* Spring 1976.

Cohn, Jules, *The Conscience of the Corporations.* New York: Praeger, 1971.

Coltman, Edward; and Metzenbaum, Shelley. "Investing in Ourselves—Public Employee Pension Fund Investment: Strategies for Economic Impact and Social Responsibility." Mimeographed, Low Income Planning Aid, 2 Park Square, Boston, Mass.: June 1979.

Conference on Alternative State and Local Policies. *New Directions in State and Local Policy.* Washington, D.C.: CASLPP, 1977.

Doeringer, Peter and Piore, Michael. *Internal Labor Markets and Manpower Analysis.* Lexington, Mass.: Heath, 1971.

Edwards, Richard C. "What Makes a Good Worker? Organizational Incentives and the Determinants of Individual Earnings." *Journal of Human Resources,* October 1976.

_____. *Contested Terrain: The Transformation of the Workplace in the Twentieth Century.* New York: Basic Books, 1979.

_____. , Reich, Michael; and Gordon, David M., eds. *Labor Market Segmentation.* Lexington, Mass.: Heath, 1975.

Faux, Jeff; and Lightfoot, Robert. *Capital and Community.* Washington, D.C.: Exploratory Project for Economic Alternatives, 1976.

Feldstein, Martin. *Lowering the Permanent Rate of Unemployment.* Washington, D.C.: Joint Economic Committee, U.S. Congress, 1975.

Fogelson, Robert. *The Fragmented Metropolis*. Cambridge, Mass.: Harvard University Press, 1967.

Freeman, Richard, ed. *The Over-Educated American*. New York: Academic Press, 1976.

Ginzberg, Eli. "The Job Problem," *Scientific American,* November 1977.

Gordon, David M. *Theories of Poverty and Underemployment*. Lexington, Mass: Heath, 1972.

————. "Digging Up the Roots: The Economic Determinants of Social Problems." *Social Welfare Forum,* 1975.

————. ed. *Problems in Political Economy: An Urban Perspective.* 2nd ed. Lexington, Mass.: Heath, 1977.

————. "Capitalism and the Historical Development of American Cities." In W. Tabb and L. Sawyers, ed., *Marxism and the Metropolis*. New York: Oxford University Press, 1978.

————. "Empirical and Methodological Issues in the Theory of Labor Segmentation." In M. Reich et al., *The Segmentation of Labor in the United States*. New York: Cambridge University Press, 1980.

————. Toward the Critique of CAPITALopolis. Manuscript in Progress, 1980.

————. Edwards, Richard C.; and Reich, Michael. "The Historical Development of Labor Segmentation in the United States." In M. Reich et al., *The Segmentation of Labor in the United States*. New York: Cambridge University Press, 1980.

Greenbaum, Joan M. *In the Name of Efficiency: Management Theory and Shopfloor Practice in Data-Processing Work*. Philadelphia: Temple University Press, 1979.

Harrison, Bennett. "Education and the Secondary Labor Market." *Wharton Quarterly,* 1974.

————. "Work and Welfare." *Review of Radical Political Economics,* Fall 1979.

————. ; and Hill, Edward. "The Changing Structure of Jobs in Older and Younger Cities." In *Central City Economic Development*. Binghamton, N.Y.: Center for Social Analysis at SUNY-Binghamton, 1978.

————. and Kanter, Sandra. "The Political Economy of State Job-Creation Business Incentives." *Journal of the American Institute of Planners,* November 1978.

————. and Sum, Andrew. "Labor Market Data Requirements from the Perspective of 'Dual' or 'Segmented' Labor Market Research." Report to the National Commission on Employment and Unemployment Statistics, 1978.

————. and Bluestone, Barry. *Capital Mobility and Economic Dislocation*. Washington, D.C.: The Progressive Alliance, forthcoming, 1980.

Herbers, John. "Nationwide Revolt on Taxes Showing No Sign of Abating." *New York Times,* August 5, 1979.

Institute for Social Research. *Quality of Worklife Survey, 1977*. Ann Arbor, Mich.: Institute for Social Research, Univ. of Michigan, 1979.

Kerr, William O. "The Effects of Unionism in a Dual Labor Market." Unpublished Ph.D. Dissertation, New School for Social Research, 1979.

89

Kieschnick, Michael. *Small Business and Community Economic Development.* Washington, D.C.: National Center for Economic Alternatives, July 1979.

Kraft, Philip. *Programmers and Managers: The Routinization of Computer Programming in the United States.* New York: Springer-Verlag, 1977.

Levine, Robert. *The Poor Ye Need Not Have With You: Lessons from the War on Poverty.* Cambridge, Mass.: MIT Press, 1970.

Litvak, Larry and Daniels, Belden. *Innovations in Development Finance.* Washington, D.C.: Council of State Planning Agencies, 1979.

Long, Larry H., "Inter-regional Migration of the Poor: Some Recent Changes," *Current Population Reports,* Special Studies, Series P-23, Number 73, November 1978.

Luft, Harold. *Poverty and Health.* Cambridge, Mass.: Ballinger, 1978.

Malizia, Emil. "Earnings, Profits, and Productivity in North Carolina." Mimeographed, University of North Carolina, May 1976.

McGahey, Richard. "The Economics of Crime: A Critical Review of the Literature." Mimeographed, New School for Social Research, 1979.

National Advisory Council on Economic Opportunity. *Eleventh Report.* Washington, D.C.: NACEO, June 1979.

National Commission for Manpower Policy, "Increasing Job Opportunities in the Private Sector: A Conference Report." *Special Report,* No. 29, November 1978.

Nation's Business. *The Years of Change: An Almanac of American Progress.* Washington, D.C.: Chamber of Commerce, 1978.

Pack, Janet Rothenberg. "Frostbelt and Sunbelt: Convergence over Time." *Intergovernmental Perspectives,* Fall 1978.

Philip, Alan Butt. *Creating New Jobs: A Report on Long-Term Job Creation in Britain and Sweden.* London: Policy Studies Institute, 1-2 Castle Lane, London SW1E 6DR, 1978.

Piore, Michael J. "Notes Toward a Theory of Labor Market Stratification." in R.C. Edwards et al., eds., *Labor Market Segmentation.* Lexington, Mass.: Heath, 1975.

————. ed. *Unemployment and Inflation.* White Plains, N.Y.: M.E. Sharpe, 1979.

Plotnick, Robert D.; and Skidmore, Felicity. *Progress Against Poverty: A Review of the 1964-1974 Decade.* New York: Academic Press, 1975.

Rainwater, Lee. *What Money Buys.* New York: Basic Books, 1975.

Rees, Albert. *The Economics of Work and Pay.* 2nd ed. New York: Harper & Row, 1979.

Rifkin, Jeremy. *Own Your Own Job: Economic Democracy for Working Americans.* New York: Bantam Books, 1977.

————. and Barber, Randy. *The North Will Rise Again: Pensions, Politics, and Power in the 1980s.* Boston: Beacon Press, 1978.

Silk, Leonard; and Vogel, David. *Ethics and Profits: The Crisis of the American Corporation.* New York: Simon and Schuster, 1976.

Sternlieb, George, and Hughes, James, eds. Revitalizing the Northeast. New Brunswick: Center for Urban Policy Research, 1978.

Tabb, William; and Sawyers, Lawrence, eds. *Marxism and the Metropolis*. New York: Oxford University Press, 1978.

Union for Radical Political Economics, ed. *U.S. Capitalism in Crisis*. New York: Union for Radical Political Economics, 1978.

Vaughan, Roger J. "Jobs for the Urban Unemployed." Mimeographed, March 1978.

————. *State Taxation and Economic Development*. Washington, D.C.: Council of State Planning Agencies, 1979.

Watkins, Alfred; and Perry, David, eds. *The Rise of the Sunbelt Cities*. Beverly Hills, Ca.: Sage Publications, 1979.

Woods, Robert. *1400 Governments*. New York: Anchor Books, 1959.

Part II

INFLATION AND UNEMPLOYMENT
SURVIVING THE 1980s

Roger J. Vaughan

INTRODUCTION

The nation is winding up the 1970s as it entered them—with a recession coupled with inflation. In fact, many analysts believe that we will suffer higher unemployment and sharper inflation in 1980 than in 1970. Between these unfortunate endpoints, we experienced the deepest recession since the disastrous 1930s, a shock that forced many already weakened local jurisdictions to the brink of bankruptcy. If past experience is any guide, the first dollars of any federal countercyclical assistance will not be distributed until 1981, by which time many state and local governments will have been forced to make painful and disruptive cuts in local services and capital expenditures. Clearly, state and local governments can no longer afford to wait for federal countercyclical programs.

Not only will federal efforts supply too little, too late, but the programs that Washington ultimately initiates are likely to be inappropriate. The true victims of recession, those with little job experience or training, will receive little benefit from countercyclical programs. High unemployment in a presidential election year may force the Federal Reserve Board to boost the money supply, setting the stage for renewed inflation during the 1980s.

So long as we rely on White House or Congressional action to combat the twin problems of recession and inflation, we are assured of continued confusion. In this paper we argue that states have many potential programs for smoothing fluctuations in employment growth and for reducing the bite of inflation. Although state governments cannot cure the nation's economic problems, they have barely scratched the surface in applying the remedies at their disposal especially when they act in a concerted fashion.

The failure of federal economic stabilization policy stems from a broader failure to solve a variety of divergent national economic problems. Increasing centralization in Washington has stunted state and local capacity to deal with regional and local development issues. Yet regional diversity in development problems renders them singularly intractable to a Washington-based solution. It is time to rethink the way we have stratified the allocation of responsibility for economic policy among the different layers of government. The Congress, the White House, and federal agencies must relinquish some of their power and build a more rational system of delegated responsibility. At the same time, state and city governments must assume a greater degree of responsibility for the economic and social well-being of all of their constituents and cease regarding the federal government as an inexhaustible source of funds. We must also rethink the way we have allocated economic objectives among alternative policies. In the confused pursuit of a "panacea policy" that can adequately respond to   *95* all objectives in all regions, we have mangled the tools at our disposal.

This paper makes a fundamental distinction between the goal of price stability, which is a federal responsibility and should be achieved through a rational monetary policy, and the goal of stimulating the economy during recessions, which is best addressed at the state and local level through countercyclical public expenditures. States do have an important role in fighting the impacts of inflation, and federal resources must be mobilized for an effective countercyclical program. But these two goals must be separated if we are to break out of the stagflation that has characterized the last decade.

Reflecting this distinction, this paper is divided into two parts: The first three chapters detail the appropriate federal, state, and local roles and policies for fighting inflation; the final three chapters examine what the federal, state and local governments can do to combat recession.

Chapter 1 examines the goal of price stability, analyzing the causes of inflation and its impacts. It distinguishes between the goal of "whipping" inflation, a federal responsibility, and the goal of ameliorating the harm done by inflation until it is controlled—both a federal and state responsibility. The failure of federal monetary policy to stabilize prices is discussed in Chapter 2. The problem is that monetary policy has been used both to stabilize prices and to stimulate the economy, an impossible double function. Chapter 3 outlines how states can help avoid the harmful effects of inflation through cost cutting, regulation review, and tax reform.

The goal of economic stability is discussed in Chapter 4. Three components are identified—absorbing excess productive capacity, providing jobs for the unemployed, and maintaining public services in the face of declining revenues. The failure of federal efforts to meet these objectives because of poor timing, poor targeting, and an overall lack of job creation is described in Chapter 5. Chapter 6 shows how states, by setting up stabilization funds which accumulate balances (from federal, state, and local sources) during expansionary years to be spent during recessions, can moderate the business cycle. Finally, a number of technical appendices provide data useful to state and local officials in designing their own economic stabilization efforts.

1
THE GOAL
OF PRICE STABILITY

Inflation is, for many Americans, our most important national problem. Yet our understanding of its causes is freighted with myth, and the most common recommendations for dealing with it are confused and contradictory. To formulate appropriate policies we must first uncover the causes of inflation, and then identify the harmful impacts that we wish to avoid—for if we cannot completely cure the disease, we can, at least, soothe its more painful symptoms. This chapter explores the roots and impacts of inflation. The following chapter describes the confusions that have caused federal price stabilization policies to fail. Chapter 3 outlines what steps states can take to help fight inflation. The major conclusions from this chapter are:

■ Inflation is primarily a monetary phenomenon, the result of a sustained increase in the money supply. Without an expansionary monetary policy, inflation is not possible.
■ The harmful impacts of inflation—especially those impacts on income distribution and real income—are the result of price rigidities, inaccurate expectations, and inadequate indexing. These factors cause problems not only with inflationary price increases, but also with relative price increases.
■ Anti-inflationary policy must include not only a stable and rational monetary policy, but also policies to reduce the harmful impacts of price changes. While states can do nothing more than concerted lobbying to help develop a sound monetary policy, they can take the lead in developing ways to ensure that inflation, or price changes, do not harm the poor.

THE CAUSES OF INFLATION[1]

Few issues have generated as much heated debate with as little clarification as inflation. Popular myth has divided the disputants into two camps: the "cost-push" school and the "demand-pull" school. The villains for each school differ. Those favoring the cost-push explanation point accusing fingers at OPEC price increases, monopolistic pricing strategies by big business, predatory and union-inspired wage increases, or the burden of proliferating government regulations. The demand-pullers blame over-extended and materialistic consumers, a bloated public sector, or an obliging Federal Reserve Board for increasing the money supply. By posing these views as an unbridgeable conflict, we ignore the very simple fact that prices are ultimately determined, albeit imperfectly and with lags, by the interaction of supply and demand. Whom you choose to blame, among the actors listed above, depends on the stage at which you enter the seamless inflationary spiral, and what direction you are facing. A wage increase could not be passed on in price increases unless consumer demand was also rising. Neither would increased consumer demand result in inflation unless producers' costs were also increasing. The stimulus for increased demand or increased costs can come from a number of sources, but will only generate inflation if all sectors participate.

Let us consider a simple example. The increase in oil prices engineered by the Oil Producing Exporting Countries (with the implicit assistance of the oil importing countries) has been widely described as inflationary. But this is not necessarily true. The initial impact of the price increase in the United States is to increase the demand for credit. Businesses require more working capital to pay for fuel and transportation. Consumers increase their monthly purchases on their gas credit cards. If the Federal Reserve took no action to accommodate these demands, the rate of interest would rise, and firms that are relatively intensive users of oil (through transportation costs, the type of raw materials used, or the energy needed as part of their production processes) would find their costs increasing relative to other firms. They would cut back their output as consumers switch to other, less energy-intensive products. The rate of interest would return to its previous level, *and only a change in relative prices would result, not any significant change in the overall cost of living.* There would be a small decline in real income in the U.S. and an increase in OPEC countries. The economy would experience a temporary rise in the unemployment rate as resources were shifted among sectors, and perhaps also among regions, depending on regional differences in the importance of oil relative to other energy sources. But this is not what happened. The Federal Reserve typically regards the rate of interest as its target variable. When the demand for credit rose, it met the demand by increasing the money supply in order to prevent the rate of interest from rising. There was more money chasing an unchanged supply of goods, and therefore all prices started to rice—not just in the energy intensive sectors, but across the board. This sets the stage for sustained inflation. Businesses, anticipating an energy induced increase in costs, raise their prices and attempt to expand inventories, i.e., buy now before prices go up further. Wage negotiators insist on a cost of living escalator clause. And all the time, an obliging Federal Reserve is raising the money supply so that banks can meet these demands. The spiral continues. The interaction between demand and supply factors was well-summarized nearly two decades ago: "The economic stalactite of inflated demand has met a sociological stalagmite of upthrusting claims; when the stalactite and stalagmite meet and fuse in an icy kiss . . . nobody on earth can be quite sure where one ends and the other begins" (Robertson, 1961).

This simple explanation obviously glosses over many parts in a complex process. But it does illustrate the central role played by the monetary policy of the Federal Reserve Board. They may not always provide the initial stimulus—although they often have—but their accommodation of rising credit demands is crucial if the upward pressure on the price level is to be sustained. In the face of a steady increase in the money supply, there is little that wage and price guidelines can do. In fact, guidelines may do more harm than good. In this example, the increase in oil prices necessitates a relative increase in the prices of energy and of energy intensive goods and services. If this relative shift does not occur, the economy must rely on alternative allocation mechanisms—rationing—which rarely works as smoothly as the price system. The basic signaling mechanism of the economy is impaired. Even allowing special fuel cost increases within the guidelines does not reflect the intricate ways in which oil price changes affect the economy.

THE IMPACTS OF INFLATION

The roots of inflation rest in expansionary monetary policy. The results, with which we are familiar, are rising prices. But is inflation harmful, and what are the problems that necessitate public policy action?

Under "ideal" conditions, inflation could be harmless. Consider an economy experiencing an annual rate of inflation of 25 percent, but where everyone perfectly anticipates the rate, all prices are free to change costlessly, and all payments are indexed to the anticipated rate. No one would suffer. Those on "fixed" incomes would receive a 25 percent cost of living adjustment. Lenders would demand an interest rate high enough to compensate for price increases, and borrowers would be able to repay through their inflation-driven increases in income. Wage settlements would include a 25 percent cost of living increase as well as a productivity increase. All contracts would reflect the steady increase in prices. Even foreign trade would proceed smoothly, as the local currency declined against those of other nations where inflation was lower.

Inflation causes problems when these ideal conditions are not met. The most important disruptive influences in the real economy arise because:

■ The prices of goods and services do not increase evenly.
■ Inflation rates are not accurately anticipated.
■ Some prices cannot adjust easily (or are not allowed to).   **99**

■ Transfer payments and tax structures are not indexed.

These are not only problems from inflation induced price changes, but also from price changes that result from structural changes in the economy. We must interpret "inflation fighting" broadly, to include not only the goal of stabilizing the rate of increase of aggregate price level but also the goal of avoiding regressive income redistribution from relative price increases.

Distribution of Price Increases   If the prices of all goods and services in all areas increased at the same rate, there would be no redistributional impacts from inflation. Unfortunately, all prices do not increase at the same rate. In recent years, living costs for the poor and for those in urban areas have risen more than they have for the relatively affluent and for those living in small towns and rural areas. This redistribution is not a result of inflation itself; it reflects underlying structural changes that have occurred at the same time as inflation. Curing inflation will not abate these redistributional tendencies. *Our price stabilization goals must include not only the stabilization of the aggregate price level, but also developing policies that ensure that structural price changes do not place an inequitable burden on those least able to bear it.*

Relative price changes serve a vital role in the operation of our economic system. A bad harvest raises wheat prices, reducing the quantity consumed, and encouraging the production of substitutes (winter wheat, other crops, imports, etc.). Without the price signal, we would have to rely on an alternative allocation system—rationing or long lines at supermarkets. Oil conservation can be effectively achieved by raising the price of oil, a move that also offers an incentive for the development of alternative energy sources. Adjustments may take time, but will be made eventually if the price system is allowed to send the right signals.

Among Income Groups. The process of adjustment is not costless nor is it borne proportionately by all members of society. A suburban household earning $30,000 a year will be able to adjust to $1.25 a gallon gasoline by purchasing a smaller automobile and taking fewer trips. Their expenditure on gasoline will rise less than proportionately with the cost of gasoline. A poor household has far fewer behavioral options and will be hit much harder.

During the relatively mild inflation of the 1960s, the poor were not harmed relative to other income groups (Hollister and Palmer, 1972). If anything, the cost of living of low income families climbed more slowly than that of more affluent households. Since 1970, however, the price of necessities—food, shelter, energy, and medical services— which comprise a very large share of the low income budget, has risen more rapidly than the price of other goods (National Advisory Council on Economic Opportunity, 1979). This change is not the result of the monetary policy pursued by the Federal Reserve Board (see Chapter 2) but of underlying structural changes in the economy: the growing world demand for U.S. agricultural output; the slow growth of petroleum supplies relative to galloping demand increases; and increased regulatory policies aimed at other social objectives such as reduced pollution and improved safety and health. Between December 1972 and December 1977, the price of necessities grew at an annual rate of 9.1 percent, while the Consumer Price Index—a weighted sum of all goods and services taken together—grew at only 7.9 percent. In the first nine months of 1978, necessities rose at an annual rate of 11.6 percent, other goods at only 6.1 percent. Table 1 illustrates the vulnerability of the poor to increases in these basic costs (Palmer, Todd, and Tuckman, 1978). Cheaper foods have inflated more rapidly than less stable items (Manchester and Brown, 1977). While anti-inflation policy will have little impact on these relative price increases, a more effective indexing policy would reduce the hardship experienced by the poor as their purchasing power is eroded.

Table 1
Expenditures on Basic Necessities by Low Income Households
1972-1973

	Lowest 10% of U.S. households	Second 10% of U.S. households	Average decile 1 and 2
Average household income	$1,559	$3,268	$2,414
Less personal taxes.................	$ 68	$ 130	$ 99
Average after-tax household income	$1,491	$3,138	$2,315
Expenditures on:			
Food	$ 663	$ 943	$ 803
(as % after-tax income)	44%	30%	35%
Energy	$ 144	$ 187	$ 166
(as % after-tax income)	10%	6%	7%
Shelter*	$ 760	$ 891	$ 826
(as % after-tax income)	51%	28%	36%
Medical care	$ 213	$ 304	$ 259
(as % after-tax income)	14%	10%	11%
Total expenditures on necessities	$1,780	$2,325	$2,054
(as % after-tax income)	119%	74%	89%

*Shelter figure differs from line item of that name in Bulletin 1992 in that payments on mortgage principal have been added in.

SOURCE: National Advisory Council on Economic Opportunity, *Eleventh Report,* July 1979, p. 3.

Table 2
Index of Intercity Differences in Living Costs for a Four-Person Family

INTERMEDIATE BUDGET, Autumn, 1977
Austin, Tex. = 100

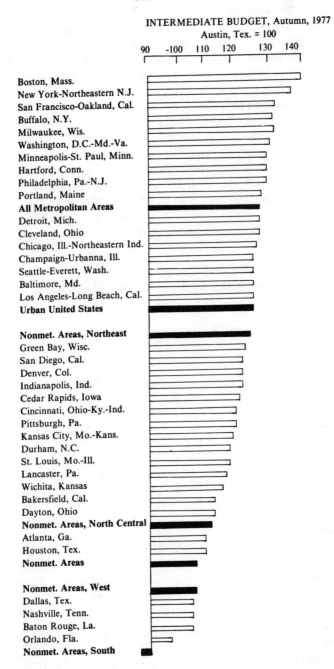

| | 90 | -100 | 110 | 120 | 130 | 140 |

Boston, Mass.
New York-Northeastern N.J.
San Francisco-Oakland, Cal.
Buffalo, N.Y.
Milwaukee, Wis.
Washington, D.C.-Md.-Va.
Minneapolis-St. Paul, Minn.
Hartford, Conn.
Philadelphia, Pa.-N.J.
Portland, Maine
All Metropolitan Areas
Detroit, Mich.
Cleveland, Ohio
Chicago, Ill.-Northeastern Ind.
Champaign-Urbanna, Ill.
Seattle-Everett, Wash.
Baltimore, Md.
Los Angeles-Long Beach, Cal.
Urban United States

Nonmet. Areas, Northeast
Green Bay, Wisc.
San Diego, Cal.
Denver, Col.
Indianapolis, Ind.
Cedar Rapids, Iowa
Cincinnati, Ohio-Ky.-Ind.
Pittsburgh, Pa.
Kansas City, Mo.-Kans.
Durham, N.C.
St. Louis, Mo.-Ill.
Lancaster, Pa.
Wichita, Kansas
Bakersfield, Cal.
Dayton, Ohio
Nonmet. Areas, North Central
Atlanta, Ga.
Houston, Tex.
Nonmet. Areas

Nonmet. Areas, West
Dallas, Tex.
Nashville, Tenn.
Baton Rouge, La.
Orlando, Fla.
Nonmet. Areas, South

Among Different Areas. Two facts about geographic differences in prices should be noted: price levels differ, and so do rates of inflation. Inflation, in the last two years, has been higher in those areas with lower living costs. It has acted to reduce inter-area cost differences. Table 2 shows an index of the cost of living in selected metropolitan areas in the United States in 1977. High cost areas tend to be cities in the Northeast and very large cities. Several factors explain these variations. First, taxes are higher in high cost areas. Employees demand higher wages to compensate for higher taxes, which drives up costs and prices. Baumol (1967) has advanced another reason. He argues that high costs in central cities, and also the high rate of price increases, may be due to the concentration of the urban labor force in sectors in which the productivity of labor grows relatively slowly. He cites teaching and culture as examples. If wages rise commensurately in all sectors, then relative costs in nonprogressive sectors must rise. The decline of manufacturing—the sector (outside agriculture) with the most rapid increases in productivity—in central cities has contributed to the urban cost disadvantage. Finally, many other costs—land, commuting time, access to recreation, for example—tend naturally to be higher in large cities.

Price levels have risen most rapidly in those metropolitan areas experiencing the fastest rates of growth and the lowest rates of unemployment (Table 3). In 1978, booming Denver suffered a 12.4 percent rise in the local cost of living, sluggish Buffalo only 8.3 percent. These differences reflect the need to offer higher wages to attract labor to tight labor markets and the pressure on even tighter housing markets. They also reflect differences in the rates of growth of local public sectors. While the fiscally distressed Northeast has been cutting public payrolls, growth areas have had to hire officials to cope with the problems of rapid development. The relatively low rate of inflation in slow growing areas will work to their advantage over time as it makes them more attractive as places to live and to do business.

Although inter-area differences in prices and price increases are necessary for the economy to adapt to structural change, they are not without their harmful impacts. Many federal programs make no allowance for cost differences. The federal tax structure includes standard deductions and tax brackets. Federal grants make no allowance for cost differences. Lack of adequate data prevents allowance of these differences from being built into federal programs. Cost of living indices are currently prepared for only 39 metropolitan areas.

Anticipation of Price Increases   When the rate of inflation is not correctly anticipated, some groups enjoy windfalls at the expense of others. If inflation soars above expectations, then borrowers gain at the expense of lenders, and   *103* employers gain at the expense of those under long term wage contracts. Empirical evidence suggests that sudden changes in the inflation rate tend to be unanticipated. Table 4 shows that the burst of inflation in 1974 far outstripped the increase in weekly earnings, while the moderate price increases in 1976 left employees with substantial gains in real income. Overall, employees and lenders have suffered most from inflationary shifts (Laidler and Parkin, 1975). The relatively affluent, because of their superior information and diverse portfolios, are able to react quickly to changes in inflationary expectations and so tend to gain relative to the poor. The middle class are less affected because their nominal assets are balanced by their nominal debts.

Price Rigidities

Inflation can lead to economic disruption when prices or wages are unable to adjust to reflect real or monetary pressures. For example, rent controls that prevent landlords from passing on fuel oil cost increases may lead building owners to cut back on maintenance expenditures in order to meet expenses. The result is a decline in building quality and even abandonment that drives up the price of other remaining housing units. A long term wage contract without a cost of living clause may

Table 3
Rate of Increase in the Local CPI, Jan. 1978-Jan. 1979 and Unemployment Rate in Jan. 1979: Selected Metropolitan Areas

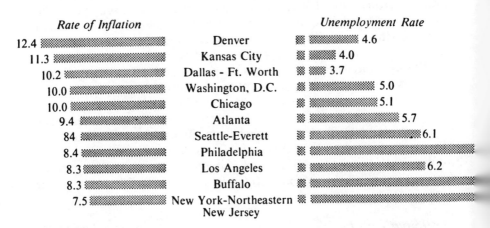

Rate of Inflation		Unemployment Rate
12.4	Denver	4.6
11.3	Kansas City	4.0
10.2	Dallas - Ft. Worth	3.7
10.0	Washington, D.C.	5.0
10.0	Chicago	5.1
9.4	Atlanta	5.7
84	Seattle-Everett	6.1
8.4	Philadelphia	
8.3	Los Angeles	6.2
8.3	Buffalo	
7.5	New York-Northeastern New Jersey	

Note: Unemployment rates are February 1979; consumer price changes are annual changes January 1978 to January 1979.

SOURCE: Bureau of Labor Statistics, various publications.

Table 4
Average Annual Increases in Money Wages and the
Consumer Price Index:
1968-1978

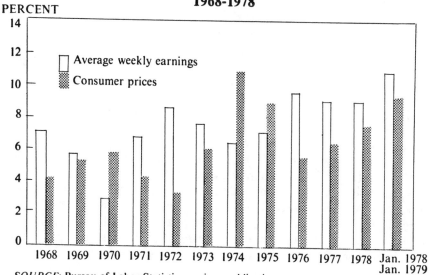

SOURCE: Bureau of Labor Statistics, various publications.

discourage workers from joining the industry, leading to reduced output. Mandatory price and wage guidelines—which do little to reduce the underlying inflationary pressures—also lead to distortions in the economy. The guidelines imposed by the Nixon Administration in 1972 and 1973 contributed to shortages in some vital primary manufacturing industries that helped to precipitate the 1974 recession. When they were relaxed, the price level soon adjusted to what it would have been without any guidelines.

There are many regulations that contribute to price rigidities that have distributional impacts. For example, Regulation Q, administered by the Federal Reserve Board, fixes the rate offered on commercial bank savings deposits. Thus, small savers earn a lower rate of return than larger savers who are able to invest in more "inflation-proof" assets. Even more harmful are usury ceilings imposed by some states on residential mortgage rates (Chapter 6). As these ceilings become binding, financial institutions cease providing mortgages and seek assets that yield a rate of return more compatible with their inflationary expectations. The result is a sudden decline in demand for homes which sends the construction sector into a tailspin.

Failure to Index

One of the major causes of inequitable income redistribution resulting from inflation is the way transfer payments and taxes are determined. Because *105* they are usually set in nominal (unadjusted for inflation) terms rather than real terms, inflation leads to falling real incomes for the poor, and a fiscal bonus for federal, state and local governments. Transfer payments and taxes are not "indexed" to the cost of living.

Transfer Payments. Some transfer payment programs are indexed. The Social Security and Supplementary Security Income payments are indexed annually to the national CPI—although not to local CPIs. This affords some protection to recipients, although, to the extent that they. tend to be low income households, indexing against the price of necessities rather than the CPI would be more appropriate. The foodstamp program, for example, is adjusted twice a year according to the rate of price increase of foodstuffs.

Many programs are not increased, and cost of living adjustments have become a luxury item in local budgets. For example, one of the first budget cuts in California in response to the passage of Proposition 13 was the scheduled cost of living increase for Aid to Families with Dependent Children recipients. New York's fiscal problems have delayed increases in welfare benefits. Increases in medical costs have not been matched by increases in Medicaid and Medicare, and patients have been forced to make greater contributions from their own pockets.

Tax Structure. Failure to index the tax structure—the value of standard deductions and tax brackets—has provided federal, state and local government with a fiscal bonus. A 10 percent increase in the cost of living increases tax revenues by more than 10 percent. Where tax rates are progressive, taxpayers are forced into a higher tax bracket, although their real income has not increased and may even have declined. The value of standard exemptions and deductions declines in real terms, and property taxes jump as property values tend to increase faster than the overall rate of inflation. The Advisory Commission on Intergovernmental Relations (1979a) calculates that states received an inflationary bonus of $1.2 billion in 1978.

Inflation acts as a disincentive to saving—thus driving down the supply of loanable funds and reducing investment and growth. A saver who earns 11 percent on a long term asset when inflation is running at 10 percent is only just ahead of the game without taxes. After taxes, he has lost purchasing power by saving. The high rate of interest reflects the inflation rate, and therefore only that yield *above* the current rate of inflation should be considered as income.

Failure to allow for inflation also erodes much of the incentive for investment. Most important, the capital gains taxes both nominal gains and real gains. For example, at a rate of about 30 percent, the capital gains tax would tax away nearly one third of the increase in value of an asset. An investor who realized a 15 percent capital gain over a one year investment when inflation was running at 12 percent would actually be worse off for having invested. His investment

Fiscal Years	Inflationary[1] Increase in Revenues Billions of Dollars	Percent of Revenues	Inflationary[2] Loss in Purchasing Power Billions of Dollars	Percent of Revenues	Net Gain[3] From Inflation Billions of Dollars	Percent of Revenues
Total State-Local						
1973	$10.3	6.8%	$ 9.4	6.3%	$ 0.9	0.6%
1974	18.0	11.4	12.4	7.5	6.5	3.9
1975	28.4	15.7	18.5	10.2	9.9	5.5
1976	19.5	9.7	13.8	6.9	5.7	2.9
State						
1973	$ 6.2	7.7%	$ 5.0	6.3%	$ 1.1	1.4%
1974	11.3	12.7	6.7	7.5	4.6	5.2
1975	17.0	17.5	9.9	10.2	7.1	7.3
1976	11.6	10.8	7.4	6.9	4.3	4.0
Local						
1973	$ 4.2	5.9%	$ 4.4	6.3%	$-0.2	-0.4%
1974	7.6	9.9	5.8	7.5	1.9	2.4
1975	11.4	13.6	8.6	10.2	2.8	3.4
1976	7.8	8.4	6.4	6.9	1.5	1.6

1. Based on regression analysis.
2. Based on percent increase in implicit price deflator for state and local purchases of goods and services.
3. Net gain equals inflationary increase in revenue minus inflationary loss in purchasing power, expressed in nominal dollars.

Time series regression analysis was computed for each level of government using fiscal year data for the period 1957-76. The model was specified as follows:

$$\Delta R = \delta + \beta_1 \Delta DEFL + \beta_2 \Delta GAP$$

ΔR = Change in own source general revenues.

ΔGAP = Change in the nominal GNP GAP.

$\Delta DEFL$ = Change in the implicit price deflator for GNP.

Regression Results

Coefficient estimated for:

	Constant	ΔGAP	$\Delta DEFL$	R^2	Durban Watson
Total	1.15	-0.12 (5.54)	236.42 (11.28)	.883	1.35
State	0.33	-0.08 (5.91)	141.21 (10.31)	.857	2.01
Local	0.82	0.04 (3.53)	95.21 (9.59)	.859	0.99

(T values are in parentheses.)

SOURCE: Advisory Commission on Intergovernmental Relations, *State-Local Finances in Recession and Inflation,* A-70, Washington, D.C., May 1979, p. 34.

yielded a negative after tax real rate of return of nearly two percent. Business tax problems do not end here. Inflation blows up the value of inventories, creating paper profits on which taxes must be paid, and shrivels the value of depreciation allowances. Tax indexing avoids this. The value of standard deductions and tax brackets is raised each year by the percentage increase in the local CPI. Three states, California, Colorado, and Arizona (the latter only for 1978), have introduced some form of indexing. The state-local sector has benefited from inflation. The inflation-induced increase in tax revenues has more than compensated for the increase in costs (Table 5). This has resulted from the fact that housing prices have outstripped the Consumer Price Index and from the failure to index tax brackets, and exemptions. This suggests that states have the resources to build stabilization funds that can increase their ability to raise expenditures during recessions, and that they can substantially improve the indexing of their transfer payment programs and of their tax structure.

IMPLICATIONS This discussion has important implications for a coordinated federal-state effort to combat inflation. First, we have distinguished between the goals of achieving stable prices and moderating the harm done by spiraling prices.

Price stability is a federal goal, and can only be achieved through a rational monetary policy. To this end, state governments must apply pressure on Congress and the Administration. We shall argue in the following chapter that high interest rates are not the *cause* but the *result* of inflation, and that slowing down inflation will necessitate even higher rates in the short run. Calls for reduced interest rates as an anti-inflationary tool by state and local governments are counter-productive.

However, helping avoid some of the more harmful impacts of inflation is a task that both state and federal governments can undertake. By indexing transfer payments and taxes, by avoiding unnecessary expenditures and costly regulations, social inequity and economic disruption can be reduced.

Footnotes to Chapter 1

1. A major review of the causes and impacts of inflation has been conducted by Laidler and Parkin (1975). In view of the divergent views of the different "schools" of inflation, we should make our own views clear in advance. We believe that inflation is primarily a monetary phenomenon. That is not to say that the Federal Reserve Board is guilty of inspiring all inflationary pressure, but that without a sustained increase in the money supply, inflation cannot continue.

2
WHY THE FEDERAL GOVERNMENT WILL NOT FIGHT INFLATION

Federal anti-inflationary policy has oscillated between monetary policy and various forms of wage and price guidelines. Neither has proved particularly effective as the soaring price level through the end of 1979 clearly attests. The failure can be traced to two major factors:

■ The mistaken belief that we face a trade-off between price stability and the rate of unemployment—popularly described as the Phillips curve.
■ An unwillingness to control the money supply because of the mistaken view that interest rates—rather than the money supply—are the appropriate target for monetary policy.

In the last few years, the weakening of the dollar in international money markets has posed an additional constraint on policy choices. These factors are examined in turn in this chapter.

THE MYTH OF THE PHILLIPS CURVE
Monetary policy has been crippled by being forced to serve two masters, full-employment and stable prices. Its dual servitude stems from a belief that there is a stable relationship between the rate of inflation and the rate of unemployment, and that monetary policy can shift the economy along the "Phillips curve" to the optimum combination of unemployment rate and inflation rate.[1] The Phillips curve is illustrated in Figure 1, and in the following quotation (First National City Bank, 1975):

> The basic assumption is that unemployment and inflation are at opposite ends of an economic seesaw. As one goes up, the other goes down, in relatively predictable proportion. Proponents of the idea point to periods when the seesaw seemed to work. At such times, when rates of unemployment were plotted on a chart against corresponding rates of inflation, the two variables met along a crescent shaped line—the Phillips curve (cc in Figure 1). One tip of the curve rose toward higher inflation as unemployment shrank; the other tip sloped down toward lower inflation as unemployment grew.

> In the early 1960s, some versions of the curve appeared to offer a range of policy options. A shift in monetary policy seemed enough to move **109**

the rate of inflation one way or another along the curve, simultaneously changing the rate of unemployment in the opposite direction.

In those halcyon days, the "discovery" of the Phillips curve played into popular demands for full employment. So long as the curve worked, a 3-5 percent rate of inflation seemed to many economists and politicians to be a bearable cost to pay for cutting the jobless rate to the minimum. Result: The policy bias in the United States was often tilted toward accelerating money growth.

Figure 1
Inflation and Unemployment
1960-1978

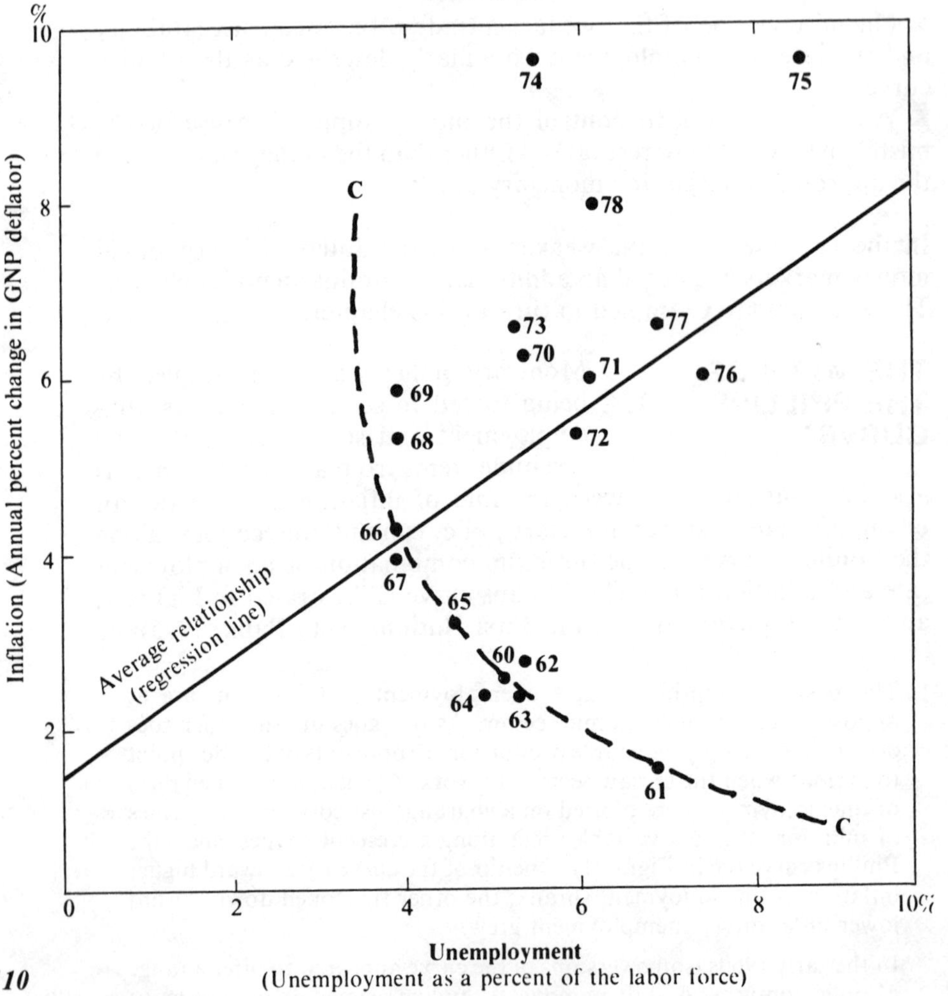

Inflation (Annual percent change in GNP deflator)

Unemployment
(Unemployment as a percent of the labor force)

But Figure 1 also illustrates that those "halcyon" days are long gone. The Phillips curve may work in the short run while households and firms suffer from a money illusion. That is, workers are tempted to accept a job by a wage offer that they think is greater than one they turned down previously; but the offer turns out to represent no real increase when inflation erodes their monetary gains; businesses try to step up output in response to a perceived increase in demand, only to find that costs have risen proportionately. As the illusion disappears, unemployment returns to its original level. Business finds the stepped up level of production unprofitable in the face of higher costs; real consumer demand falls; and employees dissatisfied with inflation-eroded wages seek better paying opportunities. Further monetary stimulus is needed in an attempt to reduce unemployment again. The nation learns to adapt to higher rates of inflation. The "stable" Phillips curve is pushed further and further from its origin at an ever increasing speed. Monetary policy has no impact on the long run rate of unemployment or on the long run rate of growth of the economy. In the short run, it does effect real growth and shifts in policy create cycles. The temporary drop in unemployment that follows from an expansionary monetary policy is followed by a burst of inflation that drowns real growth and, because all aspects of the economy cannot adjust to inflation, a recession ensues. In addition to the collapse of the money illusion, other factors have helped propel the Phillips curve into orbit. We have tried to return to the low unemployment levels of the 1960s—in spite of the fact that the behavior of the work force has changed—much as a full-grown dog still chases its tail long after its adult skeleton has ended its puppy flexibility. The broadening of unemployment insurance coverage, increases in benefit levels, the rise in the number of two-worker households and spatial shifts from the Frostbelt to the Sunbelt have all contributed to raising the "natural" rate of unemployment. The structural rate of unemployment has risen, and the frictional rate of unemployment has increased as workers hold out longer for better paying jobs. In view of these changes, our goals have been unrealistic, and our use of monetary policy to pursue them has been inappropriate.

Not only have we tried to use the money supply to control cycles, but we have also tried to use it to stimulate the economy when the economy is undergoing a real structural change. During such periods, stimulation of any sort will have little impact. The 1973 leap in oil prices is an excellent example. Karl Brunner (1979) describes the futility of the monetary stimulation that gave us the inflation of 1974 and 1975.

A large increase in the relative price of energy inputs into the production process of western countries lowers the normal output of these economies. The OPEC shock of October 1973 probably lowered   *111* the normal output of the U.S. economy by about 5 percent. The decline of 8 percent in real GNP observed from peak to trough reflected thus to a major extent *not* a ʀecession but an adjustment in normal output. Only the remaining portion of about 3 percent expresses the effect of a recession. The order of magnitude of the recession coincides thus with the patterns observed over the first fifteen years of the postwar period. The oil price shock reminds us that we cannot infer from output movements alone whether or not a recession occurred. We need additional information in order to judge whether it dropped relative to normal output. No increase in budgets or deficits and no increase in money stock whatever its magnitude will raise output again. In the other case output will rebound to the normal level provided policy does not aggravate recession by unleashing additional erratic negative shocks.

MONETARY POLICY AND INTERNATIONAL MONEY MARKETS

As if the dual role of price stabilization and low unemployment were not enough, monetary policy has also been called upon to shore up the dollar against other currencies in international money markets. As the dollar weakens, the Federal Reserve attracts foreign currency by raising the interest rate. The inflow of foreign, short term investment in response to increased yields eases devaluation pressure. With this added responsibility, can monetary policy be freed to address the problem of price stabilization? The answer is yes, but to understand why, we must examine the reasons why intervention in international money markets is necessary.

Downward pressure on the dollar arises for two related reasons: first, Americans are buying more goods from abroad than foreigners are buying from the U.S. The result is a balance of payments deficit, which is reflected in a shortage of foreign currency by U.S. importers, and a surplus of dollars in the hands of successful foreign exporters. The solution is a devaluation of the dollar, which makes foreign goods more expensive to Americans, and American goods cheaper for foreigners.

The second reason for a weakened dollar occurs when foreigners no longer regard the dollar as a secure investment and sell their investments denominated in dollars—U.S. government bills and bonds, corporate bonds, and other money market instruments—and purchase what they regard as safer investments denominated in other currencies. The Federal Reserve Board counters these expectations by raising the interest rate to make dollar investments more attractive. Defenders of this role for monetary policy argue that the massive increase in the volume of internationally mobile short term investments in the last few years, especially since OPEC countries began accumulating vast surpluses, has made the international market highly unstable, necessitating an aggressive role for the Federal Reserve Board. But this attitude begs the question of what causes shifts in expectations. They are not the product of whimsy or hysteria. They are based upon what investors feel will happen to the value of the dollar, which is determined by expectations concerning the rate of inflation. Expectations change as the Federal Reserve Board switches between "expansionary" and "tight money" policy. An expansionary policy is likely to drive up the short run U.S. growth rate beyond the capacity of U.S. industry, necessitating an increase in imports, causing a deficit and, ultimately, devaluation. It will also cause domestic inflation, making U.S. goods more expensive relative to imports, and causing an increase in imports. Monetary expansion provides a two-pronged reason for anticipating devaluation, leading to a quite rational desire to reduce dollar holdings.

The international money market has, in fact, helped dampen the more harmful tendencies of monetary policy at home. If monetary policy were not suddenly switched between its dual domestic goals of price stability and full employment, it would not be called in to rescue the dollar in international markets. If it pursued a policy of price stability at home, with no sudden surprises, then the need to intervene in international markets would be greatly diminished. In other words, using monetary policy to achieve price stability is compatible with international monetary goals.

CONTROLLING THE MONEY SUPPLY

If the Federal Reserve Board is to avoid contributing to the inflationary process, it must control the rate of monetary expansion, not the rate of interest. We saw above that if the Board pursues a low interest rate policy in spite of an increase in the demand for credit, inflation ensues. Lawrence Roos, President of the Federal Reserve Bank of St. Louis, has stated that:

> Much of the inflation that we are presently experiencing can be attributed to monetary policy directed toward the stabilization of interest rates in times of rising credit demand . . . A factor contributing to continued concentration on interest rate stabilization is a fundamental misconception of exactly what monetary policy can and cannot accomplish. Regardless of its goals and purposes, monetary policy as practiced in free market economies can directly affect only one variable, the rate of growth of the money stock.

Of course, interest rate stabilization is convenient for the Administration since it loosens the constraint on federal spending. Washington must finance its programs either through taxes, borrowing, or printing money. Since taxes are unpopular and borrowing is constrained, printing money is an attractive alternative but only in the short run. In the long run, the resulting inflation *113* precipitates a restrictive monetary policy which drives up interest rates, discouraging home purchases. Business investment also declines and the symptoms of a recession spread.

Monetary policy has little influence on the long run rate of growth of the economy but strongly influences year-to-year fluctuations in the rate of economic growth. If that influence is not to be destructive, in the sense of exaggerating cyclical fluctuations, then the rate of growth of the money supply must be controlled, and sudden shifts in policy that have characterized the post-World War II era must be avoided.

Defenders of the Federal Reserve Board argue that their ability to control their money supply has been undermined by: 1) competing definitions of which money supply they should control; 2) declining membership in the Federal Reserve System by commercial banks; and 3) technological changes that allow individuals and firms to economize on their cash balances. These defenses do not stand up to strong scrutiny.

Although there are several different definitions of the money supply,[2] the Board can determine the monthly, quarterly, or annual rate of growth of the monetary base—the total currency in circulation *plus* reserves and currency held by banks. While a target of 5 percent growth of a measure of the money supply that includes savings accounts may lead to a slightly different rate of inflation than a 5 percent increase in a measure that included only currency and bank reserves, a low rate of growth of the base will always lead to stable prices or a stable and low rate of price increase. Recent experience suggests that a 5 percent rate of growth of the monetary base—the level of bank reserves plus currency held by the public—may serve as the best target for the Board to pursue, because while innovation continues, this is likely to bring inflation down close to zero. If they use the base as the target the Board does not have to worry about the multipliers that relate the base to broader definitions of the money supply—those that encompass demand deposits and various types of time deposits. Thus, the Board does not have to worry about whether or not a bank is a member of the system or about the various technological changes that allow depositors to economize on demand deposits and switch into and out of savings deposits.[3] The shift in Federal Reserve policy announced by Chairman Volcker in October 1979 would seem to be a step in the right direction. However, it remains to be seen whether the Board will stick to this policy in the face of rising unemployment. Chairman Burns made a similar announcement in 1971, but soon gave way to demands for greater monetary stimulation.

IMPLICATIONS   The return to stable prices cannot be achieved immediately. Sudden, sharp

changes in the rate of monetary growth are economically disruptive, as our postwar experience painfully reminds us. The unexpected changes provide windfall gains to those who correctly forecast them, at the expense of those less able to understand them. Mark Willes, economist with the Federal Reserve Bank in Minneapolis, neatly summarizes how we can return to price stability:

> What policy makers do to fight inflation effectively . . . is to eliminate, whenever possible, surprises in monetary and fiscal policy. They must build a set of policies that the public has faith in and will take into account when forming expectations of future inflation and spending. In short, policy must be credible. And the only way to make policy credible is to announce it, implement it faithfully, and avoid shifting it abruptly.

The discussion should also make it clear that high interest rates are not inflationary. High interest rates are the result of inflation—lenders demand high rates to protect their assets, and borrowers are able to repay from incomes swelled by inflation. It is true that the rate of interest enters into the Consumer Price Index through the mortgage interest rate. *But accusing high interest rates of being inflationary is no more meaningful than saying that price increases cause inflation.* Inflation *is* the rapid increase in prices, and interest rates are simply the price of loanable funds. The sudden increase in interest rates as the Federal Reserve tightens monetary policy is *deflationary,* for it represents a reduction in the rate of monetary growth that will eventually lead to a lower inflation rate and lower interest rates.

Another major point to stress is that monetary restraint will only be achieved if the federal government exercises a much greater degree of control over its budget. If the federal deficit is brought into manageable dimensions through austere spending policies over the next three years, then the need to indulge in monetary finance of federal programs will be abated. But cutting spending can only be achieved if the programs themselves are more suitably designed and targeted much more carefully on those groups in society that need assistance. Without retargeting, budget cuts will impose harsh penalties on the poor and needy.

One final issue deserves discussion. It has become fashionable to seek a "supply side" solution to the problem of inflation. The theory is that if we can raise productivity there will then be more goods to absorb the increased money supply, which will moderate the increase in prices. Proponents argue for investment stimulants, and for profit sharing to induce increased labor productivity. The dramatic slow-down in the rate of productivity increase in the last decade is fingered as the major villain in the inexorable rise in inflation. Unfortunately, this approach ignores the fact that it is inflation that is largely responsible for the low rate of investment and savings. The tax system was developed in an environment of stable prices and makes no allowances for inflation. With no indexing, the personal income tax on savings interest ensures that the saver will steadily lose in real terms. **115**

The 30 percent capital gains tax becomes confiscatory—yielding a net after-tax loss in real terms on most assets. Paper profits owe their record levels to the influence of inflation on inventories. To stimulate savings and investment, Washington must index tax rates (see Chapter 3) so that the saver only pays taxes on the *real* interest, and the investor pays capital gains only on *real* gains. There is no mystery in stimulating productivity. It requires either a stable price level or an indexed tax structure. After nearly 15 years of harmful inflation it is certainly time to adopt a more rational monetary policy. But it is also time to admit that inflation is unlikely to disappear overnight, and to face up to the truth that we had better adopt a rational tax indexing policy if we are to encourage investment and, therefore, job growth.

Footnotes to Chapter 2

1. The Phillips curve is named after its discoverer, the late A.W. Phillips. His research examined the relationship between the rate of wage increases and the rate of unemployment, but the concept has popularly been applied to the relationship between inflation and unemployment.

2. There are several "definitions" of the money supply. The monetary base refers to currency in the hands of the public and to the level of bank reserves and currency reserves that are held against demand and time deposits. An expansion of reserves allows banks to acquire more liabilities and to expand deposits. A technological change (such as the use of credit cards) that allows individuals to hold less cash will leave more cash in banks and allow an expansion of deposits. These changes tend to occur steadily over time. They simply increase the multiplier relationship between base and broader definitions of the money supply that also include demand deposits (M^1) or various types of savings (time) accounts (M^2 - M^4).

3. Some of the most important technological changes include: credit cards that conserve currency; automatic funds transfers that allow accounts to be switched between demand and savings accounts; the growth of the money market that allows banks easy access to reserves so that, at the end of a business day, a bank can meet any shortfall (as might result from a large withdrawal of currency and reserves) by borrowing—thereby reducing the extent to which they must maintain surplus reserves; and repurchase agreements through which corporate accounts can invest any checking account surplus in the money market overnight, and sell it in the morning.

3
HOW STATES
CAN FIGHT INFLATION

States can do little to stop the inflationary spiral. They have not contributed to inflation, and can only fight it by lobbying for a rational and stable monetary policy by the Federal Reserve Board. *Cutting state and local government expenditures will not abate inflation. It will merely leave more spending money in the pockets of consumers, driving up prices elsewhere in the economy.* Inflation is like an expanding balloon—pressing in on one side simply extends it on another. It can only be controlled by turning off the air supply— restricting monetary growth. But that does not mean that states are unable to help either themselves or their constituents. There are several steps that states can take to reduce their operating budgets, and therefore alleviate the fiscal squeeze from inflation and recession, and there are ways in which states can cushion the corrosive influences of inflation on those least able to fight unaided. These steps are:

- Helping economic adjustment.
- A moderate appetite for public expenditures.
- An equitable and efficient fiscal structure.
- Cutting public program costs.
- Indexation to reduce the inequitable and inefficient consequences of inflation.

HELPING ECONOMIC ADJUSTMENT State economic development policy must facilitate rather than retard the adjustment of the economy to the shocks that often lead, through Federal Reserve complicity, to inflation. The structural changes that the oil price rise necessitates can be assisted by the actions of state governments. They can remove regulatory and land use barriers to the development of alternative energy sources. They can use state development finance agencies to invest in those companies that can help develop energy conservation products or new energy sources. Transition to an energy conserving environment will mean that some companies will have to expand rapidly, requiring massive capital investments. Yet rapidly growing new companies are precisely those that may find difficulty in acquiring capital from traditional sources. The energy area provides some current examples of how states should not fight inflation. Some states have attempted to roll back energy costs. This simply delays *117* adjustment and will contribute to inflation later. The correct way to protect the poor and low income families from the hardships imposed by high prices for home heating oil is to provide them with income supplementing grants, while still leaving oil prices high to encourage conservation.

There are other steps that states can take to speed up the development process and so reduce inflationary pressures. An effective labor placement and training program can reduce bottlenecks in the labor market that drive up wages. If these programs are to prove effective, then states must spend greater resources anticipating economic development trends and the implications for the demand for labor.

The state stabilization funds, proposed in Chapter 6, will also help reduce inflationary demand. By accumulating balances during periods of rapid growth, the state is cutting back on consumers' purchasing power. The resources paid into the fund would otherwise have been returned to consumers in the form of tax cuts (as they were in 1979) or have been spent on expanded public sector activity.

In other words, state development efforts must run with the direction of overall economic development—not try to fight it. Resources spent shoring up obsolete industries and inefficient behavior by consumers will be wasted. This waste will be translated into bottlenecks in the local economy, and an upward pressure on prices. An efficient state economic development effort, coupled with spending containment and cost-cutting practices, will not wipe out inflation; but it will help, and perhaps provide a useful example to the federal government over the next decade.

MODERATING THE APPETITE FOR PUBLIC EXPENDITURES

If the federal government is to reduce spending, then state governments must also curb their expenditures, for federal intergovernmental grants are bound to be affected. The economic climate of the next years will not sustain a rate of expansion in the state-local sector comparable to that of the last two decades. Government will have to re-examine its programs carefully to ensure that any shrinkage in public sector activity is made with the minimum of disruption. Increased reliance on user fees may help prune some unnecessary growth from the capital budget by curbing sprawling new development and encouraging rehabilitation and conservation of existing structures. Mortgaging future tax revenues to attract a footloose firm through tax incentives is not a wise investment. Neither is the subsidy to residential expansion implicit in the below cost extension of public services to new residential development. The long run fiscal costs of these unbalanced growth patterns outweigh any development benefits.

Rather than try to "grow" their way out of fiscal difficulty, states should try to reduce public programs in line with current levels of local economic and residential activity.

States should also review their use of mandates. Too often, new programs are mandated before a full consideration is given to their likely cost to the implementing levels of government. It is always easier to be expansionary with someone else's budget. Several states require that the costs of mandated programs be borne by the state. Others require a fiscal note to accompany any new mandates outlining its cost. This does not guarantee that only cost effective programs are introduced, but it does encourage a more informed debate.

The stabilization fund, proposed in Chapter 6, will also require all levels of government to control expenditures rather than letting a "boom" mentality pervade expenditure deliberations. Similarly, tax indexing will remove the inflationary windfall that tempts administrators and legislators to increase spending.

FISCAL REFORM   Changing the tax system can help combat the harmful impacts of inflation. This is discussed in more detail in *State Taxation and Economic Development* (Volume 1, *Studies in State Development Policy*), but the major components of a state-local anti-inflationary fiscal reform package are summarized below.

State-Local   The inroads of inflation have been sever-
Fiscal Relations   est in the largest cities, areas where a large share of the poor live. More effective targeting of state fiscal assistance would provide relief to those hardest hit. Most state revenue sharing initiatives have been regressive—collecting revenues from regressive taxes and redistributing largely on the basis of population, rather than on measures of need. Circuit breakers provide an opportunity for more targeted state assistance, and so do court decisions requiring greater state aid to education.

Income Tax   A shift to a more progressive income tax, as well as providing a more effective automatic stabilizer (Chapter 6), would also shift the burden from the poor to the more affluent. A sudden increase in progressivity that is not matched by a state's neighbors may cause affluent, mobile households to leave. This must be accompanied by indexing (see below).

Sales Tax   The regressivity of the sales tax can be lessened by including exemptions for necessities, food, clothing, and medical supplies. These are the very items that have been attacked most severely by the recent burst of inflation. The exemptions will not abate inflation but will afford some relief to the poor.   *119*

Property Taxes   The property tax—the least popular source of revenue—should be changed to to reduce its inflationary burden on the poor and to respond to public dissatisfaction expressed in the taxpayers' revolt. First, states should finance circuit breakers that prevent low income households—both owners and renters—from paying more than a fixed fraction of their incomes in property taxes. An explosion of property values has left many elderly and poor households with staggering property tax bills or rents driven up by property taxes. Local jurisdictions rarely have the resources to assist these households, and local financing would unduly penalize cities and counties with large concentrations of the poor. Circuit breakers must be a federally assisted state responsibility.

Second, states must work with local jurisdictions to improve property tax assessment and collection techniques. Assessment in many areas is primitive and inequitable. It must be in the hands of professional appraisers, computerized, and annual assessments clearly publicized. Fair and prompt assessment practices will increase taxes in rapidly growing areas and reduce them in declining ones—a shift that will improve equity. States will become more deeply involved in property taxes as the repercussions of *Serrano v. Priest* are worked through in all states. They may use the opportunity to follow the example of Florida, which requires that assessors publish revenues, the tax base, the tax rate, and the programs that have necessitated revenue increases.

Finally, some consideration should be given to shifting the property tax burden from structures onto land so as not to deter housing rehabilitation and upgrading. This will help reduce prices in the long run by encouraging better maintenance of our existing housing stock, thereby reducing the need for wasteful and expensive new development.

User Fees   User fees provide an excellent opportunity for states and local areas to reduce expenditures and also to avoid the costs of growth and development from raising the tax burden of all local residents. The administrative problems in devising the fee schedule are not insuperable. The failure to charge fees for new development has serious cost implications. For example, until recently, builders of summer homes in Vermont were required to pay only $19 for electricity hook up, although the cost to the state was $1,350 (National League of Cities, 1975). All state taxpayers helped to subsidize these new homes. And in California, as a result of Proposition 13, the expanding suburb of Petaluma near San Francisco now charges developers and "impact fee" of $3,000 per acre. Charging fees will help control costs and control wasteful spending.

User fees of this sort will drive up the cost of new homes, although
only by a modest amount. However, they will reduce the tax burden

that is currently borne by all homeowners. To the extent that this leads to a more compact pattern of residential settlement, the cost of delivering public services will be reduced in the long run. A general principle is that fiscal policies should never be pursued merely to cut taxes. The criteria of efficiency and equity, established in *State Taxation and Economic Development,* should be the guide.

COST CUTTING

The opportunities for cost cutting in public service delivery are too numerous to examine in any detail here. Volumes have been written on improved management, sunset laws, procurement, and the administration of public utilities. All we can do in this section is to suggest a number of directions to act as a check list to fiscally pressed local administrators.

Personnel Management

Although it offers short run gains, low salary increases may not cut long run costs. States will lose their ability to hire the caliber of administrators and technicians needed to run state programs. However, some savings can be enjoyed by switching from direct salary payments to fringe benefits. For example, Texas has switched to paying the entire Social Security tax for its employees. The state avoids the additional tax that it would have had to pay had it given an equivalent amount in salary increases. Part-time employees and volunteers can also be used to reduce costs.

Financial Management

States can reduce the interest cost and transactions costs on local bond issues by packaging them together and issuing them as a state bond issue or through a state bond bank. States can also offer cash management services to local governments, allowing them to invest their idle balances at higher yields through an investment pool.

Sunset Laws

Many regulations and regulatory agencies outlive their usefulness because a busy legislature has failed to review their effectiveness. Sunset laws guarantee that laws and agencies will be reviewed by allowing them to die after a prescribed period unless explicitly reauthorized. Not all activities can or should be sunsetted. Indeed, the zero-based budget movement, which essentially requires all programs to be evaluated each year, has withered as states realize the massive increase in workload it entails. However, states should consider applying the sunset principle where it is appropriate.

Rulemaking Oversight

A lot can happen to a program when it passes out of the hands of the legislature and into the hands of administrators. Rules and regulations of different agencies can work at cross purposes, raise costs, and erode the business climate. Systematic legislative oversight can avoid some of these problems.

Simplifying the
Permit Process

The proliferation of regulatory activity, both state initiated and federally mandated, has increased business costs. By making federal, state, and local regulations compatible, ensuring there is not duplication in the paper work, and providing for a regulatory ombudsman, these costs can be reduced. This is an important area, since regulatory constraints seem likely to expand in the future. Building codes can be modified where they needlessly raise costs and discourage cost-saving innovation. At the same time, codes can be used to encourage energy conservation. The city of Portland, Oregon, has devised an extensive energy conservation plan which uses such techniques as requiring double glazing for a house to pass building inspection—a necessary step in securing a mortgage. The danger in such conservation efforts is that the costs of conservation far outweigh the value of the energy saved. No program can be justified on conservation grounds alone, but must be shown to be cost-effective.

Antitrust Activity

Many of the goods and services purchased by state and local governments are highly specialized, and may be dominated by a few firms—activities that range from highly technical medical services to garbage collection. States can use both legal recourse and their purse strings to discourage firms from charging monopoly prices.

Procurement

The state can use its size and influence to assist local areas to reduce procurement costs. Packaging the procurement needs of several small jurisdictions can reduce their costs. The state can also act as a clearinghouse of information on procurement costs for materials and services from its component jurisdictions. It may also use its financial sources to obtain long term and large scale purchases of materials (such as heating oil and building materials), passing on the savings to local governments. It can also encourage energy savings by purchasing energy efficient equipment.

Utility Rate Regulation

Most electric utilities have practiced the energy wasting pricing policy of declining block rates. Peak load pricing—a system which prices electricity consumed at seasonal or daily peak periods above electricity consumed at other periods—may reduce energy costs by spreading the demand allowing more efficient capacity utilization. A similar pricing structure should be applied to water use and mass transit fares.

States can also use their rate regulatory powers to ensure that cost effective energy conservation programs are in place before permission is granted to expand generating capacity or to raise rates across the board.

Health Care

The rapid expansion of medicaid, medicare, and medical insurance, has sent medical costs skyrocketing. Many people are price insensitive to medical costs—those that are sensitive, the poor, are unable to deal with the problem. States have many avenues to help contain health costs. The principle objective should be to reduce the capital intensity of the health system by closing hospitals and assisting local clinics. Outpatient care is much cheaper than in-patient care. They can use their licensing powers, regulatory agencies, and massive budgets to coordinate the delivery of health care services.

Cooperatives

The new federal legislation setting up a national cooperative bank provides states with a vital tool to assist low income communities cut the costs of one basic necessity—food. By providing technical assistance to community groups, state and local governments can help them set up food cooperatives that may yield substantial savings. The state is in the unique position of being able to coordinate the efforts of buyers, most of whom will be urban groups, with suppliers in rural areas.

INDEXING

Indexing offers an opportunity to mitigate the harmful effects of inflation, such as economic disruption and eroding purchasing power. Indexing is essentially an accounting technique that ties prices, interest rates, and wages—*nominal terms*—to the overall price level, usually measured by the consumer price index. Its purpose is to promote a more effective adjustment of the economy to inflationary forces. The private sector already indexes extensively. Most long term contracts, such as long term loans, supply agreements, and wages, are tied to escalator clauses. Interest rates are allowed to fluctuate, supply prices rise, and wages adjust according to the strength of inflationary impacts.

Indexing is needed in the public sector, particularly in the tax structure. Inflation has driven nominal wages up along with prices, so that wage earners find themselves in higher tax brackets with no real gain in income. Two years of inflation at 14 percent, even if wages fully adjust, is equivalent to a 10 percent increase in tax rates at a time of stable prices. Real disposable income declines by 1 percent each year. Unfortunately indexing is not a miracle cure for inflation. It involves real economic costs—price adjustments are never costless—which make it less preferable than no inflation at all. The key areas for indexing are:

■ *Interest income on saving.* Inflation has driven savings down to a record low share of personal income—less than 5 percent, compared with about 15 percent in other developed countries. The real yield on most forms of saving is now negative. Only that portion of savings income that represents a real rate of return over and above the inflation rate should be subject to taxation.

■ *Capital gains.* Similarly, only that part of capital gains that represents an increase above the inflation rate should be subject to taxation.

■ *Corporate income.* Inflation generated increases in the value of inventories should not be counted as taxable income.

■ *Tax deductions and tax brackets.*

States can play only a limited role in rationalizing the tax structure. They must alter their own tax structures and apply pressure to Washington to rationalize the federal system.

Another problem stems from imperfections in published price indices. The representatives of the population to which an index refers and the samples used to reflect that population—fixed weights for the various components of consumer expenditure, differences between list and actual transaction prices, and inadequate allowances for quality changes—all these may cause measured indices to diverge from the true index. Moreover, even if the measured indices are flawless, they are still after the fact, and thus adjustments can only be made with some time lag. However, most firms have judged that benefits outweigh costs and have adopted it voluntarily. The public sector and certain government-regulated portions of the private sector will need enabling legislation to allow them to use this practice. The rates of interest paid on short and long term government bonds, personal tax brackets, personal exemptions and standard deductions for the personal income tax, the bases for calculation of capital gains and depreciation for both the personal and corporate income tax, and the book values of inventories for the latter should all be subject to continuous adjustment to reflect changing price levels. Any other government payments that are fixed in nominal terms, such as wages and pensions, should also be indexed. For government-regulated private industries, legislation should be enacted to repeal any existing legal roadblocks to the adoption of indexing—anti-usury laws, restrictions on variable-term mortgages, other limits on interest rates payable on deposits of financial intermediaries or chargeable on loans, and ceilings on the prices charged by public utilities, airlines, and interstate truckers. Without indexing, especially by the federal government, the prospects for any substantial increase in investment are dim.

4
THE GOAL
OF COUNTERCYCLICAL
ECONOMIC POLICY

The goals of countercyclical economic policy are quite distinct from those of anti-inflationary policy. Countercyclical policy is concerned with the problems caused by a temporary decline in demand for goods and services. It is not concerned with the problems caused by a structural change in the economy. This is an important distinction: unemployment resulting from a temporary lull in demand may be reduced by an effective countercyclical spending program; that resulting from structural adjustment may not.

The major conclusions that are reached in this discussion of the goals of countercyclical policy are:

■ Recessions arise from a variety of causes and therefore must be addressed through a variety of policies. Not every increase in unemployment or negative growth rate in output signals a business cycle downturn, but may result from structural shifts in the economy. Policy must not discourage these adjustments.

■ The most important cycle impacts which determine the goals of countercyclical policy are: under-utilized productive capacity, long term unemployment of low income individuals; public service cutbacks necessitated by declining revenues.

■ Each of these objectives must be addressed by a distinct countercyclical program. Idle capacity can be employed through increased capital expenditure; unemployment through publicly subsidized jobs and training; and public service cutbacks through fiscal assistance.

WHAT CAUSES RECESSIONS?

Fluctuations in the rate of economic activity occur for many reasons, and can, at best, be only partially explained by the tools of economic theory. Differences among economic forecasts testify to the variety of cycle theories, and their inaccuracies show how inadequate these theories are. Even the term *cycle,* against which recessions are measured, is by no means unambiguous.

Definitions[1]

A brief review of the literature reveals at least five major types of cycles, each distinguished from others principally by its average duration.

Business Cycle. The basic definition of this cycle is provided by Burns and Mitchell (1946):

> Business cycles are a type of fluctuation found in the aggregate economic activity of nations that organize their work mainly in business enterprises: a cycle consists of expansions occurring at about the same time in many economic activities, followed by similarly general recessions, contractions and revivals which merge into the expansion phase of the next cycle; this sequence of changes is recurrent but not periodic; in duration business cycles vary from more than one year to ten or twelve years; they are not divisible into shorter cycles of similar character with amplitudes approximating their own (p. 3).

The National Bureau of Economic Research has developed an index of twelve indicators that are used to measure the path of economy and has based considerable research on this concept. Business cycles have an average duration of three to four years.

Growth Cycle. The definition of this cycle is similar to that of the business cycle, except that it is based upon economic fluctuations "adjusted for their long term trends" (Mintz, 1974, p. 7). Growth cycles therefore are based upon deviations from long run growth rates. Growth cycles tend to coincide with business cycles although, unlike a business cycle, a growth cycle can occur with no decline in output.

Juglar Cycle. Juglar cycles are defined as cycles in the average growth rate. They last approximately ten years. Burns and Mitchell refer to them as "hidden cycles." Relatively little empirical examination has focused on them.

Kuznets', or Trend, Cycle. These are cycles in the rate of growth of production and prices. They last about 20 years and have been identified in several countries (Abramovitz, 1961). They may be linked to major transportation investments (Isard, 1942) or to population changes (Kuznets, 1958).

Kondratieff Cycle. These cycles have only been vaguely defined in terms of growth rates. They typically last between 40 and 60 years (Schumpeter, 1935). However, evidence for such swings has not stood up to more detailed statistical analysis, and interest has waned (American Economic Association, 1965) until recently. Walter Rostow believes we are on the verge of an upswing in a long cycle, while MIT economist Jay Forrester believes we are on the downturn (*Business Week,* 9/10/79).

From the perspective of countercyclical policy, we are concerned with business cycles. Nevertheless, it should be noted that other types of cycles may contribute toward the pattern of economic behavior during business and growth cycles although exactly how is not yet understood.

Figure 2 shows downturns or contractions shaded in grey, and plots the rate of growth of Gross National Product adjusted for price

Figure 2
Unemployment and Real GNP Growth Rate Since 1948
During Recession and Expansion

(Recessions are shown shaded with the dates of peaks (p) and troughs (t) indicated)

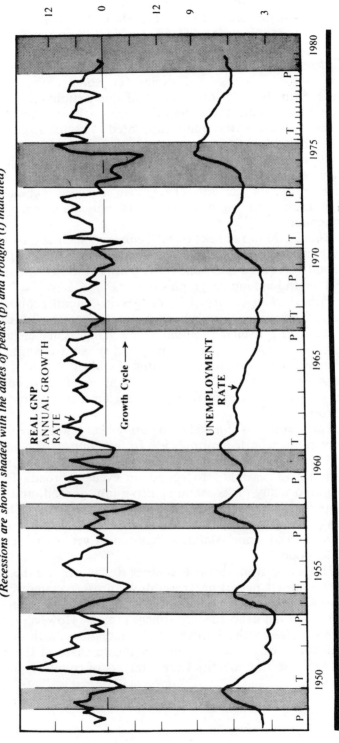

increases. Prior to the present recession, the U.S. had experienced six postwar major recessions, of which the one in 1974-75 was the deepest, and one growth cycle, 1966-67.

Causes

There is no one, simple explanation for cycles. To some extent, each cycle is unique, in that the combination of international and national economic developments and public policies—the ingredients that lead to recession—are never quite duplicated. The following factors have contributed to past recessions.

Business Expectations. If businesses anticipate a decline in sales, they respond by cutting new investment orders and running down inventories. In general, changes in business expectations are a response to growing price instability, anticipated changes in federal economic policy.

Shocks. Major shocks to the economy, such as a bad harvest, the outbreak or cessation of war, or oil price changes, often lead to a period of reduced economic activity while resources are shifted among sectors and among geographical areas.

Policy Changes. Abrupt changes in federal economic policy— particularly monetary changes (see Chapter 2)—can be very destabilizing. Even if no actual policy change is made, the fact that the federal government may or may not make a change, can lead to destabilizing shifts in expectations. As Mark Willes of the Minneapolis Federal Reserve Bank has argued, an effective countercyclical policy must be based on removing the element of surprise from federal actions.

The future is unlikely to bring us fewer shocks or much improvement in federal policies. In fact, improved communications and the growing importance of world trade may have increased the nation's vulnerability to economic events abroad. The U.S. has exported many of its manufacturing jobs abroad, and is providing more and more service functions for foreign nations. The impacts of this growing interdependence and international specialization on the nation's economic stability have not yet been recognized or understood.

The lesson from this is that some downturns are the result of *real* structural change. For these downturns, countercyclical action, however prompt, is unlikely to significantly reduce unemployment, and may even delay the adjustment process. However, action can be taken to lessen the burden of the recession on those sectors and individuals who bear a disproportionate share of the burden. The following section identifies these targets of countercyclical policy.

THE IMPACTS OF RECESSION

The goal of countercyclical policy is, in fact, composed of three components:

■ Providing jobs for the cyclically unemployed suffering the worst hardship.

■ Absorbing excess productive capacity.

■ Maintaining public services in the face of declining revenues. By examining each of these targets in more detail, we can identify the appropriate policies to reach these goals.

Cyclical Unemployment

Defining the need for countercyclical policy has been confused by the quest to find "the natural rate of unemployment" —the El Dorado of macroeconomists. Searchers have reasoned that, if they could define the natural rate, then, by comparison with the actual rate, they could determine exactly how much countercyclical stimulus was needed. To understand the futility of this quest, it is worth examining—if only briefly—the different types of unemployment, and how they vary over time. The targets of countercyclical programs are those who have become unemployed because of a decline in the level of aggregate demand—demand-deficient unemployment. Three major categories of unemployment can be identified in addition to cyclical unemployment. These are: frictional, structural, and institutional unemployment.[2] The existence at "full employment" of a pool of unemployed at a rate of between 2.5 and 4.0 percent of the labor force is attributed to these secular causes rather than to cyclical causes.

Frictional Unemployment. Frictional unemployment results from a number of reasons. The competitive operation of the economy, which causes some companies within any industry to succeed and grow while others decline and eventually close down, leads to unemployment since new companies are rarely set up next to ones that have closed, and workers from declining or dead companies must spend some time searching for the new openings in their industries. Second, households may choose to migrate among regions for noneconomic reasons, and time must be spent at the new locations seeking a job. Third, workers may voluntarily quit their jobs to search for better paying employment. These periods between jobs are categorized as frictional unemployment.

Frictional unemployment may vary cyclically and secularly. For example, frictional unemployment has been high during the 1970s because growth companies are located in the South, far from the closing and contracting companies in the North.

Structural Unemployment. While frictional unemployment can be regarded as an intra-industry phenomenon, structural unemployment results from structural changes in the economy that necessitate a shift of labor and other productive factors among economic sectors. These changes are made necessary because the economy experiences shocks **129** or "once-and-for-all" changes.

As the economy experiences these shocks, some jobs are lost and others are created but with a lag. Workers and capital relocate in regions whose advantages have been enhanced. New types of equipment are installed and new labor skills are developed. However, these adjustments do not occur instantaneously. There is inertia within the system, due in part to the costs of making the adjustments, to the fact that full information is not always available, and to the fact that the changes themselves may occur gradually.

There are three important aspects of structural unemployment that should be noted. First, the level of structural unemployment is not constant; it depends upon the number, magnitude, and types of the shocks that the economy has received. The recent rapid increase in energy prices, coupled with the introduction of environmental protection laws, might be expected to lead to a higher rate of structural unemployment than would have otherwise occurred. Second, the adjustments themselves are necessary if the economy is to maintain or regain economic efficiency in the face of changes in factor and commodity prices. Third, a countercyclical public works program may have little or no impact on the level of structural unemployment. A public works program will not reduce the extent of regional and sectoral adjustments occurring at any given time, and it may even slow down the adjustment process by delaying the decision to migrate.

As with frictional unemployment, structural unemployment does not remain constant over time. Therefore, separating its contribution to total unemployment during a recession in order to identify the demand-deficient unemployed presents problems. Changes in the rate of structural and frictional unemployment may cause changes in the rate of demand-efficient unemployment. For example, an increase in structural unemployment may be interpreted by some businesses as the beginning of a recession and may lead them to scale down their investment plans, thereby creating a recession through multiplier and acceleration effects.

Institutional Unemployment. There are a number of institutional aspects of the labor market that may contribute toward the level of unemployment. For example, a labor union may succeed in raising the wage rate that is paid to its members. As a result, the number of people wishing to work will increase and the quantity of labor demanded will decline. Ultimately, the expected annual earnings of union members will tend to equal the expected annual earnings of those with comparable skills in non-unionized sectors, with the higher skills being equalized by a reduced probability of finding work. An increase in the level of demand for workers in the unionized sector will be compensated for by an inmigration of labor from other sectors. Thus, a high unemployment rate among union members will reduce their
130 expected income to that in non-unionized industries.

Similarly, a union that is able to restrict membership (through appenticeship programs and other measures that limit the quantity of labor supplied to an industry) may create a bottleneck that causes workers in complementary trades to become unemployed. For example, if the supply of bricklayers were not increased as demand for new construction increased, plumbers and carpenters might not be able to find jobs.

Federal policies, too, may affect the number of institutionally unemployed. The minimum wage law may result in reduced employment opportunities for teenagers and unskilled labor. The costs and returns of education determine whether a member of the labor force seeks a job or enters college—which will affect the level of unemployment. The level of welfare payments may also affect the willingness of a person to enter the labor force and seek employment.

Cyclical Unemployment. The target of countercyclical policy is the cyclically unemployed. But, since public resources are limited, special efforts must be made to identify those who suffer the worst hardship during a recession. Unemployment is an inadequate measure. Employees in a cyclically volatile industry do experience more unemployment, but this is not necessarily a measure of hardship. They tend to be compensated both by higher wages when they are working and by generous supplementary unemployment benefits. The high wages in the construction sector are a result of the fact that construction workers cannot expect to work a full 52 week year. In fact, four out of ten male job losers between 25 and 64 during 1974, the height of the last recession, were on lay-off (Rosanna, 1979). Less than one quarter actively sought alternative employment.

Second, unemployment insurance benefits have taken some of the sting out of unemployment—although some physical and psychological problems do occur, particularly for those workers either not covered by UI and supplementary employee benefits or without the guarantee of re-employment.

Third, the way that unemployment insurance premiums are levied has actually increased cyclical unemployment. Most state funds levy unemployment insurance at a basic rate and use a formula to determine how much contributions increase in relation to a firm's turnover. But high-turnover firms typically do not pay a premium that fully reflects their employees' above average demands on the UI fund. Further, because firms know that laid-off employees will not be financially compelled to seek immediately alternative employment, they are more willing to layoff workers.

These caveats reinforce the concern, identified in this chapter, with the hard-to-employ, upon whom the cycle falls especially hard. They are more likely to be fired rather than laid-off, and unlikely to have jobs in other sectors. With these caveats in mind, let us turn to an analysis of how recessions affect different groups in the labor market *131* and different industries.

The cyclically unemployed constitute only a fraction of the unemployed even during a national recession. Vernez et al. (1977) measured cyclical unemployment as the difference between the employment level at cycle trough and the level at the preceding cycle peak, calculating that more than 75 percent of the increase in the total number of unemployed from peak to trough were cyclically unemployed (p. 53ff). This measure does not include new entrants into the labor force, but is a better measure of cyclical unemployment than is the aggregate unemployment rate.

A worker may become unemployed in four ways:

- Involuntary termination (job losers).
- Quitting a job (job leavers).
- Unsuccessful labor force re-entry.
- Unsuccessful labor force entry.

Job losers are between 36 percent and 55 percent of total annual unemployment (see Table 6). This group is also the most cyclically volatile. Between 1973 and 1975, the number of unemployed rose by 3.5 million. Those involuntarily unemployed rose by 2.7 million, job leavers by 0.15 million, unemployed re-entrants by 0.5 million, and unemployed new entrants by 0.17 million. Job losers accounted for 75 percent of the increase in unemployed during the recession. In absolute numbers, re-entrants exhibit a slight procyclical behavior, while new entrants and job leavers exhibit no cyclical tendencies (Gilroy and McIntire, 1974). However, these data may be misleading. Unemployment behavior may change in response to changes in the availability, level, and duration of benefits from unemployment insurance (UI). If UI coverage and duration of benefits improve, workers may hold out longer before accepting a job at a firm that pays a lower wage than the "reserve" wage which they feel they can obtain.

Preliminary estimates indicate that layoffs would decline by about one half if the UI incentive were eliminated (Feldstein, 1976a). Therefore, the impacts of cycles and countercyclical programs may be difficult to separate from the effects of changes in unemployment insurance benefits. For example, during early 1974, the UI program placed a time limit on the period during which benefits could be received (between 20 and 36 weeks, depending on the state).[4] However, the Emergency Employment Act of 1974 (Federal Supplement Program) extended this time period.[5] In addition, the Special Unemployment Assistance program and the Unemployment Assistance Act of 1974 extended insurance coverage to those not previously covered.[6] Both measures may be expected to result in increased unemployment.

About half of the increase in the unemployment rate during a

Table 6
Unemployment Characteristics of the Nonagricultural Labor Force, 1968 to 1976

Year	Unemployment Rate	Involuntary Part-time Employment Rate[a]	Percent of Work Force Experiencing Unemployment[b]	Number of Unemployed (thousands)	By Reason				By Duration (Weeks)				Average Duration (Weeks)
					Job Losers	Job Leavers	Re-entrants	New Entrants	<5	5-14	15-26	>26	
1968	3.6	1.1	12.4	2817	38.0	15.3	32.3	14.4	56.6	28.8	9.1	5.5	8.5
1969	3.5	1.2	12.5	2831	35.9	15.4	34.1	14.6	57.5	29.3	8.5	4.7	8.0
1970	4.9	1.4	15.3	4088	44.3	13.4	30.0	12.3	52.3	31.6	10.4	5.7	8.8
1971	5.9	1.4	16.3	4993	46.3	11.8	29.4	12.6	44.7	31.6	13.3	10.4	11.4
1972	5.6	1.3	15.4	4840	43.2	13.1	29.8	13.9	45.9	30.1	12.3	11.6	12.1
1973	4.9	1.2	14.2	4304	38.7	15.7	30.7	14.9	51.0	30.1	11.0	7.8	10.0
1974	5.6	1.4	17.6	5076	43.4	14.9	28.4	13.3	50.6	31.0	11.1	7.3	9.7
1975	8.5	1.8	NA	7830	55.4	10.4	23.8	10.4	37.0	31.3	16.5	15.2	14.1
1976	7.7	NA	NA	7288	49.7	12.2	26.0	12.1	38.3	29.6	13.8	18.3	NA

NOTE: NA means not available.

a Includes those persons in the nonagricultural labor force who usually work full time working less than 35 hours a week because of slack work, job changing, material shortages, inability to find full-time work, etc., expressed as a percentage of the total nonagricultural labor force.

b This is the percentage of the work force experiencing at least one spell of employment during the year.

SOURCE: Bureau of Labor Statistics, *Handbook of Labor Statistics 1976*, Bulletin 1905, U.S. Department of Labor, Washington, D.C., 1976.

recession results from prolonging the periods of unemployment of those who experience difficulty in finding work even during the best of times. The remainder of the increase comes from an increase in the numbers of workers experiencing unemployment. Distinguishing between a *deepening* of the unemployment experience (the first case) and a *broadening* (the second case) has important implications for countercyclical programs. To the extent that recessions fall upon the chronically unemployed, the need for training programs, counseling services, and other measures aimed at improving the employability of participants is increased. On the other hand, if a recession results primarily in a broadening of the unemployment experience, the income maintenance and net job-creation aspects of countercyclical programs are more important.

During the 1969-1971 cycle, more than half the increase in unemployment was attributable to the more acute unemployment experience among the chronically unemployed. While the unemployment rate rose from 3.5 percent to 5.9 percent, an increase of 68.6 percent, the percentage of the labor force experiencing at least one period of unemployment during the course of the year rose from 12.5 percent to 16.3 percent, an increase of only 30.4 percent (see Table 6). Warren (1977) estimated that 45 percent of the changes in the unemployment rate between 1969 and 1975 were explained by changes in the duration of unemployment, while 55 percent of the changes were attributable to changes in the flow of persons into unemployment. A recession increases the average duration of unemployment. For example, between 1973 and 1975, the average duration of a spell of unemployment rose from 10 weeks to 14.1 weeks (Table 6). Those unemployed for less than five weeks fell from 51.0 percent in 1973, a peak year, to 37.0 percent in 1975, a trough year, while those unemployed for 15-26 weeks increased from 11.0 percent to 16.5 percent, and those unemployed more than 27 weeks, rose from 7.8 percent to 15.2 percent.[7]

During a recession, many workers are affected through forced reduction in working hours as well as through outright unemployment. The involuntary part-time employment rate behaves procyclically (see Table 6). In 1969 and 1973, which were peak years, 1.2 percent of the total nonagricultural labor force was involuntarily working less than 35 hours a week. In the recession years of 1971 and 1975, this rate climbed to 1.4 percent and 1.8 percent, respectively.

Although the level of part-time employment is considerably less than the unemployment rate (between one-third and one-quarter of the latter), it is an important indicator of cyclical effects for two reasons. First, changes in the rate of part-time employment are a leading indicator of cycle turning points (Bednarzik, 1975a). Bednarzik found that the changes in this rate consistently led both

unemployment cycles and business cycles at peaks and troughs.

**Idle Productive
Capacity**

All sectors are not equally sensitive to changes in the national rate of employment growth. The construction and manufacturing sectors typically experience cycles of much higher amplitude than all sectors taken together (Bednarzik, 1975a; Marston, 1976; Vernez et al., 1977). Mining, finance, insurance and real estate, selected services, and the government sector are the least cyclically sensitive. Between November 1973 and June 1975, construction employment fell by 7.0 percent and manufacturing employment declined by 9.6 percent. By contrast, employment in mining rose by 17.6 percent, in finance, insurance and real estate by 4.1 percent, and in services by 7.7 percent. Past research has shown that those sectors and industries most cycle-prone are construction and durable goods manufacturing. A public works program—increased spending on capital projects during a recession—would target on these industries.

If a public works program is to be a component of a countercyclical strategy, then it is important to know how those industries that provide materials for construction projects behave over the cycle. Vernez et al., (1977) identified 18 industries that were major suppliers to public works projects (listed in Table 7) and examined the timing and amplitude of these industries' cycles compared with national employment cycles. In unpublished research, they also examined the relationship between monthly growth rate of employment by these industries.[8] The results of these two analyses appear in Table 7. Major findings are summarized below. The construction sector is discussed separately.

The timing of turning points differs among the 18 supplying industries' employment cycles.[9] At the *initial downturns* of the last two national classical cycles (1970-1971 and 1974-1975), all supplying industries led the nation by two to eighteen months. The leads have been longer in the more severe cycle of 1974 to 1975. The industries that typically displaced the largest leads (two quarters or more) are: fabricated metal producers (SIC 34); transportation equipment (SIC 37); and textile mill products (SIC 22). The general building contractors industry (SIC 15) has also exhibited a lead of a quarter or more in each of the three post-1960 classical cycles.[10]

At *upturns*, all major supplying industries led the nation in recovery during the 1960-1962 cycle, while most trailed the nation in recovery during the 1970-1971 cycle—except furniture and fixtures (SIC 25), which led the nation in recovery.

Responsiveness indicates the magnitude of the change in an industry's employment growth rate in response to a given change in national employment growth. For example, the results in Table 7 indicate that a one percentage point increase in employment growth at the national level will tend to lead to a 2.48 percentage point increase in **135**

Table 7
Cyclical Behavior of Major Industrial Sectors, 1960-1975

SIC	Description	Responsiveness (Coefficient) β_i	Secular Growth α	R^2	Leads (-) and Lags (+) in Months at Cycle Turning Points				Relative Amplitude at National Upturns	
					Downturn		Upturn			
					1970-71	1974	1960-62	1970-71	Nov. 1970	June 1975
14	Mining	.7203	-.0986	.11	NA	-7	NA	+15	8	6
15	General Building Contractors	2.034	-.2806	.30	-3	-14	0	-2	3	26
16	Heavy Construction Contractors	1.282	-.0724	.11	$	-7	$	$	NA	19
17	Special Trade Contractors	1.411	-.1011	.32	0	-7	-2	-6	3	21
24	Lumber and Wood Products	1.732	-.3695	.42	-12	-5	-2	+9	10	18
25	Furniture and Fixtures	2.019	-.2505	.60	-11	+3	-3	-11	8	23
32	Stone, Clay, and Glass Products	1.646	0.2426	.55	-3	-9	-2	+4	5	17
33	Primary Metal Products	2.480	-.3543	.73	-5	-9	-1	+9	11	18
35	Non-Electrical Machinery	2.353	-.2620	.55	0	+1	-1	+7	10	11
36	Electrical Equipment	3.235	-.6350	.44	-5	-8	-6	+8	15	21
37	Transportation Equipment	1.637	-.1132	.64	-7	-14	-2	+11	21	16
38	Instruments and Related Products	1.431	-.2836	.62	-7	-2	-2	+5	8	9

22	Textile Mill Products	.8069	-.0612	.44	-8	-18	-2	+4	5	16
26	Paper and Allied Products	.7809	-.0185	.46	03	-8	-2	+7	3	13
28	Chemicals and Allied Products	4.261	-.1473	.07	-8	0	-2	+14	3	13
29	Petroleum Products	2.065	-.1080	.41	$	$	$	$	NA	NA
30	Rubber and Miscellaneous Plastics	1.661	-.1905	.25	-2	-8	-2	+2	7	21
	Durable Goods	2.7441	-.4348	.86	-7	-09	-1	+9	12	15
	Nondurable Goods	.8481	-.1163	.66	-7	-9	-2	+9	4	10
	Total Manufacturing	1.922	-.2977	.89	-7	-9	-2	+9	9	12

SOURCE: The Rand Corporation from Monthly Employment Series of the Bureau of Labor Statistics; and Georges Vernez, Roger Vaughan, Burke Burright, and Sinclair Coleman, *Regional Cycles and Employment Effects of Public Works Investments*, The Rand Corporation, R-2052-EDA, January 1977, Tables 7.2 and 7.5.

a For a discussion of the basic model, see Appendix A.

$ indicates that the sector skipped the cycle.

the primary metal products industry (SIC 33). Overall, most suppliers of public works projects respond to an increase (or decrease) in national employment by a larger increase (decrease) in their own employment. The most responsive industries were: electrical equipment (SIC 36); fabricated metal products (SIC 34); primary metal products (SIC 33); and nonelectrical machinery (SIC 35). A one percentage point change in national employment growth will, on average, result in at least a two percentage point change in the employment growth rates of these industries.

The industries vary in cyclical amplitude, measured as the percentage change in employment from cycle peak to cycle trough. A number of industries have experienced consistently large relative amplitudes in all post-1960 cycles: lumber and wood products (SIC 24); transportation equipment (SIC 37); and rubber and miscellaneous plastics (SIC 30). Their relative amplitudes have consistently been higher than the average for total manufacturing employment (Vernez et al., 1977, pp. 170-176). Also, a number of industries have consistently experienced relatively mild cycle amplitudes: mining (SIC 14); chemicals and allied products (SIC 28); and petroleum refining (SIC 29).

The coefficient of determination (R^2) reported in Table 7 measures the extent to which variations in industry growth rates can be explained by variations at the national level. Industries exhibiting a high degree of conformity include: primary metals (SIC 33); fabricated metal products (SIC 34); furniture and fixtures (SIC 25); transportation equipment (SIC 37); and instruments (SIC 38). With the exception of the last mentioned, these are also highly responsive industries. Low-conformity industries are heavy construction contractors (SIC 16) and chemicals (SIC 28).

The construction sector is of particular importance because the on-site labor demanded by public works projects must be provided, for the most part, by the cyclically unemployed in this sector. Over the course of a cycle, employment in the construction sector behaves differently from aggregate employment. Employment in this sector tends to lead national growth but shows low conformity to the nation as a whole.

At actual turning points, construction industries have tended to lead the nation. All construction industries led the nation during the 1974 downturn; general contractors (SIC 15) by fourteen months, the others by seven months. Special trade contractors (SIC 17) consistently led the nation at all upturns since 1960. The relationship between the timing of construction sector employment and total employment cycles varies widely among labor market areas. Nevertheless, in a majority of labor market areas, construction leads at cycle downturns. There is no strong tendency for a lead at cycle upturn.

Construction industries tend to be relatively responsive to changes in the national growth rate of total employment. A one percentage point change in national growth will be reflected in employment growth with a change greater than one percentage point in the same direction, in each of the three construction industries.

There are considerable differences in cyclical amplitude among construction industries. General building contractors (SIC 15) have relatively high cyclical amplitude, greater than that of total employment, while heavy construction tends to experience cycles of low amplitude. *A countercyclical public works program should concentrate on building rather than on heavy construction projects.*

State and Local Fiscal Activities in Recession The business cycle affects state and local fiscal behavior. First, state and local governments act countercyclically to dampen the cycle through both automatic and discretionary stabilizers in much the same way as the federal government does. The record suggests that their actions have proved quite effective. Second, recessions increase the demand for services while reducing tax revenues, placing states in a fiscal squeeze.

State Local Countercyclical Behavior. State and local governments have traditionally been accused of acting perversely over the business cycle, contributing to overheating during expansions, and to reduced demand during recessions. The evidence suggests otherwise. Table 8 shows that expenditures have grown more rapidly during recessions than during expansions, and revenues have grown more slowly during periods of slow growth than during booms. The result has been that surpluses have acted countercyclically. Although the tendency is less pronounced, state-local employment has acted more countercyclically than federal hiring (Table 9).

The countercyclical behavior of state surpluses has arisen, in large part, inadvertently. The Advisory Commission on Intergovernmental Relations (May 1979) explains it in this way:

First, most state and local governments operate on either one or two year budget cycles. Revenue estimates are made and expenditures are planned for the entire budget period. If revenues fall short of estimated amounts, there is a time lag before expenditure adjustments can be made. Most of the recessions since World War Two have not lasted long enough for state and local governments to cut expenditures.

A second and probably more important factor is that state and local governments are expected to have balanced budgets. Since these governments must at least plan a balanced budget, their tendency is to estimate revenues conservatively. If the economy is booming these conservative estimates may understate actual collections and result in unplanned surpluses. During recessions it appears that state and local

139

Table 8
State-Local Fiscal Behavior:
Average Quarterly Rates of
Growth of Expenditures, Receipts, and Surpluses
1957-1977

During Recessions

Contraction[1] (peak-trough)	Expenditures (average quarterly rate of growth in percent)	Receipts (average quarterly rate of growth in percent)	Surplus (average quarterly change: billions of dollars)[2]
1957: III-1958: I	2.9%	1.7%	$-0.55
1960: I-1960: IV	2.1	1.9	-0.10
1969: III-1970: IV	3.2	2.8	-0.46
1973: IV-1975: I	3.3	2.6	-1.32

During Expansions

Expansion[1] (trough-peak)	Expenditures (average quarterly rate of growth in percent)	Receipts (average quarterly rate of growth in percent)	Surplus (average quarterly change: billions of dollars)
1958: I-1960: I	1.5%	2.4%	$0.34
1960: IV-1969: III	2.4	2.5	0.08
1970: IV-1973: IV	2.5	2.9	0.80
1975: I-1977: I	1.8	2.9	2.95

1. Peak and trough quarters are used for real GNP, as identified by the U.S. Department of Commerce, Bureau of Economic Analysis (BEA).
2. Total expenditures, receipts, and surplus were used to compute the above, hence federal aid and trust fund amounts are included.

SOURCE: Advisory Commission on Intergovernmental Relations, *State-Local Finances in Recession and Inflation,* A-70, Washington, D.C., May 1979, p. 7.

governments draw down these surpluses, enabling them to maintain or increase expenditures.

However, the data suggest that the countercyclical influence of the state-local sector is declining as its growth rate declines and as the importance of federal aid—*which has not been used counter-cyclically*—increases (ACIR, May 1979a). Since state governments are, with few exceptions, constitutionally precluded from operating a budget deficit, they can only regain their countercyclical influence by setting up a stabilization fund (along the model of Michigan). They can no longer rely on the automatic stabilizing influence of reduced revenues and increased expenditures.

Recession and State-Local Fiscal Conditions. A recession can create serious fiscal problems for local governments. They are squeezed between the increasing demands for services and income transfers for those rendered jobless and indigent by the slowdown, and shrunken revenues from reduced personal and business income. The extent of the fiscal problem will depend upon the depth of the local recession and by the local tax structure. Appendix A shows that a recession is not borne equally by all areas. Neither does a one percent decline in personal income translate into the same decline in revenues in all areas. The elasticity of taxes differs. The revenues from a highly progressive personal income tax will be highly volatile, or "elastic," in response to changes in local personal income. A motor fuel tax will be less responsive. There have been many attempts to compute the elasticity of the major state and local taxes. The Advisory Commission for Intergovernmental Relations (May 1979a) calculated the middle

Table 9
Private and Public Sector Employment, 1957-76
(Full-Time Equivalent Employees)

During Recessions

Contraction[1] (peak-trough)	Private Sector (average annual growth in percent)	Public[2] Sector (average annual growth in percent)	Federal[2] (average annual growth in percent)	State-Local (average annual growth in percent)
1957-58	-4.0%	0.0%	-3.8%	5.1%
1960-61	-1.0	3.4	2.0	4.7
1969-70	-0.9	-0.3	-5.8	4.3
1973-75	-1.4	1.8	-0.6	3.1

During Expansions

Expansion (trough-peak)	Private Sector (average annual growth in percent)	Public[2] Sector (average annual growth in percent)	Federal[2] (average annual growth in percent)	State-Local (average annual growth in percent)
1958-60	2.4%	1.9%	-0.1%	3.9%
1961-69	2.9	3.7	2.9	4.4
1970-73	2.6	0.5	-4.7	4.3
1975-76	3.6	0.3	-1.0	1.0

1. Calendar year peaks and troughs chosen to most closely reflect employment at peak and trough months as measured by BEA.
2. Includes military.

SOURCE: Advisory Commission on Intergovernmental Relations, *State-Local Finances in Recession and Inflation*, A-70, Washington, D.C., May 1979, p. 9.

141

range estimates of income elasticity for four major tax sources and estimated tax revenue loss due to the recession in 1975:

Tax	Elasticity	Loss ($ billions)
Personal Income Tax	1.7	3.42
Corporate Income Tax	1.1	0.68
General Property Tax	0.98	4.74
General Sales Tax	1.0	4.67
		Total Loss 13.51

This hypothetical loss amounts to 10.5 percent of actual state-local tax collections in 1975. The more volatile taxes should provide the basis of contributions into a state stabilization fund, proposed in Chapter 6.

Public perception of the fiscal crisis has focused on the problems of large, old central cities. While the recession of 1974-75 raised concern over the ability of these cities to bring expenditures in line with revenues, their basic problem was one of long run erosion in the tax base, a secular rather than a cyclical problem. In fact, at least one study estimates that states suffer two-thirds of the revenue loss caused by a recession, with other jurisdictions accounting for the other one-third. This is a result of the state reliance on the personal income tax (ACIR, May 1979a). Although states tend to have more fiscal padding than many central cities, many are facing a growing fiscal strain (ACIR, February 1977). Many cities are severely affected. In the most severely affected cities (which also tend to be the largest cities), capital expenditures are the first category to be cut (U.S. Congress, 1977). This accentuates the need for a public works and fiscal assistance component of a state based countercyclical program. Recent analysis by the ACIR (1978) has shown that there is a wide range in the fiscal strength of state governments—some can reasonably be expected to help their distressed cities, others do not have sufficient fiscal strength. Thus, some form of federal assistance may be necessary.

IMPLICATIONS The preceding discussion establishes three distinct goals for a countercyclical policy, goals that are related to the dual purposes of moderating the depths of recessions and helping those most harmed. In trying to smooth out fluctuations in economic activity—fluctuations that arise from the inexorable rhythms of the business investment cycle or from shocks such as a sudden increase in energy costs, the declaration of peace, or political uncertainty—stabilization policy embodies three components:

■ Absorbing excess productive capacity;

- Providing employment for those rendered jobless;
- Maintaining public services.

While these goals are not mutually exclusive, they are distinguishable and must be met through separate programs. For example, a public service employment program may provide jobs for the cyclically unemployed, but will have little impact on idle productive capacity. A fundamental mistake in federal stabilization strategy has been the failure to implement separate programs for these separate goals. For example, during the 1973-75 recession, the Comprehensive Employment and Training Administration (CETA) program was stepped up to meet two goals—providing the unemployed with jobs and to help maintain public services. Few of the unskilled were hired and the maintenance of public services was hampered by the restrictive regulations. A single program cannot meet more than one goal successfully. This does not mean that a program targeted at one goal will have no impact on other goals. It means that a program should never be justified or modified to address a secondary goal. Just as an airplane has one set of controls for vertical movement and one set for lateral movement, *a stabilization strategy must include a separate program for each goal.*

The three objectives outlined above can be met by three major programs:

Goal	Program
Reducing idle capacity in construction and manufacturing	Increased capital spending (public works)
Providing jobs for the cyclically unemployed and the hard to employ	Public employment and training
Maintaining public services	Antirecessionary revenue sharing

Other programs can also help meet each of these goals and are discussed in Chapter 6. However, these three programs are the most important in developing a state based countercyclical strategy.

Public Works

The construction industry, and industries providing materials for construction activity, are among the most cyclically volatile of all sectors. A well-designed and well-timed public works program is an important component of a countercyclical strategy. It can easily be incorporated in state and local government policy because of the large volume of publicly funded construction. While the transportation equipment *143* sector is also volatile, it can be assisted less easily because of the relatively small role of the public sector in total sales, and because of the very long duration of publicly funded transportation equipment projects. Three factors should be considered in the design of a counter-cyclical public works program:

The cycle in construction employment does not coincide with the cycle in total employment; therefore, public works investments must be tied to the level of construction sector unemployment, not the prevailing aggregate unemployment rate. Construction typically leads the total cycle, and for this reason public works should be undertaken before other countercyclical expenditures. Federal public works have usually lagged behind the cycle and have contributed to inflationary pressure during the economic recovery.

A countercyclical public works program should concentrate on short duration, general construction projects. The heavy construction industry rarely behaves cyclically and projects are lengthy which makes the industry an unsuitable target for countercyclical purposes.

In order to ensure timely implementation, state and local governments must have "pre-planned" projects on the shelf, ready to carry out as the local economy softens.

Public Employment and Training Programs

A major cause of the increase in the unemployment rate during a recession is the prolonged unemployment of those who find it difficult to secure regular employment even during the best of times. These tend to be the young, the unskilled, and the inexperienced. An effective and equitable countercyclical program must reach out to enroll the hard-to-employ in training and work experience programs. Improving the quality of the labor force can help reduce cyclical volatility in the long run. Employers are less willing to layoff skilled and able workers during a recession for fear that they will be unable to rehire them during the ensuing recovery. They will "hoard" labor which will dampen employment fluctuations. Again, three considerations should guide the design of a countercyclical public employment and training program.

First, the program must be separated from the program aimed at assisting state and local governments to maintain public services. A major flaw in the 1975-77 countercyclical component of the Comprehensive Employment and Training Act (CETA Titles II and VI) was that it confused public service maintenance with work experience and training. The result, quite naturally, was that hard-pressed local governments used the funds to hire the relatively skilled to fill regular public sector slots. The unskilled were rarely able to get these jobs.

Second, at the expense of speedy enrollment, the program must embody strict eligibility requirements to ensure that participants are truly those in need.

Third, an effective program demands coordination with the private sector to ensure that the skills and experience imparted are relevant to the needs of local industry. Failure to do this will make it difficult for participants to find permanent, unsubsidized employment. Public employment should only be regarded as a temporary measure.

Antirecessionary   Many jurisdictions, particularly large
Fiscal Assistance   cities with a heavy concentration of their
                         workforce in durable goods manufacturing, suffer acutely during national recessions. Revenues decline sharply and the demand for public services grows rapidly. Long term economic decline has effectively removed any "fiscal padding" in their budgets and they are ill-equipped to face the additional strains imposed by a cyclical downturn. In the long run, these troubled jurisdictions must adjust their revenue structure and the menu of services offered to reflect their smaller size and altered economic base. In the short run, they require fiscal assistance to help weather the recession. An antirecessionary fiscal assistance program must deliver the aid where it is most needed and, at the same time, not remove the underlying incentives for long run fiscal adjustment. These, then, are the bare bones of stabilization policy. In the following chapter we examine why the federal government has failed to meet these objectives. In the final chapter, we outline how states can implement an effective stabilization strategy.

Footnotes to Chapter 4

1. This subsection is adapted from Vaughan (1976), pp. 22-23.

2. Institutional unemployment refers to those who are unemployed through aspects of the labor market that create a pool of unemployed. For example, minimum wage legislation and unionization may have the effect of creating institutional unemployment.

3. This group includes those who have been temporarily laid off and those permanently separated.

4. Most states pay UI benefits up to 26 weeks. Puerto Rico pays only 20 weeks of benefits, while the District of Columbia pays more than 26 weeks. The value of benefits varies considerably among states.

5. The amended Federal Supplemental Benefits Program now provides 65 week coverage to states whose insured unemployment rates have exceeded 6 percent for the most recent 13 weeks, and 52 week coverage for states whose unemployment rate has been between 5 and 6 percent.

6. For a period of 39 weeks (*Employment and Training Report of the President, 1976*). In 1975, 1.2 million of the unemployed, or 15 percent, received benefits under these special federal provisions.

7. The dramatic increase in the share of this latter category in 1975 may be attributable in part to the extension of UI benefits, discussed above.

8. The form of the model is described in a footnote to Table A.2 and is the same as that used to examine the relationship between local and national employment growth rates. See Vernez et al., (1977, Sec. III).

9. Vernez et al., (1977, Table 8.2), p. 169.

10. The industries are referred to by their Standard Industrial Classification Code (SIC), employed by the Bureau of Labor Statistics. A *classical cycle* is a period marked by a fall in the level of employment followed by an increase. A *growth cycle*, on the other hand, is a period of relatively slow growth followed by a period of faster growth.

5

WHY THE FEDERAL GOVERNMENT CANNOT FIGHT RECESSION ALONE

Washington has built several automatic stabilizers into the fiscal system. Unemployment insurance, welfare payments and foodstamps automatically increase the flow of federal dollars as economic conditions worsen. The progressive income tax ensures that revenues fall more proportionately than income. These programs are largely effective in dampening cycles, although they are not, and cannot be, targeted to meet local needs. The problem with federal countercyclical policy lies in its discretionary programs—temporary programs initiated during recessions and designed to stimulate the economy. The federal government has tried tax cuts, tax rebates, tax credits, public works, public employment, and special revenue sharing grants. No set of programs could wipe out fluctuations completely. But these tools have been ill-timed, have failed to generate jobs, and have rarely provided aid where it is most needed:

■ *Policy Delays.* The onset of a recession is not immediately recognized, and must be geographically widespread to be politically accepted. Political debate and administrative activity use up valuable time. Thus, policies are implemented tardily, not when they are needed.

■ *Displacement.* Because of uncertainty over the policy, federal countercyclical grants to state and local governments often do little other than substitute federal for local funds with no increase in total public expenditure.

■ *Targeting.* Areas differ widely in their cyclical behavior. Federal targeting often does not reflect these differences, and the jobs created by federal programs are rarely created in those areas beset by the greatest cyclical unemployment.

The analysis of federal programs in this chapter is based upon our experience in the most recent recessions. The Local Public Works program (LPW) is no longer active, but might be reactivated, in some form, if the present recession deepens. The Comprehensive Employment and Training Act (CETA) countercyclical programs (Titles II and VI) have also been substantially altered during the 1978 reauthorization. Some of the problems identified in this discussion are peculiar to the particular programs, but, overall, we have identified problems *147* that are innate to any federal discretionary countercyclical program. The solution is to develop a state-based countercyclical strategy.

THE TOOLS OF A COUNTER-CYCLICAL STRATEGY[1] Countercyclical policies, listed in Table 10, are those that attempt to increase federal spending or reduce revenues during recessions, and cut spending or increase revenues when the economy is heated. Some programs are automatic—they switch on and off without congressional debate. For example, unemployment insurance outlays automatically increase during recessions, and the progressive personal income tax guarantees that federal revenues decline more proportionately than income. Other programs are discretionary—a cut in the tax rate or a public works program. Automatic programs have been much larger than discretionary programs in all the postwar recessions. Table 11 shows that, in 1976, a recession year, automatic

Table 10
Federal Stabilization Programs

Automatic

> Expenditure Increasing
>> Unemployment Insurance
>> Public Assistance
>> Food Stamps
>> Housing Assistance

> Revenue Reducing
>> Income Taxes (corporate and personal)
>> Payroll Taxes

Discretionary

> Expenditure Increasing
>> Public Works
>> Public Employment
>> Anti-Recessionary Fiscal Assistance
>> Increased Federal Procurements

> Revenue Reducing
>> Investment Tax Credits
>> Tax Cuts
>> Tax Rebates

programs increased federal outlays by nearly $18 billion, compared with 1974, an expansionary year. By contrast, discretionary programs increased by only $12.9 billion, of which $10.7 billion was attributable to tax cuts.

Automatic stabilizers are largely income redistribution programs, and cannot easily or equitably be fine-tuned to provide a counter-cyclical stimulus. Our discussion will therefore focus on discretionary programs.

Increasing Expenditures During Recessions[2]

The countercyclical use of public works began in the 1930s. Between 1933 and 1942, while the unemployment rate never dipped below 13 percent, the federal government spent $19 billion ($80 billion at today's price level) on public works and public employment programs. No public programs since have employed as many workers as the Emergency Administration of Public Works (PWA) and the Works Progress Administration (WPA) programs. PWA employed over 600,000 at its peak in 1934, and WPA employed over three million in 1936.[3]

Despite four national recessions during the 1940s and 1950s, it was not until the recession in early 1960 that the first postwar counter-cyclical public works program (APW) was implemented, and not until 1971 that the first postwar countercyclical public service employment program was created, the Public Employment Program (PEP). The 1970-71 recession also marked the first time since World War Two that federal countercyclical actions provided for a combination of public works and public service employment programs, a strategy that was repeated again during the 1974-75 recession. Table 12 shows that the federal outlays for these programs were generally proportional to the amplitude of the cycles, but not sufficient to create job opportunities for more than 10 percent of those idled by the reduction in economic activity.[4]

The countercyclical use of public works and public employment programs since World War Two has been slight because, despite the real achievement of the 1930s programs,[5] their image remains one of inefficient "make work" activity. Instead, we have relied more on monetary policy—the control of the interest rate through the rate of increase in the money stock to stimulate or reduce aggregate demand, which, we saw in Chapter 2, has been inappropriate and inflationary. Also, social welfare programs, including social security, unemployment insurance and Aid to Families with Dependent Children, provide relief to a majority of those idled during recessions, reducing the pressure for job creation programs. Finally, postwar recessions have been short, making these slow acting programs less desirable than tax rebates.

Since the 1930s, programs have moved from partial to full federal **149**

Table 11
Outlays of Discretionary and Automatic Countercyclical Programs: 1974 to 1977
(in billions)

Program Type	Expansion Year	Recession Years			Increase from 1974		
	1974	1975	1976	1977[u]	1975	1976	1977
Planned Countercyclical Programs							
Public Works[b]	0.94	—	—	1.28	—	—	1.24
Public Service Employment[c]	0.55	1.26	2.75	2.83	0.71	2.20	2.28
Tax Reductions[d]	—	10.56	10.70		10.50	10.70	
Revenue Sharing[e]	—	—	—	1.25	—	—	—
Subtotal	0.59	11.76	13.45	5.36	11.21	12.90	4.77
Automatic Countercyclical Programs							
Unemployment Insurance	5.21	12.22	17.61	14.28	7.01	12.40	9.07
Public Assistance[f]	6.83	8.67	9.80	10.18	1.84	2.97	3.35
Foodstamps	2.73	4.36	5.27	4.39	1.63	2.54	1.66
Subtotal	14.77	25.25	32.68	28.85	10.48	17.91	14.08
Manpower Programs[g]	3.44	4.60	5.48	6.18	1.16	2.04	2.74
Total	18.80	41.61	51.61	40.39	22.81	32.81	21.59

NOTES: Figures may not add to totals because of rounding.

a Estimated outlays.

b Includes the Public Works Impact Program (1974 appropriation), the Local Public Works Program and additional grants for construction of waste treatment plants under the Environmental Protection Agency (1977 estimated outlays).

c Includes the public service employment portion of the Emergency Employment Assistance (1974, 1975); Comprehensive Manpower Assistance, CETA Titles I, II, III (1975, 1976, 1977); Temporary Employment Assistance, CETA VI (1975, 1976, 1977); Job Opportunities Program (1975, 1976, 1977); and Work Incentives (1974 to 1977).

d Includes the refund of 1974 taxes to individuals (1975), increase in standard deductions (1975, 1976), general tax credit (1975, 1976), earned income credit (1976), tax credit for home purchase (1976), investment tax credit (1975, 1976), and corporate tax rate deductions (1975, 1976).

e "Countercyclical" revenue sharing assistance to state and local governments (1977 appropriations).

f Includes the Aid to Families with Dependent Children, Aid to Families with Dependent Children and Unemployed Father, and Supplemental Security Income programs.

g Includes all federal training and unemployment programs other than public service employment; on-the-job training; institutional training; vocational rehabilitation; work experience; and labor market services.

Table 12
Major Countercyclical Public Works and Public Service Employment Programs Since 1930

Excessive Years	Annual Average Amplitude[a]	Public Works		Public Service Employment	
		Description	Outlays ($ billions)	Description	Outlays ($ billions)
1933-1942 (Depression)	9.3	Emergency Relief and Construction Act (FY 1933)	.30b		
		Federal Civil Works Administration (CWA, FY 1934)	.95		
		Emergency Work Relief Program (EWRP, FY1934-1935)	1.30		
		Emergency Administration of Public Works (PWA, FY 1934-1938)	6.08c	Works Progress Administration (WPA, FY1936-1942)	9.58d
1960-1961	2.5	Accelerated Public Works Program (APW, FY 1962-1963)	1.70e	NONE	
1970-1971	2.5	Public Works Impact Program (PWIP, FY 1972-1973)	.13	Emergency Employment Act (PEP, FY1972-1974)	1.62
1974-Present	NA	Local Public Works Program (LPW, FY1977)	6.00f	Comprehensive Employment and Training Act CETA I, II, III. (FY 1975-1977) CETA VI (FY 1975-1977)	1.94 4.00

NOTE: NA means not available.

a Defined as

$$\frac{1}{2} \times \left(\frac{\text{Employment at initial downturn minus employment at upturn}}{\text{Number of years of decline}} + \frac{\text{Employment at end peak minus employment at upturn}}{\text{Number of years of rise}} \right)$$

Cycle Base

where cycle base is defined as the average monthly employment over the cycle.

b Another $1 to $0.5 billion was also made available to finance self-liquidating public works projects—i.e., projects whose costs could be recouped within a reasonable period through user charges. This fund was not used and eventually transferred to other uses.

c Includes state and local shares. Federal share was approximately $.82 billion.

d Includes federal, state and local shares. The initial FY1936 allocation was $4.38 billion.

e Includes an initial FY 1973 allocation of $3.3 billion.

f Obligations. An estimated $.8 billion is expected in outlays in FY1977.

g Includes only outlays in the public service employment component of CETA.

SOURCE: Georges Vernez and Roger Vaughan. *Assessment of Countercyclical Public Works and Public Service Employment Programs*, R-2214-EDA. The Rand Corporation. September 1978, p. 4.

153

financing and from centralized to decentralized administration. The Emergency Relief and Construction Act of 1933 provided only low interest loans to state and local governments. As the depression grew longer and deeper, the federal government assumed greater direct financing responsibility. The federal share increased to 50-75 percent under the APW program and reached 100 percent under the 1976 Local Public Works (LPW) program. The government has always asssumed full financing of public service employment programs. By contrast, program administration has been steadily decentralized. Public works programs in the 1930s were controlled, coordinated and administered by specially created federal agencies. Under the more recent public works programs, legislated authority for direct federal construction projects was limited (APW) or nonexistent (Public Works Impact Program (PWIP) and LPW). Only projects sponsored by state and local governments were eligible. Public service employment programs evolved through three phases. Under WPA, administration was centralized, with funds used directly on federal projects or allocated to local governments, bypassing states. Until 1973, public employment programs were centralized, categorical programs designed to serve specified subgroups of the population. Since 1973, CETA block grants have decentralized and decategorized federally sponsored employment programs. Thus, some administrative capability for a state-based countercyclical program is already in place.

Eligibility has also changed. Prewar programs were restricted to those unemployed and on relief. Postwar public works construction has typically been subcontracted to private contractors subject to no restrictions. In contrast, all public service employment programs restricted program participation to those unemployed at least one week (PEP) and one month for CETA II and VI (later reduced to two weeks). In addition, these programs specify groups that receive special consideration for employment: veterans, the underemployed, the long term unemployed, welfare recipients, and members of minority groups. The 1978 amendments to the CETA program greatly improved the targeting of its countercyclical component (Title VI). Eligibility was limited to those from poor households, receiving assistance, and unemployed for 10 of the 12 previous weeks.

Cutting Taxes

Cutting taxes, providing tax credits, or even giving tax rebates, have been popular weapons in Washington's countercyclical armory. Their popularity is based not on their effectiveness, but on their political expediency. Personal income tax rates were cut in 1962 and 1975, in response to rising unemployment, and were raised in 1968 to cool off the war-heated economy. Corporate income tax rates have also been shifted for countercyclical purposes, although investment tax credits have proved a more popular investment stimulus. However, neither personal consumption nor investment expenditure have proved easy to manipulate countercyclically. Any response to a permanent tax cut takes several quarters to fully influence behavior. Consumption spending is determined by what households perceive to be their permanent income rather than their money income at the time (Eisner, 1969). Transitory increases in income that a tax cut or rebate causes tend to be reflected in saving or dissaving. Thus the Ford Administration's well-publicized attempt to fight the 1974-75 recession with an income tax rebate led households to reduce personal indebtedness and had little impact on consumption (Modigliani and Stendel, 1977).

Investment is even less tractable. Investment decisions are typically long term construction projects which are not sensitive to either corporate income tax changes or investment tax credits. The destabilizing exception is inventory levels (both of inputs and finished output). A business slowdown will lead to a run-down in inventories which aggravate the recession. This was a major component of the precipitous decline in employment in 1975. Tax changes have no effect on inventory decisions. Discretionary changes in the level of tax credits may have a perverse, destabilizing influence (Eisner, 1969). While Congress debates whether to increase investment tax credits in the face of a slowdown, business defers as much investment as possible to ensure that it receives the maximum credit. The result is a sharper slowdown.

DELAYS IN COUNTER-CYCLICAL POLICY

Federal stabilization programs have been ineffective because they are undertaken too late. To be effective, a countercyclical program must be timed correctly. Expenditure must increase as soon as possible after a cyclical downturn, and choked-off as soon as possible after overheating starts. The record at the federal level has been poor. Discretionary measures have not actually created jobs until between two to four years from cycle downturn.

Delays occur at four stages: 1) recognizing that a cyclical downturn has occurred; 2) passing the appropriate legislation; 3) taking the appropriate administrative action once the legislation has passed; and 4) enrolling program participants. Table 13 shows the length of each of these lags under recent public works and public employment programs.

Lag in Public Initiation

The time between the beginning of a national recession and the introduction of countercyclical legislation in Congress has varied from 8 to 22 months for public works and from 7 to 11 months for public service employment (Table 13).[6] The Kennedy

Table 13
Lag in Job Creation from Date of Recessionary Downturn
(in months)

Lag In	Public Works			Public Service Employment		
	Accelerated Public Works 1962	Public Works Impact Program 1971	Local Public Works-I 1976	Emergency Employment I Act 1971	Comprehensive Employment and Training Act, 1973 Title II 1973	Title VI 1974
Initiation of policy action[a]	22	8	19	17	—	11
Legislative action[b]	6	6	14	16	8	4
Subtotal	28	14	33	13	—	15
Federal administrative action[c]	1	4	5	11	5	1
Outlays until half the jobs have been created[d]	12	12	12	16	8	6
Total	41	30	50	22	—	22

NOTES: Dashes mean not applicable. CETA II was part of the "Comprehensive Employment and Training Act of 1973" designed to consolidate and decentralize all previous manpower programs. It was not originally intended as a countercyclical program, and was signed into legislation one month after the November 1973 recessionary downturn.

a Time lag between date of recessionary downturn—as dated by the National Bureau of Economic Research (NBER)—and date the program was first introduced in Congress in the form of legislation.

c Time lag between introduction of initial legislation and presidential signing of passed legislation.

c Time lag between the presidential signing of passed legislation and the allocation of funds to state and local governments.

d Time lag between allocations of funds to state and local governments and half the number of direct jobs created. For public works, it includes any lag occurring between project selection and start of construction.

SOURCE: George Vernez and Roger Vaughan, *Assessment of Countercyclical Public Works and Public Service Employment Programs*, R-2214-EDA, The Rand Corporation, September 1978, p. 49.

Administration did not ask Congress for funds to stimulate the economy until February 1962, well after the trough of the 1960 recession.[7] Congressional public works action was not initiated until three months after the trough of the 1970-71 recession (PWIP); action coincided with the trough of the 1974-75 recession (LPW I), but still 19 months after the downturn.

A large part of the delay arises because of the political difficulty in admitting that a recession is imminent. A new Administration generally has a mandate to stimulate the economy. After two or three years in power, it is difficult to admit that the economy is turning sour. Congress can rarely admit to a recession without admitting that past policies have been incorrect although a political scapegoat (such as OPEC) makes facing up to the statistics somewhat easier. Another reason for the delay is the difficulty encountered in anticipating the duration and severity of a predicted recession. Although we are now able to predict recessions with somewhat greater confidence, we are still unable to distinguish between a mild "pause" requiring little federal action and a sharp recession requiring special programs. Given present forecasting capabilities, some delay in the initiation of countercyclical policy action is unavoidable, making it imperative that legislative action not be delayed. The delay in initiation is likely to be less at the state level because the geographic area involved is smaller. While Congress waits for the whole nation to experience a recession, a state government can respond to local indicators. The imprecision of currently available state and local data may lead to some "false starts" under a state based program, but the development of better data over time (which a state based countercyclical strategy may hasten) should help to overcome this.

Legislative Lag

The lag between the initiation of policy action in Congress and final enactment has varied between six and fourteen months for public works programs, and between four and eight months for public service employment (Table 13). Delays have been even longer for tax rebate legislation: the Revenue Act of 1962 was delayed in Congress for 18 months, and the Revenue Act of 1964 for 13 months (Portney, 1976). The former provided a 7 percent investment tax credit for depreciable machinery and other equipment; the latter, reductions in both personal and corporate income tax rates. Delays occur whether or not the program has executive support.

The legislative lag could be shortened. Portney (1976) suggested a resolution settling in advance controversial program distributional provisions. Congress might be able to act more promptly on proposed public works, public service employment, or tax rebate if it had already settled how program funds would be allocated among areas, projects, and so on, perhaps based on local indicators of counter- *157* cyclical need. The political problems involved in determining an equitable and efficient allocation formula in Congress cannot be overestimated (see below). That is why the state stabilization fund approach, outlined in the following chapter, advocates that federal funds be allocated as matching grants.

Bakke (1972) suggested three ways in which a countercyclical program could ensure a timely release of funds:

■ The funds could become available automatically when economic indicators reached certain specified values, subject to legislative review and veto.
■ The funds could become available automatically when economic indicators reached certain specified values, unconditionally.
■ The executive could be granted full discretionary authority to use the funds under legislatively defined conditions.

The second option is the most likely to result in timely policy action. The "trigger" approach has been a proposed component of most proposed public service employment since the 1960s, but was actually enacted only once—under the Emergency Employment Act of 1971. The Anti-Recessionary Revenue Sharing program has also tied the level of outlays to national economic indicators. Triggering is attractive because the size of the program can be related directly to the level of unemployment by specifying the release of additional funds as the rate of unemployment increases. This principle is employed in determining expenditures from the state stabilizing fund outlined in Chapter 6. Defining the appropriate trigger mechanism raises a number of issues.

First, can we expect Congress (or the state legislature) to set aside funds until specified conditions are met during expansionary periods when programs that may need additional funds are being cut back in pursuit of budget cutting and inflation fighting? The political difficulties, while great, are not insuperable. As we shall see in the following chapter, Michigan has set up a stabilization fund which sets aside resources for countercyclical purposes, and Alaska has set up a "permanent fund" for its oil revenues.

Second, what economic indicator or set of indicators should trigger the release of countercyclical funds? The rate of unemployment is often proposed. But the national unemployment rate ignores variations among areas, sectors and labor groups. Other triggers include duration of unemployment, level of unemployment, or number of layoffs. Public works and public service employment countercyclical programs target on different triggers. A state program employing separate indicators for each expenditure component could be much more sensitive to local needs (see following Chapter).

Finally, it is necessary to choose a time period over which the indicator will have the specified value—a month, quarter, or year. Title II of CETA used an absolute level for allocation of funds among prime sponsors' areas—a 6.5 percent rate of unemployment for three consecutive months. The countercyclical component of CETA under the reauthorized legislation (Title VI) triggers funds based upon the national unemployment rate, and allocates funds based on the local unemployment rate. The change-in-indicator approach was proposed in 1962 by President Kennedy, when he asked for standby authority to commit funds for public works when the seasonally adjusted unemployment rates had risen by at least 1 percent during the period, three out of four (or four out of six) consecutive months. These design issues are addressed below in the discussion of a state-based program. The selection of indicators and the degree to which an allocation formula can be designed to meet local needs is, of course, limited by the availability and quality of data.

Lags in Administrative Action and in Enrolling Participants   Both types of lags have been generally shorter for public service employment than for public works programs (see Table 13). Administrative action reflects the time required after legislative enactment to: 1) draw up regulations by the appropriate federal implementing agency; 2) prepare project applications; 3) process and review project applications; and 4) allocate funds among sponsoring agencies. The lag in program outlays, or external lag, reflects the time required for the allocated funds to be actually spent, i.e., for jobs to be created and filled.

Public Service Employment. The administrative lag for a public service program employing about 250,000 people may be as low as one month and the delay between outlaying funds and actually creating jobs may be about six months. The administrative lag depends on the allocation rules, and the external lag depends on the fiscal situation of state and local governments, eligibility restrictions, the size of the program, and the political pressure for rapid job creation.

Public Works. The administrative lag for a public works program can be as long as five months, and the lag until at least half the total on-site jobs are created has averaged 12 months. The length of the administrative lag has depended on administrative requirements and allocation procedures. Under the APW program, less than one month elapsed until the first project was approved, while four and five months elapsed under the PWIP and LPW programs, respectively. Two factors appear to account for the faster allocation under APW. First, coordination for the APW program was entrusted to the Area Redevelopment Administration (ARA) in the Department of Commerce, created especially to carry out the Area Redevelopment Act of May 1961. Individual projects were filed and processed by federal agencies with primary operating responsibilities, and the ARA acted as the *159* coordinating unit stressing speed of implementation. In contrast, the PWIP and LPW were implemented by the Economic Development Administration (EDA) in addition to its regular activities, using guidelines developed by the EDA in Washington, D.C., but with EDA regional offices responsible for field implementation.

The second and perhaps more important factor was the procedure adopted for the allocation of funds. APW funds were allocated as applications came in, on a project-by-project basis, rather than under the "once-and-for-all" procedure used under PWIP and LPW I.

Jobs were created with about equal speed under the APW, PWIP, and LPW I programs. 40 to 50 percent of total funds were distributed in four quarters. This delay in distribution includes the time to start up construction. Because most PWIP projects were approved at the same time and APW projects were approved one at a time, this is unexpected. It may reflect a shorter average time lag between approval and start of construction under APW than the 114 days averaged under PWIP (Sulvetta and Thompson, 1975, p. 272). Most projects under APW and PWIP were completed two years after initial allocation. Under PWIP, the average time from start of construction to completion was 308 days.

The result of these lags is a tendency for federal grants to state and local governments to behave procyclically (ACIR, July 1978).

SUBSTITUTION AND DISPLACEMENT   The ability of the federal government to stimulate economic activity by increasing public sector expenditures during a recession is impeded by substitution—the crowding out of private sector investment by federal borrowing to finance countercyclical spending—and by displacement—reductions in state and local financing in response to federal grants. Both substitution and displacement mean that a job created by federally financed programs does not represent a *net* increase of one job in the economy, since private sector and local public sector employment is reduced. Substitution is probably not a major problem—most studies suggest that federal borrowing of $20 will only reduce private spending by $1 or $2 (Hendershott, 1975). Displacement is a major obstacle to the implementation of federal programs that are channeled through state and local governments, such as CETA and LPW. Total public sector spending increases by much less than the value of the federal grant. Estimates of displacement suggest that displacement within one quarter of receiving federal funds is between zero and 30 percent and may approach one hundred percent after two years.[8] State and local governments are not "guilty" for creating the problem of displacement. The problem is that no regular countercyclical program has been set up. When the federal government at last reacts to a recession and hastily allocates funds for public works or public employment,

160

there is little that can be done at the state or local level within the federal time constraints other than undertake projects that were already on the drawing board, or hire employees for slots that already existed. This means that there is little increase in public capital expenditures, nor are the expenditures retimed from expansionary years to recession periods. A state stabilization fund strategy described in the next chapter would not involve any increase in spending; rather it would *retime* spending to increase during recessions.

The countercyclical Local Public Works (LPW) programs probably suffered from close to a 100 percent displacement rate, that is, it had little impact on state-local construction expenditure (Gramlich, 1978). From the first quarter of 1976 to the first quarter of 1977, total state and local construction expenditures fell by $7.7 billion in current dollars. At the same time, federal capital grants for highways and sewers rose by over a billion dollars, real income grew by 4.5 percent, and state and local bond rates fell by almost 1 full percentage point. This apparently puzzling decline of 27 percent in real terms can be blamed on the passage of the Local Public Works Act in August 1976, after nearly a year of protracted deliberation in Congress. Local officials had ample notice of forthcoming federal funds and an incentive to delay their own construction in the hope that the federal government would pay for some of their projects, although, until regulations were issued and the allocation formula determined, they did not know which projects. The Economic Development Administration received $22 billion worth of applications for the initial $2 billion allocation. Many projects would have been built regardless. Rather than stimulating the economy, LPW actually *delayed* the economic recovery during late 1976 and early 1977.

TARGETING FEDERAL COUNTER-CYCLICAL ASSISTANCE

The third reason why federal countercyclical programs have failed is that they have not been targeted in a way that reflects local cyclical behavior. This failure arises from three factors:

■ There is a wide variation in cyclical behavior among states, and even among areas within a state. Since federal countercyclical programs are triggered by national indicators, aid is often inappropriately timed for local cyclical problems.
■ The process of creating a congressional consensus leads to allocation formulas that do not reflect local needs.
■ Many of the jobs created by the spending of funds in a given area spill over across geographical boundaries and, therefore, do not help the targeted local economy.

**State-Local Variations
in Cyclical Behavior**

Appendix A analyzes variations in cyclical behavior among states and labor market areas (LMAs). LMAs correspond to standard metropolitan statistical areas in most states. Table 14 summarizes the relative performances of states and LMAs in each census region, with respect to four characteristics of local cyclical behavior. However, these general regional tendencies in cyclical performance mask very different patterns from cycle to cycle. *Since it is difficult to predict which states will be affected most acutely by a recession, states must plan for several contingencies.* For the most part, the regional characteristics as defined by states and by LMAs are similar. They differ markedly in some cases: in the New England, South Atlantic, and East-South Central regions, states indicate close or very close conformity of their economic performance with that of the nation as a whole; and LMAs indicate low conformity, high responsiveness to changes in national growth, and very low employment growth rates. The Mountain region is the reverse; it leads the nation and exhibits very low conformity and responsiveness and high secular growth trends. Other regions are not as easy to characterize. The West-North Central and West-South Central are mixed. The mixed pattern in the West-North Central region is due to a clearly defined North-South division. The eastern part corresponds closely to the East-North Central regions, and the western states correspond to the Mountain region. The Pacific region is also divided into two distinct areas. LMAs in the northwestern portion exhibit high responsiveness combined with low growth; LMAs in the southwestern portion exhibit low responsiveness and high growth.

**Targeting Through
Grant Allocation
Formulas**

Because of the necessity of achieving a political consensus in federal grants programs, allocation formulas rarely target funds where they are needed. All areas want a piece of the action. The result is a tendency for small areas, and areas not severely impacted by a recession, to receive a disproportionately large share of a countercyclical grants program. The same tendency will exist at the state level. For this reason, the structure of the state stabilization fund outlined in Chapter 6 encourages a matching fund approach so that only those areas which had committed resources to the fund would receive expenditures. Noncyclical areas would probably not regard the contributions as worthwhile.

The Antirecessionary Fiscal Assistance (ARFA) program has proved the most effectively targeted of federal programs. Table 15 shows the state and local share (by state) of ARFA allocations, and provides an estimate for each state of the state-local share of total state-local revenue loss. The estimates are based on the responsiveness

Table 14
Summary of State and Labor Market Area Cyclical Characteristics, by Region*

Region		Leads or Lags	Conformity	Responsiveness	Relative Sectoral Growth
New England	States	One state lags, all others coincide	Close	Mixed	Very low
	LMAs	Mixed	Low	Mixed	Very low
Middle Atlantic	States	All coincident	Very close	Low	Very low
	LMAs	Some lags, mostly coincident	Very close	Low	Very low
East-North-Central	States	All coincident	Very close	Very high	Very low
	LMAs	Some lags, mostly coincident	Very close	Very high	Very low
West-North-Central	States	3 states lag, 1 state leads	Average	Mixed	Low
	LMAs	Most lag	Mixed	Mixed; Many very low	Mixed
South Atlantic	States	All coincident	Very low	Very high	Low (except *Florida*)
	LMAs	Most lead	Low	Mixed	Low
East-South-Central	States	All coincident	Very close	High	Low
	LMAs	Most lead	Low	Mixed	Low
West-South-Central	States	1 state leads, 1 state lags	Low	Low	Mixed
	LMAs	Most lead	Mixed	Mixed	Mixed
Mountain	States	3 states lead	Very low	Very low	Very high
	LMAs	Most lead	Very low	Very low	Mixed
Pacific	States	2 states lead	Mixed	High Northwest: High Southwest: Low	Low Northwest: Low Southwest: High
	LMAs	Most lead	Mixed		

*The component states of these regions are: *New England:* CT, MA, ME, NH, RI, VT; *Middle Atlantic:* NJ, NY, PA; *South Atlantic:* GA, NC, SC, FL, VI, WV, MD, DE, DC; *East North Central:* IL, IN, MI, OH, WI; *East South Central:* KE, TN, AL, MP; *West North Central:* KA, IO, MN, MO, SD, ND, NE; *West South Central:* OK, LA, AK, TX; *Mountain:* MT, WY, ID, CO, NM, AZ, NV, UT; *Pacific:* CA, OR, WA.

SOURCE: Georges Vernez et al., *Regional Cycles and Employment Effects of Public Works Investments*, R-2052-EIA, The Rand Corporation, January, 1977, p. 97.

163

Table 15
Proportional Revenue Losses From GAO Simulated Recession and Antirecession Fiscal Assistance, By State

Revenue Loss—GAO Simulated Recession

States	Millions	Proportion of Total Loss	Percentage of Total ARFA Disbursed Through the Sixth Quarter[1]
U.S., Total	$2,531.4	100.00	100.00
Alabama	29.5	1.16	1.09
Alaska	7.8	0.31	0.42
Arizona	18.4	0.73	1.26
Arkansas	16.5	0.65	0.78
California	351.2	13.87	13.14
Colorado	32.8	1.30	0.78
Connecticut	43.8	1.73	2.09
Delaware	6.7	0.26	0.50
D.C.	—	—	0.55
Florida	69.0	2.73	4.89
Georgia	58.0	2.29	2.10
Hawaii	22.1	0.87	0.62
Idaho	5.9	0.23	0.46
Illinois	118.0	4.66	3.68
Indiana	59.3	2.34	1.59
Iowa	25.2	0.99	0.53
Kansas	21.1	0.83	0.48
Kentucky	40.9	1.62	0.98
Louisiana	30.3	1.20	1.30
Maine	8.8	0.35	0.70
Maryland	60.6	2.39	1.37
Massachusetts	105.0	4.15	3.70
Michigan	134.0	5.29	6.12
Minnesota	73.5	2.90	1.19
Mississippi	25.6	1.01	0.76
Missouri	48.3	1.91	1.28
Montana	3.9	0.15	0.48
Nebraska	12.1	0.48	0.42
Nevada	6.7	0.26	0.52
New Hampshire	5.4	0.21	0.47
New Jersey	62.7	2.48	5.30
New Mexico	6.5	0.26	0.66
New York	309.4	12.22	12.74
North Carolina	62.8	2.48	1.63
North Dakota	—	—	0.38

Table 15 continued

Revenue Loss—GAO Simulated Recession

States	Millions	Proportion of Total Loss	Percentage of Total ARFA Disbursed Through the Sixth Quarter[1]
Ohio	112.0	4.42	4.58
Oklahoma	22.7	0.90	0.76
Oregon	23.5	0.93	1.57
Pennsylvania	144.6	5.71	5.40
Rhode Island	11.3	0.45	0.69
South Carolina	32.4	1.28	0.98
South Dakota	1.3	0.05	0.33
Tennessee	35.1	1.39	1.17
Texas	62.0	2.45	2.83
Utah	16.2	0.64	0.52
Vermont	6.1	0.24	0.47
Virginia	58.0	2.29	1.30
Washington	32.5	1.28	1.98
West Virginia	14.6	0.58	0.76
Wisconsin	73.3	2.90	1.34
Wyoming	4.0	0.16	0.33

1. The sixth ARFA quarter ended December 31, 1978.

SOURCE: Advisory Commission on Intergovernmental Relations, *State-Local Finances in Recession and Inflation,* A-70, Washington, D.C., May 1979

of the state-local tax base to a simulated recession—a fair comparison since ARFA is aimed at maintaining state and local public services. At one extreme, Florida experienced an estimated 2.73 percent of the total state-local revenue loss, but received nearly 5 percent of ARFA allocations. At the other extreme, Wisconsin experienced nearly 3 percent of the revenue loss but received only 1.34 percent of allocations.

Table 16 compares the allocation of funds by state for the three most recent countercyclical public works programs—Public Works Impact Program and Local Public Works Program, Rounds I and II—with the number of cyclically unemployed[9] to determine how well the distribution matched *cyclical* unemployment problems, and with the total number of employed to determine how well the distribution matched local *aggregate* unemployment problems.

There are considerable variations among states in the dollars allocated per unemployed. Under the PWIP program, $62 were allocated per cyclically unemployed person nationally, and $13 per unemployed person. The corresponding allocations of LPW I 165

Table 16
Allocation of Public Works Funds Per Cyclically Unemployed and Unemployed Person, By State, 1972 and 1976

Region[1] and State	PWIP Project cost per cyclically unemployed person[2]	PWIP Project cost per unemployed person, 1971[3]	LPW I Obligations per cyclically unemployed person[2]	LPW I Obligations per unemployed person, 1976[3]	LPW II Allocation per cyclically unemployed person[2]	LPW II Allocation per unemployed person 1976[3]
Region I						
Connecticut	39	16	676	356	1120	580
Maine	87	16	507	227	1503	716
Massachusetts	67	24	1049	153	2672	508
New Hampshire	115	47	887	394	2727	1200
Rhode Island	30	11	668	246	1314	901
Vermont	32	5	1188	435	3750	1579
Region II[5]						
New Jersey	46	7	577	306	1262	633
New York	11	6	719	296	1548	622
Region III						
Delaware	82	33	618	434	1878	1307
Maryland	5	15	843	149	1637	307
Pennsylvania	28	15	473	184	1031	449
Virginia	5	12	489	149	879	297
West Virginia	5	58	771	202	2308	588
D.C.	5	28	5	369	5	400
Region IV						
Alabama	353	29	391	145	696	334
Florida	$	10	575	66	670	501
Georgia	$	15	281	123	661	428
Kentucky	$	23	603	140	1154	370
Mississippi	$	33	296	143	911	514
North Carolina	$	8	301	122	489	286
South Carolina	$	42	208	105	458	348
Tennessee	302	36	380	159	464	278
Region V						
Illinois	11	$	330	155	463	270
Indiana	7	$	151	109	266	270
Michigan	26	12	775	282	1048	572
Minnesota	25	$	290	159	529	279
Ohio	12	$	385	146	1274	425
Wisconsin	49	22	619	147	995	285
Region IV						
Arkansas	$	55	245	136	714	484
Louisiana	73	14	1241	215	1733	343
New Mexico	$	37	$	300	$	957
Oklahoma	108	19	$	230	$	784
Texas	$	11	1115	171	1825	287
Region VII						
Iowa	14	3	735	153	1875	566
Kansas	13	7	387	193	1164	658
Missouri	72	17	275	128	523	275
Nebraska	$	6	$	256	$	127?

Region VIII					
Colorado	$	20	440	198	1092	431
Montana	$	54	$	376	$	1649
North Dakota	na	20	na	700	na	na
South Dakota	$	68	1495	738	4971	3163
Wyoming	$	102	4968	1263	15,000	4286
Utah	76	11	1771	269	5047	1044
Region IX					
Arizona	$	14	412	145	2532	671
California	27	6	1589	269	3057	540
Hawaii	6	6	a	375	na	711
Nevada	$	10	$	348	$	1169
Region X					
Alaska	na	54	na	464	na	3507
Idaho	$	24	$	379	$	1456
Oregon	64	15	1176	275	2269	556
Washington	22	11	4628	284	6802	578
National mean	62	13	740	223	2381	1799
Mean for states	66.3	22.6	869.0	274.5	2008	857
Standard dev. for states	82.6	19.7	982.1	204.2	2497	865
Ratio standard dev. to mean	1.23	0.87	1.13	0.74	1.24	1.01

NOTES: na means data unavailable on state absolute amplitude; $ means state skipped cycle.

1. Regions correspond to CETA region definitions.

2. Total project cost (PWIP) or obligations (LPWP) divided by the number of cyclically unemployed. Cyclically unemployed defined by absolute amplitude of employment cycle, 1970-1971 for PWIP, 1974-1975 for LPWP, from Vernez et al. (1977), Table C.5.

3. Total project cost (PWIP) or obligations (LPWP) divided by the number of unemployed, defined as the annual average level of unemployment for each state (ETRP, 1976).

4. Weighted by the state's share of total national cyclical unemployment or by state's share of total national unemployment.

5. Excludes Puerto Rico.

6. Hawaii received no PWIP funds.

SOURCE: Georges Vernez and Roger Vaughan, *Assessment of Countercyclical Public Works and Public Service Employment Programs*, R-2214-EDA, The Rand Corporation, September 1978, p. 74.

---

obligations are $740 per cyclically unemployed and $223 per unemployed, and for LPW II, $2381 and $1799. The range among states is considerable—Hawaii received no PWIP allocations, while Alabama received $353 per cyclically unemployed. Wyoming received $1263 per unemployed person under LPW I and $4286 under LPW II, while Florida received only $66 and $501, respectively. The allocation among states is more equal with respect to total unemployed than with   *167* respect to cyclically unemployed for PWIP and both rounds of the LPW program.

PWIP projects were concentrated in small towns and rural areas. Towns with populations of less than 25,000 and rural areas received over 60 percent of total funds allocated while containing less than 48 percent of the population. By contrast, large cities with populations in excess of 100,000, where nearly 28 percent of the nation's population lives, received only 12 percent of the funds.

The Local Public Works program was much more heavily concentrated in larger areas; these areas with populations in excess of 100,000 received 30.3 percent of the allocations under LPW I and 35.4 percent under LPW II. By contrast, areas with populations less than 25,000 received only 40.7 percent of LPW I funds and 32.8 percent of LPW II funds.

Table 17 shows the allocation of countercyclical funds by state per cyclically unemployed and per unemployed worker for public service employment programs (CETA II and VI). These data show considerable variation in funds per unemployed among states. Not surprisingly, because total rather than cyclical unemployment was used in the fund distribution formula, inequalities are greater per cyclically unemployed worker than per unemployed worker.

Average allocations per *cyclically* unemployed person were $454 under CETA II and $960 under CETA VI in 1975-1976. Corresponding allocations per unemployed person were $137 and $289, respectively. The variation among states was large—and larger per cyclically unemployed person than per unemployed person. For example, the state of Washington received $3640 under CETA II per cyclically unemployed person, while Wyoming received only $48.

Targeting of Program Impacts

Program impacts can be targeted less effectively than program allocations. Not all jobs resulting from a countercyclical public works program are created where the funds are spent. Some supplies and some labor will be provided by other regions. Spillovers will be small for public service employment programs since vacancies will be filled from the locally unemployed. Spillovers from public works projects will depend on the extent to which special skills required for the project are available in the local labor force. The greater the reliance on highly skilled workers, the more likely some of the labor will have to be imported from outside the region. The lower the unemployment rate in the local construction industry, the more jobs will be filled by those from outside the area. The probability of local bottlenecks in available skilled labor has been aggravated by the allocation of public works grants according to aggregate unemployment rates. Public works expenditures must be determined by unemployment rates in the construction sector.

Table 17
Allocation of CETA Title II and Title VI Funds for Cyclically Unemployed and Unemployed Person, by State, 1975 and 1976

Region and State[1]	CETA Title II		CETA Title VI	
	Allocations[2] per Cyclically Unemployed[3]	Allocations[2] per Unemployed person[4]	Allocations[2] per Cyclically Unemployed[3]	Allocations[2] per Unemployed[4]
Region I				
Connecticut	257	135	547	288
Maine	390	174	692	310
Massachuetts	1154	167	2063	300
New Hampshire	164	73	568	253
Rhode Island	347	127	787	290
Vermont	587	239	887	362
Region II				
New Jersey	339	180	597	317
New York	388	160	754	311
Region III				
Delaware	165	115	405	284
Maryland	361	63	1186	209
Pennsylvania	270	104	697	270
Virginia	207	63	741	227
West Virginia	527	137	1265	337
Washington, D.C.	$	278	$	413
Region IV				
Alabama	161	60	615	229
Florida	137	84	420	252
Georgia	115	65	483	273
Kentucky	429	99	1000	232
Mississippi	142	69	457	220
North Carolina	145	59	769	312
South Carolina	141	61	524	263
Tennessee	156	65	537	225
Region V				
Illinois	178	84	450	210
Indiana	167	120	419	301
Michigan	536	196	907	331
Minnesota	506	278	673	369
Ohio	342	103	875	263
Wisconsin	544	129	1127	269
Region VI				
Arkansas	150	83	515	285
Louisiana	1345	234	2277	395
New Mexico	$	220	$	390
Oklahoma	$	55	$	187
Texas	412	63	1368	210
Region VII				
Iowa	159	33	775	162
Kansas	52	29	306	152
Missouri	132	62	493	230
Nebraska	$	53	$	220

Region VIII				
Colorado	119	54	446	201
Montana	$	251	$	430
North Dakota	NA	322	NA	374
South Dakota	98	49	429	211
Utah	946	144	1743	264
Wyoming	48	12	719	183
Region IX				
Arizona	309	109	819	289
California	1206	204	2139	362
Hawaii	NA	368	NA	520
Nevada	$	185	$	348
Region X				
Alaska	NA	308	NA	445
Idaho	$	127	$	312
Oregon	391	91	1282	300
Washington	3640	223	6668	409
National Mean	454	137	960	289
Weighted Standard Deviation for State	598	132.8	985	290
Standard Deviation for States	598	84.6	1029	78.1
Ratio of Standard Deviation to Mean	1.37	0.64	1.04	0.27

NOTES: NA means data not available on state absolute amplitude; $ means state skipped cycle.

1. Regions correspond to CETA region definitions.

2. Allocations combine FY 1975 and FY 1976.

3. Total allocations divided by the number of cyclically unemployed. Cyclically unemployed defined by absolute amplitude of employment cycle, 1974 to 1975, derived from Vernez et al. (1977). Table C.5, Appendix C.

4. Total allocations divided by the number of unemployed, defined as the annual average level of unemployment for each state (*Employment and Training Program of the President,* 1976).

SOURCE: Georges Vernez and Roger Vaughan, *Assessment of Countercyclical Public Works and Public Service Employment Programs,* R-2214-EDA, The Rand Corporation, September 1978, p. 72.

The demand for materials will be felt in those areas with industries producing construction supplies. The distribution of these demands is difficult to anticipate. Some measure of the degree of these spillover effects can be gained from the employment multipliers estimated by Vernez et al. (1977). While they estimated that 0.2 jobs would be created within a labor market area for each on-site job created, three jobs would be created in the nation as a whole. Contrary to widely accepted belief, the ability of public works to serve local cyclical needs may be limited. To some extent, these jobs will be created in highly cyclical supplying industries, which tend to be concentrated in the Northeast and North-Central regions. Thus, although large industrial areas have tended to receive a relatively small allocation of funds per unemployed person, they may benefit from the creation of indirect and induced jobs as the projects are carried out in other areas.

The geographic distribution of the impacts of non-targeted programs—such as tax cuts and investment tax credits—is often perverse. Cutting income tax rates will raise disposable income in relatively affluent areas which tend to be less prone to high amplitude cycles. It also increases the inequity of income distribution by providing the greatest benefit to those households who are the least harmed by a recession. Similarly, investment tax credits provide the greatest boost to firms in those areas that are growing, and relatively little assistance to slow growing firms, the very companies most prone to cyclical decline.

POLICY IMPLICATIONS

States can learn a great deal from federal attempts to combat recession—lessons that can be applied to the design and implementation of a state-based countercyclical program.

The first, and most obvious, lesson is that states cannot expect much improvement from Washington. Displacement, delays and ill-targeting cannot easily be improved by fine tuning. Can a state-based program avoid these problems that have rendered federal efforts so ineffective? The answer is yes, providing the state-based program is designed correctly.

Displacement

Displacement can be avoided in a state-based program by setting up a permanent countercyclical program that identifies in advance specific projects and activities that will be undertaken when the local economy slows down. The problem of displacement in federal programs is that it leads to little increase in spending during a recession. If specific projects are identified in advance by state governments, then there is still displacement *over time,* but there is an increase in public spending when it is needed, during a recession. The purpose is not to increase aggregate spending over the course of the cycle, but rather to shift *171* expenditure from good to lean years. An ongoing stabilization program—which federal efforts are not—would reduce displacement, and specific project identification in advance would eliminate it.

Timing

Nothing can be done to avoid delays in recognizing a recession, although they will be shorter at the state level than at the national level because at the state level there is less of an aggregation problem than at the national level. A "lead" state will have experienced unambiguous indications of a recession long before the nation as a whole.

To avoid local legislative delays, the program should be designed to function as automatically as possible. The countercyclical fund proposed in the following chapter should undertake expenditures automatically when target economic indicators cross threshold levels.

To avoid administrative delays, states should work with local governments to ensure that there are suitable countercyclical projects "on the shelf," ready for immediate implementation during a recession. Planning for a public works or training project takes time. It must be coordinated with local economic development strategies, must meet environmental and affirmative action requirements, and acquire the necessary zoning actions and other regulatory permits in advance. And, it must be designed to maximize job creation impacts.

Targeting

Many of the problems of targeting will exist at the state level as they do at the federal level. The political machinations necessary to achieve consensus can just as easily lead to ineffective and inequitable allocation formulas. A state-based program will only be successful if it is designed and operated with the full cooperation of, and contributions from, local jurisdictions. We believe that by encouraging localities to buy into the stabilization fund, thus providing some measure of local control over allocations, and by allowing local participation in the program design and implementation process, the allocation mechanism can perform well. However, federal "strings" may be necessary to ensure an equitable allocation of funds among jurisdictions and to ensure that the programs reach out effectively to those really in need.

Footnotes to Chapter 5

1. This discussion of timing, displacement and targeting is based on Georges Vernez and Roger J. Vaughan, *Assessment of Countercyclical Public Works and Public Employment Programs*, R-2214-EDA, The Rand Corporation, September 1978.

2. A number of detailed historical accounts of countercyclical public works and public service employment programs are available: see Tobin (1975); Briscoe (1972); and Manpower Report of the President (1975).

172 3. At a time when there were nearly 9 million workers unemployed.

4. Determining the appropriate size of these programs relative to the numbers of unemployed is a key issue. Today, unemployment insurance and welfare payments provide some relief for the cyclically unemployed, as does the high relative wage in cyclically volatile industries. This allows greater emphasis to be placed on the productivity of jobs created under countercyclical programs.

5. Under the WPA program alone, 651,000 miles of road, 16,000 miles of water and sewer systems, 85,000 public buildings, 2,877 utility plants, 3,085 playgrounds and athletic fields were built (Briscoe, 1972).

6. The longer delay on public works programs may be because they are regarded as the least desirable approach to countercyclical job creation.

7. This proposal resulted in the Public Works Acceleration Act of 1962. It was signed by the president in September 1962, authorizing an appropriation of $900 million.

8. See Fechter, 1974; Gramlich and Galper, 1973; Johnson and Tomola, 1975 and 1976; Manvel and Calkins, 1975; and National Planning Association, 1974.

9. Measured as the net number of jobs lost between the cycle peak and the following recession. This is an imperfect measure at best, but may reflect local cyclical (as opposed to secular) problems more accurately than does the aggregate number of unemployed.

6

HOW STATES
CAN FIGHT RECESSION

A state's own economic stabilization strategy is certain to be more effective than federal efforts in softening the blows of recessions. It will not wipe out recessions; indeed, it will only make a modest dent in the economic problems that a recession causes. But it will lead to a more rational deployment of countercyclical resources and provide more targeted assistance to those affected by an economic slowdown. The preceding chapters have provided some indication of what such a strategy would look like. This chapter spells it out in more detail. The first step is to set up a stabilization fund—following the Michigan model—which is built up during periods of relatively rapid growth and spent during recessions.[1] The fund would be used to finance three types of countercyclical programs: public works, public employment and training, and intrastate antirecessionary fiscal assistance. These programs would function automatically, subject to legislative review, with funds released when local economic indicators crossed predetermined thresholds. Each program would be keyed to a different indicator since each program is addressing a different countercyclical goal. But this is not the full extent of a countercyclical strategy. There are other measures, including tax reform, long term economic development financing, and regulatory review, that can help reduce local cyclical volatility.

The stabilization fund offers state governments many advantages:

■ *It requires no increase in state and local spending.* Through the fund, state and local spending is retimed and redistributed more evenly over the course of the cycle. Public works are concentrated in times of slack demand for construction activity, and the high level of transfer payments that a recession entails are paid for, in part, during boom years. Expenditures, therefore, reflect *average* revenues over the cycle rather than the present year-to-year budgeting which has led to such a switchback in public spending.

■ *It maintains the integrity of appropriations during recessions.* All too often, recession-induced shortfalls in revenue necessitate the cutting back (or even the cutting out) of programs for which the legislature has appropriated funds. The stabilization fund avoids the need for such wasteful surgery.

■ *It reduces the temptation during good years to expand public programs beyond a sustainable level or to temporarily cut taxes.*

Surging revenues during economic booms, when social services are at a low level, often encourage the expansion of existing programs or the addition of new programs that would not be undertaken if the budget constraint were tighter. A state surplus frequently leads to political pressure to cut taxes. From the perspective of the overall cycle, these surpluses are not "real." They are matched by potential deficits during slumps. The stabilization fund avoids the appearance of such surpluses.

■ *It may actually reduce spending in the long run.* By encouraging a longer term approach to budgeting, reducing the full impact of recessions, and retiming capital expenditures, the fund may actually help reduce state and local expenditures.

The concept of the stabilization fund can be extended beyond the goal of fighting cyclical downturns. States can design a fund to avoid long term problems such as the decline in revenues from severance taxes or depletable natural resources. The State of Alaska is currently designing a permanent fund into which oil revenues will be deposited. If invested profitably, the annual interest from the funds investments will provide a permanent source of revenues from which to meet operating expenses. Any state with substantial revenues from severance taxes should take similar steps to avoid the catastrophic adjustment problems that will otherwise occur when these resources are exhausted.

We must stress that the recommendations made in this chapter are exploratory and intended for guidance only. States have widely varying economies and must design their funds to suit local conditions. Research, thought, imagination and experience will improve the design of stabilization funds.

A STATE STABILIZATION FUND

To finance the necessary countercyclical programs, and to reduce excessive growth in spending during periods of rapid expansion and inflation, states must set up stabilization funds. Contributions would be accumulated while the economy—and state and local revenues—grows at above average rates, and would be withdrawn and spent when growth—and revenues—falter. The fund would not necessarily be reduced to zero during every recession. Some recessions are deeper than others. By maintaining some reserve during a shallow decline, the fund would be larger when a deep recession threatens.

Setting up such a fund is essential. States will not set aside surpluses for a rainy day without a special program. The natural tendency to run surpluses during good years generates political pressure to either cut taxes or start new programs, leaving little fiscal flexibility to face the ensuing recession. While the taxpayers' revolt maintains a head of steam, this pressure is unlikely to abate. In 1979, as the nation's economy neared recession, many states undertook wholesale tax reductions. Property taxes were reduced in 22 states, assessments curbed in four; personal income taxes were cut in 18 states, and sales taxes in 15. The principal beneficiaries of these tax cuts will be the relatively affluent. The equity and efficiency of the state-local tax system have been reduced, and as the recession makes inroads into revenues, these same states will demand federal assistance. In fact, the basic lesson from the discussion in this book is that the surplus is not really a surplus at all. The gap between spending and revenues should not be judged on a year to year basis but over the full cycle. Enough of the expansion years' bonuses should be set aside to allow for the continued operation of state and local services and to fight recession during the bad years.

We propose a stabilization fund with four sources of contributions:

■ *Federal Matching Funds.* Instead of current countercyclical programs (LPW, ARFA, and fluctuating CETA VI appropriations) federal grants should be made to stabilization funds of $3-$4 billion annually (at a minimum), allocating according to each state's own contribution, with allowance for local fiscal conditions.
■ *State Tax Revenues.* The cyclical component of a volatile tax such as the personal income tax.
■ *State Borrowing.* Bond issues for designated countercyclical projects, in those states in which this is permitted.
■ *Contributions from Local Jurisdictions.* Payments by local jurisdictions into a "recession insurance" fund, from which they could draw as revenues fell.

These sources are discussed, in turn below. But before discussing these sources of funds we must analyze how big these funds should be, and what triggers should be used to turn on contributions and expenditures. Following this discussion, some of the institutional issues involved in setting up such a fund are analyzed.

The Size of Stabilization Funds

How big should a state stabilization fund be, and at what rate should states contribute during good years? Ultimately, the best answer to these questions will be provided by experience accumulated through the operation of stabilization funds. The only experience thus far has been with the Michigan stabilization fund and that has been in existence for only two years. Until experience is gained, however, some "ballpark" estimates may provide some initial guidance as well as some insight into the likely impact of the program. The following subsection discusses the institutional issues relevant to the determination of contributions and expenditures. This subsection analyzes only the aggregate questions of fund levels and accumulation rates.

Let us assume that full scale countercyclical expenditures from the fund are required in one year out of four.[2] Expenditures would not cease as soon as the economy turned upward. During one or two quarters after the end of a recession, expenditures would run close in volume to contributions. And even during the best years, expenditures might run at 20 percent of contributions as the state provided assistance to local areas with cyclical problems out-of-phase with the overall state economy. Therefore, expenditures in the three non-recession years would probably run at an average of 25 percent of contributions.

Total state spending from the fund during the one bad year would be about $20 billion if all states participated (see below). Total federal contributions over the four year period would be $16 billion, of which the states would have spent $3 billion during the inter-recession years when expenditures from the fund were running at about one quarter of contributions. Assuming that there are only small state and local contributions during the recession (made to leverage federal contributions), then state contributions during the inter-recession years must average about $4.5 billion (of which one quarter would be spent) each year. This would range from perhaps only $1 billion during the first post-recession year, as the recovery gained momentum (1976, for example), to $7 billion during the peak year (1978). A hypothetical four year period and aggregate contributions and expenditures are shown in Table 18.

Why $15-$20 billion? The estimate is not random. The 1974-75 recession was particularly severe, and is unlikely to be duplicated by most recessions because of the severity of the impact of the rise in oil prices. Experience in that recession thus provides an upper limit for an estimate of the appropriate level of spending on each component. Estimates of state-local revenues lost because of the high rate of unemployment in 1975 range from $5 billion to $20 billion (ACIR, May 1979). Perhaps $6-$8 billion should be set aside for antirecessionary fiscal assistance. In the same year, state-local construction expenditure was about $4 billion in real terms below what it would have been in the absence of a recession, and private construction declined by 20 percent, an abnormally sharp decline. Between $5 and $7 billion should be set aside for public works. Finally, $4 to $5 billion should be set aside to provide employment and training opportunities for the hard-to-employ.

How should this total be allocated among states? This will depend on relative state contributions. But for the sake of illustration, let us assume that all states participate, and that state funds are proportional to their share of national cyclical unemployment and total state-local revenue loss. Table 19 shows how a $16 billion accumulated total *177*

Table 18
Economic Conditions and the Behavior of Hypothetical State Stabilization Funds

	YEAR 1	YEAR 2	YEAR 3	YEAR 4	TOTAL
			Peak	Trough	
ECONOMIC CONDITIONS	Weak Recovery	Strong Recovery		Recession	($ billions)
State Stabilization Funds ($ billions)					
Federal Contributions	4	4	4	4	16
State-Local Contributions	1	4	7	1.5	13.5
(Borrowing)		(1.5)	(2.5)	(1)	(5.0)
Expenditures	4	2	2	20	28
Accumulated Fund Balance (End of Year)	1	7	16	1.5	

would be distributed among the 50 states, assuming that about $9 billion is set aside for public works and public employment and $7 billion for antirecessionary fiscal assistance. It also shows each state's contribution when total contributions run at annual rate of $1 billion.[3] The most obvious fact revealed by this table is that states will differ in the relative importance of revenue sharing and public works and employment programs, depending upon the relative cyclical volatility of their revenues and employment. For example, California experienced only 5.5 percent of the cyclical unemployment in 1975, but, in a GAO simulated recession, experienced 13.9 percent of the cyclical decline in state-local revenues. The California strategy would concentrate on the fiscal assistance component (ACIR, May 1979). By contrast, Indiana suffered 5.3 percent of the employment decline and only 2.3 percent of the revenue decline. Their efforts will have to focus on job creation. These differences result from differences in economic and fiscal structure.

We should stress that these numbers are only indicative. Each recession is, in some ways, a quite distinct experience, and local incidence differs from recession to recession (Appendix A).

Triggering   States may either adopt an automatic triggering mechanism in which both contributions and expenditures are triggered by the performance of the state and local economies relative to threshold indicators, or may make contributions or withdrawals each year on a discretionary basis. The examination of federal programs in the preceding chapters suggests that an automatic procedure leads to more rapid response than a discretionary procedure. Politically, too, an automatic trigger lessens the temptation to indulge in short run tax cutting or spending increases rather than accumulating a necessary surplus. The Michigan fund (see inset) determines contributions based upon the growth in real personal income, and triggers the release of funds for budget balancing (antirecessionary fiscal assistance) based upon real income growth, and for economic stabilization (public works and public employment) based upon the state unemployment rate. Based upon our previous discussions we suggest the following triggers:

■ *Contributions.* The trigger should be an indicator that is most closely correlated with total revenues, perhaps personal income, unemployment rate, or employment growth. The pay-in trigger should be a measure of the secular growth rate or level (a 2.0 percent growth in real income in Michigan). The best trigger will differ from state to state according to economic and fiscal conditions. States must undertake research to determine the triggers that are best suited to their local economy.

Table 19
Hypothetical State Stabilization Funds Accumulated Before a Recession and Annual Contributions

State	State Share of Total (percent)		State Stabilization Fund Accumulation at Cycle Peak[a]	State Stabilization Fund Accumulation at Cycle Peak ($ millions)			State Contribution per $1 billion of Total State Contributions	Accumulation at Cycle Peak as a percent of State Expenditures
	Cyclical Unemployment in 1975	Decline in State-Local Revenues		For Public Works and Public Employment[b]	For Fiscal Assistance[c]	Total		
Alabama	1.7	1.2	1.5	153	84	237	14.8	12.7
Alaska	—	—	no fund	—	—	—	—	—
Arizona	1.1	0.7	0.9	99	49	148	9.3	15.3
Arkansas	1.5	0.7	1.2	135	49	184	11.5	19.4
California	5.5	13.9	9.2	495	973	1468	91.7	14.8
Colorado	0.9	1.3	1.1	81	91	172	10.8	13.6
Connecticut	0.9	1.7	1.2	81	119	200	12.5	12.4
Delaware	0.5	0.3	0.4	45	21	66	4.1	13.9
D.C.	—	—	no fund	—	—	—	—	—
Florida	8.2	2.7	5.8	738	189	927	57.9	32.1
Georgia	4.0	2.3	3.3	360	161	521	32.6	24.6
Hawaii	—	—	no fund	—	—	—	—	—
Idaho	—	0.3	0.1	—	21	21	1.3	4.5
Illinois	6.8	4.7	5.9	612	329	941	58.8	16.5
Indiana	5.3	2.3	4.0	477	161	638	39.9	34.5
Iowa	0.5	1.0	0.7	45	70	115	7.2	8.3
Kansas	0.9	0.8	0.9	81	56	137	8.6	12.0
Kentucky	0.9	1.6	1.2	81	112	193	12.1	9.7
Louisiana	0.7	1.2	0.9	63	84	147	9.2	6.4
Maine	0.7	0.4	0.6	63	28	91	5.7	15.7
Maryland	0.9	2.4	1.6	81	168	249	15.6	11.8
Massachusetts	1.7	4.2	2.8	153	294	447	27.9	13.2
Michigan	7.1	5.3	6.3	639	371	1010	63.1	21.0
Minnesota	1.8	2.9	2.3	162	203	365	22.8	18.0

State							
Mississippi	1.2	1.0	1.1	108	70	178	11.1	15.7
Missouri	2.5	1.9	2.2	225	133	358	22.4	20.6
Montana	—	0.2	0.1	—	14	14	.9	2.4
Nebraska	—	0.5	0.2	—	35	35	2.2	5.1
Nevada	—	0.3	0.1	—	21	21	1.3	5.9
New Hampshire	0.4	0.2	0.2	18	15	33	2.1	7.2
New Jersey	6.1	2.5	4.5	549	175	724	45.3	21.2
New Mexico	—	0.3	0.1	—	21	21	1.3	3.2
New York	11.2	12.2	11.6	1008	854	1862	116.4	22.8
North Carolina	3.3	2.5	2.9	297	175	472	29.5	21.6
North Dakota	—	—	no fund	—	—	—	—	—
Ohio	4.3	4.4	4.3	387	308	695	43.4	17.6
Oklahoma	—	0.9	0.4	—	63	63	3.9	4.5
Oregon	0.9	0.9	0.9	81	63	144	9.0	10.3
Pennsylvania	6.2	5.7	6.0	558	399	957	59.8	15.5
Rhode Island	0.9	0.5	0.7	81	35	116	7.3	18.1
South Carolina	2.3	1.3	1.9	207	91	298	18.6	19.1
South Dakota	0.3	0.1	0.2	27	7	34	2.1	7.9
Tennessee	2.3	1.4	1.9	207	98	305	19.1	16.6
Texas	1.8	2.5	2.1	162	175	337	21.1	6.6
Utah	0.2	0.6	0.4	18	42	60	3.8	8.0
Vermont	0.3	0.2	0.3	27	14	41	2.6	11.0
Virginia	1.6	2.3	1.9	144	161	305	19.1	12.4
Washington	0.4	1.3	0.8	36	91	127	7.9	5.6
West Virginia	0.5	0.6	0.5	45	42	87	5.4	7.7
Wyoming	0.1	0.2	0.1	9	14	23	1.4	8.1
U.S. TOTAL[e]	100	100	100	9000	7000	16,000	1000	15.5

a Total expressed as a percent of fund accumulations for all states.

b Share of cyclical unemployed x $9 billion.

c Share of revenue loss x $7 billion.

d As a percent of total state expenditures, FY 1977.

e Columns may not add to totals due to rounding.

SOURCE: Calculations of state share of total cyclical unemployment use estimates of cyclical unemployment in Vernez et al. (1977, p. 252); share of decline in state-local revenues are from ACIR (May 1979, p. 27).

Michigan State Stabilization Fund

As enacted, the countercyclical budget and economic stabilization fund is designed to attack the two problems of cyclically low revenues and high unemployment. The law establishes formulas by which money is deposited in the fund and by which withdrawals can be made. (Included in Appendix B of this paper.) Major provisions of the law are as follows:

Budget Stabilization

1. All transfers into or out of the fund will be based upon the annual growth of adjusted Michigan personal income (MPI) in the current calendar year.

2. Adjusted Michigan personal income is defined to mean total state personal income minus transfer payments (nontaxable income received from the government) deflated by the Detroit Consumer Price Index so as to remove any inflationary bias. Transfer payments are deducted so that the full impact of the cycle is identified.

3. When the adjusted MPI grows by more than the *pay-in* trigger level of 2 percent, the percentage excess will be multiplied by the total general fund/general purpose revenue accruing to the current fiscal year to determine the amount to be transferred from the general fund to the stabilization fund in the *coming* fiscal year.

4. When the annual change in adjusted MPI is less than the *pay-out* trigger level of 0 percent, the percentage deficiency will be multiplied by the total general fund/general purpose revenue accruing to the current fiscal year to determine the amount to be transferred from the stabilization fund to the general fund in the *current* fiscal year.

Examples: If GF/GP revenue is assumed to be $3 billion and the adjusted MPI change from the prior year is assumed to be: *Case 1:* + 7 percent; *Case 2:* + 1.5 percent; *Case 3:* -4 percent, application of the formulas would be:

Case 1: 0.7 - .02 = .05 x $3 billion = $150 million pay-in to fund next FY,

Case 2: .015 is between .000 and .02 = no pay-in or withdrawal.

Case 3: -.04 x $3 billion = $120 million withdrawal during current FY.

It was not intended that the budget stabilization fund would entirely eliminate the problems posed by revenue fluctuations. Its purpose is to ameliorate the problem by reducing the extreme peaks and valleys.

Economic Stabilization

1. In any quarter following a quarter when unemployment averages 8 percent or more, the act provides that an amount may be appropriated from the fund for countercyclical policy as shown below:

Percent Unemployed in Most Recent Quarter	Percent of Fund Available for Economic Stabilization During the Following Quarter
8.0 - 11.9 percent	2.5 percent
12.0 percent and over	5.0 percent

Example: If the stabilization fund balance is assumed to be $200 million and the rate of unemployment is 9 percent for the quarter ending March 31, 1979, the fund could be used as follows in the April-June quarter: .025 x $200 million = $5 million for countercyclical programs.

2. The funds appropriated for economic stabilization may be used for capital outlay, public works and public service jobs, refundable investment or employment tax credits against state business taxes for new outlays and hiring in Michigan, or any other purpose the legislature may designate by law which provides employment opportunities counter to the state's economic cycle. Obviously, the latter purpose is subject to very broad interpretation.

In brief, the law states that payments will be made into the fund when the adjusted MPI annual growth rate exceeds 2 percent, and, withdrawals from the fund may be made in four situations: (1) the real MPI decreases, (2) quarterly unemployment exceeds 8 percent, (3) revenue falls short of statutory estimate (without change in the tax rate or base), and (4) in an emergency upon two-thirds vote by each house.

Source: Council of State Governments (1979).

■ *Expenditures.* Each of the three program categories requires a different trigger since each is targeted on a different goal:
   ■ Public Works—the unemployment rate in the local construction industry;
   ■ Public Employment—the number of eligible participants;
   ■ Fiscal Assistance—an indicator correlated with revenues, perhaps as in Michigan, the same indicator that is used to trigger contributions.
Unlike the other two programs, public employment and training is an entitlement program, for which the volume of spending is determined by the number in need. The hard-to-employ will be enrolled in CETA funded programs even during the best of times, but as their number increases during the recession, increased funding will be made available to CETA prime sponsors from the state stabilization fund.

Local jurisdictions may wish to develop their own triggers to determine their contributions to the stabilization fund, depending upon the cyclical behavior of their revenue base. The property tax tends not to be cyclical, and cities may find a measure of the cyclical component of expenditures (i.e. the unemployment rate) may prove more effective. Expenditure triggers should be *local* so that the state can determine the appropriate location for its public works and the distribution of the local part of its fiscal assistance. We would expect that local jurisdictions are more likely to favor making discretionary contributions. We urge that they attempt to develop automatic indicators to avoid the temptation to spend excessively during good years.

Federal Matching Funds   Washington should allocate the $3 to $4 billion a year it has spent on discretionary countercyclical programs among state stabilization funds according to states' own contributions in the form of a matching grant. During the early years of this policy, when only a few states have such funds, it will be necessary to fix a match rate. When almost all states participate, the total $4 billion would be divided among the states according to how much they have contributed—leading to a lower match rate when state contributions are large, and a high rate when they are small. We have argued that little can be done to improve the effectiveness of federal counter-cyclical programs. Poor timing has led to long delays in recognizing a recession and in taking the appropriate legislative and administrative action. The on-off approach to countercyclical policy, which changes from one recession to the next, has stunted the development of local stabilization capacity. It has also meant that federal expenditures have little stimulative effect because they tend to displace state-local funds. The short time schedule given state and local governments to spend the federal largesse virtually ensures that the projects funded must already be in the pipeline. Neither does the uncertainty about the level of federal funding encourage, or even allow, rational budgeting by other levels of government.

The federal contribution is important because it increases the attractiveness to local voters of a stabilization fund as an alternative to a state tax cut. By spreading federal outlays evenly over the course of the cycle, the tendency for the federal countercyclical spending to be concentrated in inflationary periods, and therefore to contribute to inflation, will be abated.

Allocation Formula. By providing funds only to those states that have set up stabilization funds, there is automatically some targeting. States that do not experience cycles will not find it worthwhile to participate. Under a straightforward matching grant system, each year a state would receive a share of the federal allocation that is equal to its share of total state contributions to all stabilization funds. However, this would make no allowance for differences among states in their ability to pay. Some weighting system, or allocation formula, is required. No variables or indices have been devised that reflect "ability to pay" to the satisfaction of all observers, but experience suggests that some simple "needs" variables could help. Two possible variables could be applied: indices of the state unemployment rate and the local effort in paying for welfare assistance relative to national averages. These variables would be used to weight the value of states' own contributions. For example, a state whose average unemployment rate was ten percent above the national average in a given quarter (6.6 percent against a national rate of 6.0 percent, for example) and whose own source welfare payments absorbed a percentage of state personal income that was twenty percent above the average for all states (0.90 against 0.75 percent) would be treated as if it had contributed $1.32 (= $1.0 x 1.1 x 1.2) for each dollar it actually contributed into its fund. Other variables which could be included to measure the extent of local fiscal capacity include per capita income, state and local taxes per $1000 of local taxes, and the poverty rate.

Federal Conditions. The allocation of $4 billion of federal funds to state stabilization funds runs the danger of becoming a mere extension of the General Revenue Sharing program unless conditions are attached concerning state expenditures from the stabilization funds. It would defeat the entire countercyclical purpose if states used the resources acyclically to address problems of long term economic decline, or simply to meet operating expenses. At the same time, if states could only make expenditures according to some national unemployment rate above 7 percent for two quarters—the program could no longer meet *state and local* countercyclical needs. Or, if it were required that funds only be spent in counties whose unemployment rate exceeds 8 percent, then the program would be one addressing long-run economic decline rather than cyclical unemployment. Two conditions that are both administratively feasible and would encourage the development of the right type of stabilization fund expenditure triggering mechanism are:

■ Expenditures from a stabilization fund cannot exceed 25 percent of contributions in 10 out of 16 quarters. Federal contributions would be reduced by the percent that states exceeded this limit. This allows states to make at least some expenditures in any period to address local cycles but ensures that overall, expenditures are concentrated in one time period.

■ Expenditures can only be made in areas (counties, cities, or townships) whose unemployment rate has exceeded 125 percent of its two year average for two successive quarters. Again, states that ignored this would be penalized by the loss of federal contributions.

It is also desirable to include some federal conditions to ensure that state efforts are effectively targeted on those most in need. Many state and local governments have needed federal prodding into the areas of affirmative action and income transfers. The public employment component of state stabilization expenditures will be channeled through the existing CETA prime sponsors, and will be subject to current regulations. Therefore, some minority set aside provision for public works projects and an equitable allocation formula for the fiscal assistance program could be required. The simplest administration procedure would be to require federal approval of the stabilization fund design before it became eligible for federal matching grants. This type of procedure has been used by the CDBG program and for various types of education assistance.

State Tax Revenues   Total state-local contributions over the four year cycle total $13.5 billion, of which about $5 billion may be borrowed. How much should come from state revenues and how much should come from local revenues is up to the individual states. Two considerations should guide these deliberations. First, the share should be related to the share of each level of government in total revenues, which varies among states, averaging about 50-50 nationwide. But the state share should be greater than the local share because state revenues tend to be more cyclical than local revenues. The property tax provides much more stable revenues than income taxes. Second, the share of contributions should be related to the relative distribution of antirecessionary fiscal assistance grants. Since states are likely to take a disproportionately large share of this component because of their volatile revenues, state contributions should be larger. Also, states are able to use their broader tax base to redistribute resources from rich to poor *185* jurisdictions. To do this effectively, they must make the major share of state-local contributions.

Setting up a fund will be more difficult for those states with relatively regressive tax structures, since they tend to have less cyclically volatile revenue sources—a regressive income tax, or a sales tax, is less volatile than a progressive income tax. The stabilization fund provides a complementary policy for those states taking steps to improve the equity of their tax structure since it will help dampen the increased cyclical volatility of their revenues.

State Borrowing

Since about a third of the expenditures are for capital projects, those states that are able should finance a part of their stabilization fund by issuing bonds. Many states, however, are constitutionally precluded from borrowing, and will have to make their full contributions from tax revenues. Those states and jurisdictions that can borrow should prepare a number of long term capital projects that can be delayed with little harm until the economy weakens. Bonds should be issued to finance these projects under conditions that: "the project shall be undertaken when the unemployment rate in the local construction sector has increased for two consecutive quarters and has reached a rate in excess of 140 percent of its average level in the preceding six quarters" or similar language. To ensure coordination between state and local countercyclical efforts, the state should act as a packager for the bond marketing. In fact, the state could contribute part of the cost of locally funded projects in order to ensure local participation and cooperation.

There are several reasons for borrowing early to finance counter-cyclical public works. First, bond issues take time. If the state waits until a recession, or a construction slowdown is clearly indicated, expenditures will not be made until the worst is passed. Second, by "setting aside" a number of projects, the problem of displacement is minimized, and thus one of the major problems inherent in the federal system is overcome. Third, cycle peaks and the first year of recessions have been accompanied by record inflation and interest rate levels (Figure 3). Further, high interest rates usually lead financial institutions to reduce their portfolios of tax exempt bonds as they seek more effective shelters, which further increases the cost of public sector borrowing. Funding countercyclical public works during good years will cut borrowing costs. Finally, voters may be more willing to approve a bond issue during good times than when afflicted by recession-induced frugality.

A major advantage of borrowing is that it allows a rapid increase in stabilization funds. However, since it is tied directly to public works projects, it should never provide more than about one-third of the state contributions to the fund.

Yields on Selected Long Term Securities (1930 to present)

(Recessions are shown shaded, with peaks (p) and troughs (t) indicated)

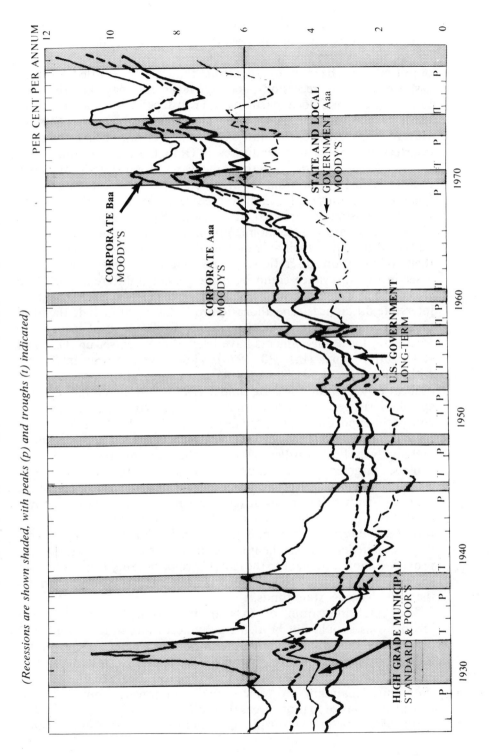

Local Contributions   Participation by local jurisdiction is essential to ensure: a) accountability of the state fund to its component jurisdictions; and b) prudent budgeting by local governments to avoid becoming "fiscal junkies." These objectives can be met by requiring that, to be entitled to fiscal assistance during recessions, local governments pay into the state fund. The extent of local participation will depend on the allocation of fiscal responsibility between the state and local governments. In Hawaii, for example, the state government is responsible for three quarters of state-local expenditures; in Ohio, less than one third. This would operate very much in the same way as total state-local contributions paid into the fund leverage federal matching grants. Thus, local contributions paid would leverage state allocations from the fund when a recession necessitated withdrawals. By making contributions, cities would learn that economic booms are not the norm, and would be forced to reduce their average spending level (which would reduce their reliance on discretionary and uncertain federal and state assistance). Allowance could be made for local differences in fiscal effort just as allowance would be made by the federal government for interstate differences. The allocation formula might include the local unemployment rate and local taxes per $1000 of local income. In Michigan, local governments have been allowed to set up their own stabilization funds (P.L. 30, 1970). They have not been integrated within the state fund. The advantages of integrating local countercyclical funds within the state fund are: 1) state-local countercyclical spending can be coordinated—operating under consistent triggers and consistent expenditure program design; and 2) the broad state revenue base allows the state to redistribute resources toward relatively poor and highly cyclical jurisdictions so that the state countercyclical effort can be targeted to the most needy areas. However, a major metropolitan area with cyclical needs very different from the rest of the state and with sufficient local resources may wish to set up its own fund, either metropolitan wide or only the central city. In this case, the role of the state would be to make matching funds available in the same way as the federal government makes matching funds to states. Some provision should be made in the federal program to distribute a limited share of funds directly to local jurisdictions' funds—treating them on the same basis as state funds.

The total allocation of expenditures from the fund among jurisdictions should not be tied rigidly according to local contributions, since this would remove the important element of flexibility. Each jurisdiction would be guaranteed expenditures equal to what it had contributed plus some allowance for local fiscal conditions. The state must maintain an "emergency" component from which to provide assistance to those areas that suffer unusually deep recessions. A rule of thumb, at least during the initial years of operating the fund, would be to keep, say, 25 percent of the cumulative total within each of the three components of the fund as a "discretionary" allocation.

The state may also wish to provide assistance in the form of short or medium term loans to local jurisdictions suffering from acute fiscal distress. This will encourage those jurisdictions to deal with their fiscal problems rather than become permanently dependent on emergency assistance.

Institutional
Design Issues
Setting up an effective stabilization fund raises two other important design issues: How is the fund administered? And what is the role of the state legislature?

Fund Administration. Those administering the fund must perform several tasks:

■ Managing contributions, including those from local jurisdictions.
■ Coordinating bond issues for countercyclical public works projects.
■ Controlling short term portfolio investments to maximize the rate of return on the accumulated balance.
■ Administering the distribution of expenditures among jurisdictions and programs.
■ Managing federal receipts and ensuring compliance with federal regulations.

To ensure local participation, representatives from those participating jurisdictions should be included on the administrative board, together with representatives of the relevant state agencies, the governor, and the state legislature. Voting on geographic allocation issues could be on the basis of the value of accumulated contributions into the fund.

Expenditure allocation procedures must be set up in advance of a recession, to avoid administrative delays, with legislative approval if required.

The accumulated fund balance should be invested in secure, short term investments that yield the highest possible rate of return—money market certificates, federal government securities, even state and local bonds providing their maturity does not exceed the date at which fund expenditures are most likely to be necessary. The fund cannot be used to further local development finance efforts since such investments are unlikely to be liquid, especially during a recession.

Role of the Legislature. The legislature will be called upon to remove statutory blocks to setting up a stabilization fund as well as shaping the enabling legislation. There may even be constitutional amendments to be overcome. The Council of State Governments summarizes the legal aspects in Michigan:

Michigan's constitutional provisions prohibiting continuing appropriations, or accumulation of funds for future use, limiting fund transfers except as accomplished by legislative appropriations, and requiring an annually balanced budget are common to many states. In Michigan, an opinion of the attorney general states that creation of a trust fund and legislative appropriations to the fund for a valid public purpose meet the constitutional requirements.

Passage of the necessary amendments and legislation is most likely while the impacts of a recession are still fresh in the memories of the public and the legislature.

The legislature will also play a role in administering fund contributions and expenditures. Although difficult to achieve, the legislature's role should be one of oversight through a standing committee or subcommittee—not one of prior approval. In this way, control could be effective without the time-consuming process of seeking approval before action is taken.

PUBLIC WORKS

The major function of public works projects is to develop economic and social infrastructure. The public works component of the countercyclical strategy is targeted at providing employment for idle resources in the construction and building supplies industries. Special construction projects should not be undertaken solely to provide jobs for the unskilled or inexperienced. There are two reasons for this: 1) the average duration of low-skilled jobs on public construction projects has been about 2 weeks; 2) because of skill requirements and the nature of the construction labor market, few jobs for the unskilled are generated on site. The hard-to-employ are the target of the public employment and training programs described in the following section. Appendix C provides estimates of the number of jobs and the type of participants in past public works projects and public employment programs.

Triggering Expenditures

A project for which the finances had already been raised would be started when unemployment in the local (county or city) construction sector shows a cyclical downturn. Because monthly local employment and unemployment data are not always reliable, there is something of a trade-off between waiting for sufficient monthly data to be sure that a downturn has occurred, and creating jobs as quickly as possible. Employment and unemployment data, while providing confusing signals, are, along with housing permits, the only data available in a timely fashion at the local level. States will have to experiment on developing efficient leading indicators of construction downturns. Until satisfactory analyses have been undertaken, we would suggest the following indicator:

■ Pre-selected public works projects will be undertaken in an area (county, city, special district) when the unemployment rate in construction increases for two successive quarters and averages a rate for three months that is 140 percent above its average rate in the preceding twelve months.

The indicator must be based on the behavior of the construction sector since this does not necessarily coincide with total employment and public works are specifically targeted to construction. In order to avoid labor supply bottlenecks, the predicted number of on site jobs created by a project should not come within more than 66 percent of the estimated number of unemployed construction workers within easy access of the project site.

Type of Public Works Projects   Public works projects undertaken as part of state stabilization policy should be those that are compatible with the area's overall economic development strategy and public infrastructure needs. There is little that can be gained in selecting special labor intensive projects since these are unlikely to provide the unskilled worker with more than two or three weeks work which does next-to-nothing for his skills, work experience or income maintenance. Make-work construction projects leave the local taxpayer with bond-servicing costs and little of permanent value by way of reward. There is little cyclical behavior in the type of public construction projects undertaken by state and local governments and so state-local patterns provide no basis for selection of project type most suitable for counter-cyclical purposes (Vernez and Vaughan, 1978).

Heavy construction projects—flood control, dams, levees, water supply facilities and water treatment plants—are rarely suitable for countercyclical purposes because the heavy construction industry does not behave cyclically. The 1974-75 downturn was an exception. Moreover, the equipment and skills needed on such projects are highly specialized, and may have to be imported from other areas and states, which will reduce their local job generating ability. However, some heavy construction projects should be kept "on-the-shelf" in case of a repeat of the 1975 experience. Sewer projects have the advantage of being relatively quick to complete (Table 20).

For timely implementation, the planning for countercyclical projects must have been completed in advance, so that time consuming public hearings and lawsuits do not delay getting construction firms to work on the projects. Pre-selection is obviously a difficult issue. If the project is essential to the delivery of public services, then delay may be costly and disruptive. On the other hand, construction projects should never be undertaken simply in order to create jobs. Developing the planning capacity at the state and local level to set aside capital projects for countercyclical implementation will take time, and involve *191* a new function for state and local planning agencies, and will add a new dimension to capital budgeting (see Volume 9 in Studies in State Development Policy, *The Capital Budget*).

The energy crisis has led state and local governments to investigate the feasibility of using energy conservation projects as a means to create jobs. It seems doubtful that many low-skilled and unskilled jobs can be created in this way. Even relatively straightforward construction and rehabilitation projects embody a very high percentage of skilled workers—plumbers, carpenters, electricians, for example. Overall, only 13 percent of those in the construction industry are unskilled; 56 percent are craftsmen. Craftsmen are in short supply during most of the business cycle, and depending on local cyclical behavior, may not be readily available even during a recession. Since as many as four craftsmen are needed for each laborer, few unskilled jobs can be created.

PUBLIC EMPLOYMENT AND TRAINING

The increased duration of joblessness by the chronically unemployed constitutes about half of the increase in the unemployment rate during a recession. This group also suffers most acutely; they are less likely to receive unemployment insurance or other benefits, have any accumulated savings, or have other wage earners in the household. They are therefore the special target of the public employment and training component of the countercyclical strategy. Unlike public works, expenditures from the fund would not be determined by local economic indicators, but by the numbers of eligible participants. Eligibility would be the same as for Titles II and VII of the newly re-enacted CETA program, and expenditures from the fund would be made to local CETA prime sponsors as their ranks of participants were swelled by the recession. The stabilization fund would, essentially, allow states to accumulate CETA funds to cope with a recession, since Washington has proved unwilling to appropriate sufficient funds during recessions to provide for the number of eligible unemployed.

Eligibility

The program must focus on those most harmed by cyclical fluctuations—those who find it difficult to secure employment even in the best of times. These include:

■ Those who have drawn unemployment insurance for more than 15 weeks or have exhausted their benefits
■ Welfare recipients (AFDC, Home Relief, etc.)
■ Disadvantaged new entrants to the labor market who have unsuc-
cessfully searched for at least 15 weeks, including those released from

prison or the armed forces, and those from households earning below the poverty level.

Strict enforcement of eligibility is necessary. Prior to the 1978 reauthorization, those enrolled under countercyclical CETA programs were all too often employed on the day prior to entry, were relatively skilled and well educated, would have been eligible for unemployment insurance, and, in all likelihood, would only have been unemployed for a short period of time. Although strict enforcement slows down the rate of job creation, the trade-off can be worthwhile if it effectively targets on the needy.

Type of Program   Experience suggests that there is no simple formula that guarantees success in training the hard-to-employ. States and localities are developing programs that are best suited to their problem clientele and to their economic structures under Title II and VII of the new CETA legislation. Their approaches include: 1) public employment; 2) training; and 3) wage subsidies.

Public Employment. Although the CETA experience has led some commentators to criticize public employment as an effective job-creating device, it may be the only effective way to reach out to "high risk" cases—just as loan guarantees are the only way to reach certain high risk businesses. And, as in the case of capital market failures, the problem is one of transactions costs. A private firm may find it very expensive to search for, screen, and train an ill-educated, inexperienced member of the labor force. A firm employing 20 people can scarcely invest in a personnel office skilled in the techniques necessary to bring such individuals into the workforce. The public sector, because it already has data in the eligible population, because it has been administering training programs, and because of its size and its diversity of employment opportunities, can make a greater outreach effort.

But public employment should be regarded, in part, as a *screening* system—a way of identifying those who are and those who are not suitable for private sector training and employment. A public sector jobs program should not be regarded as an end in itself, unless participants can move into permanent public sector employment.

Training. A recurring failure in publicly administered training programs has been the inappropriate skills imparted to many of their participants. Evaluations of pre-CETA manpower programs suggest that few participants "were placed in areas of growing demand, in jobs with real potential for advancement" (Perry et al., 1976, p. 77).

Greater effectiveness may result from a coordination of training efforts with private employers. By training eligible participants for slots needed by private employers, or even subsidizing private firms to train eligible participants (but without the type of red-tape that has   *193*

Duration of Construction, by Type of Public Works Project

Building Construction	Average Duration in Months (with Percentage of Total Jobs Generated by Quarter)	Total Duration in Months	Total On-site Man-hours[a]	Range of Construction Time
Private one-family housing		4.8	37.5	NA
Public housing	10.4 / 21.6 / 27.3 / 23.2 / 15.1	14.8	52.9	NA
Schools	15.6 / 26.9 / 32.6 / 22.2	12.0	39.3	NA
Hospitals	6.5 / 12.4 / 16.5 / 19.3 / 17.6 / 14.9 / 9.8	21.0	43.4	10-47
Nursing homes		13.4	42.0	NA
College housing	11.1 / 22.4 / 31.3 / 25.4 / 9.6	13.4	43.7	4-22
Federal office buildings	6.8 / 15.3 / 20.5 / 23.0 / 21.8 / .6	16.8	41.9	9-31

Scale: 3 6 9 12 15 18 21

Heavy Construction		Total Duration in Months	Total On-site Man-hours[a]	Range of Construction Time
Sewer lines	27.0 / 41.1 / 26.4 / 5.5	9.5	45.0	NA
Sewer plants	45.7 / 47.3	6.5	43.4	NA
Land operations[b]	27.5 / 33.5 / 26.0 / 13.0	11.1	52.2	2-30
Dredging[c]	39.5 / 44.0 / 16.5	6.7	82.3	2-16

4

NOTES: Figures in italics indicate percentage of total on-site man-hours spent in quarter. NA means not available.

a For each $1.000 of contract costs, measured in 1974 dollars.

b Land operations, as defined by the Bureau of Labor Statistics, include 28 civil works projects: large earth-fill dams (1 project), small earth-fill dams (3 projects), local flood protection (3 projects), pike dikes (5 projects), levees (7 projects), revetments (5 projects), and four miscellaneous projects—channel improvement, jetties, outlet channel, and sea wall extension.

c Dredging includes 15 projects, of two different types: hydraulic, in which a dredge equipped with a cutterhead pumps soft material through a pipeline to a disposal area, usually on-shore; and the second type, in which soft or broken hard material is loaded into scows and taken to a disposal area, usually in deep water. The sample projects are the same as those used in the Haveman and Krutilla study.

SOURCE: Labor and Material Requirements for Construction of Private Single-Family Houses, 1972, BLS Bulletin 1755, p. 5: Labor and Material Requirements for Public Housing Construction 1968, 1974, BLS Bulletin 1821, pp. 6-7: Labor and Material Requirements for School Construction, June 1968, BLS Bulletin 1586, pp. 7, 17: Labor and Material Requirements for Hospital and Nursing Home Construction, 1971, BLS Bulletin 1691, pp. 14-15: Labor and Material Requirements for College Housing Construction, May 1965, BLS Bulletin 1441, pp. 24-25: Labor Requirements for Federal Office Building Construction, 1962, BLS Bulletin 1331, pp. 26-27: Labor and Material Requirements for Sewer Works Construction, 1966, Bulletin 1490, p. 18: Labor and Material Requirements for Civil Works Construction by the Corps of Engineers, 1964, BLS Bulletin 1390, p. 19-20.

impeded WIN), the unskilled may be prepared more effectively for unsubsidized employment. The Private Industry Councils (PICs) financed under CETA Title VII may become a model for an expanded state-based countercyclical effort. There may also be opportunities to expand the level of apprenticeship programs to provide skill training to the uneducated. European nations make much more use of apprenticeship programs than does the U.S.

Wage Subsidies. Jobs can be created by reducing the cost of hiring additional labor. A wage subsidy could take several forms. One approach could be modeled on the new Targeted Jobs Tax Credit which is applicable only to the hard-to-employ, and can be taken by business as a credit as well as a reduction in taxes. During its initial nine months, the program has been poorly publicized and has encountered severe administrative problems. But it could provide the basis for an effective state effort. An alternative would be to provide employment vouchers to unemployed individuals, based upon their past income and unemployment experience. An employer could redeem these vouchers—either for cash or reduced business payroll taxes—for each week that they provided the worker with a job. The cash value, or subsidy, would decline over time as the subsidized worker gained work experience. Additional subsidy would be provided to employers providing vouchered workers with training programs. However, accumulated experience with wage subsidies has not shown them to be overwhelmingly successful. Whether this is due to poor program design or to an inelastic demand for unskilled labor has not yet been established.

The sobering conclusion is that there is no easy way to provide either effective training or private sector employment to the economically disadvantaged. With the greatly improved targeting in CETA and the growth of Private Industry Councils, the capacity to assist those in need will, we believe, be improved. The ability of the stabilization fund to inject an additional $7 billion into the delivery system when demands increase will encourage the development of a targeted countercyclical component to the CETA program.

ANTI-RECESSIONARY FISCAL ASSISTANCE

Fiscal assistance must serve two purposes: 1) it must provide short run assistance to help the state and local jurisdictions that suffer sudden negative cash flows; and 2) it must allow state and local governments to meet public service demands and maintain the integrity of appropriations.

The fiscal assistance component would offer two types of aid: grants released by a trigger indicator, and short term loans made to jurisdictions suffering from a sudden and harsh combination of reduced revenues and increased expenditures.

Triggering   The trigger to release grants for state and local fiscal stabilization must be an economic indicator related to the extent of fiscal stress—the combination of declining revenues and increased social service expenditures. Michigan uses the adjusted personal income growth rate. When this falls below zero, funds are released to the state government at a rate proportional to the shortfall of the indicator (see above). The best indicator will differ from state to state, depending on the economic and fiscal base, and upon the level and type of social services. States must conduct research to determine which variable, or set of variables, is most closely related to fiscal outcomes. Other variables that might be included are: the welfare caseload; the unemployment rate; the number of unemployed; the number of long term unemployed; and the change in employment. The trigger should be some level of an indicator that is only exceeded in recessions, and that is proportional to the level of cyclical—rather than secular—fiscal stress. The trigger would be used, each quarter, to determine the volume of counter-cyclical grants available to state and local governments.

Allocation   The distribution of these grants between state and local governments, and among local governments, is a key issue. The record of many state governments with respect to fiscal assistance and state-based revenue sharing is not encouraging. Neither is it possible to develop any rules that can be applied to all states. The state of Hawaii collected 75 percent of total state-local revenue and would require a much larger share of the countercyclical component than the state of Ohio, which collects barely 30 percent of state-local revenue. However, two aspects of the design of the state stabilization fund will help in overcoming these difficulties. First, federal approval of the fund's operating procedures would be required to make the funds eligible for federal matching grants. Second, and more important, local governments would participate in the state stabilization fund, both by making contributions and by sharing in its administration. We suggest a two stage allocation procedure. In the first stage, the trigger determines the total volume of fiscal assistance available for a given quarter. This is allocated between the state and local levels of government according to some pre-agreed share. In general, state governments would receive more than half of the allocations because their revenues constitute about half of the state-local total and because their revenues are much more cyclical. In the second stage, the local share is allocated among local jurisdictions. This could be done either according to local indicators—for example, a city might receive an amount proportional to its share of the total state welfare case-load—or according to the city's own previous contributions to the stabilization fund. The latter method could take into account local fiscal effort in much the same   *197* way as federal matching grants make allowance for state fiscal effort (see above). Jurisdictions, through allocations from all three components, would be guaranteed expenditures more than equal to their accumulated contributions. The second allocation method is more attractive since it would encourage local areas to adapt to fiscal realities—the most cyclically volatile would face an incentive to make large contributions. This would reduce their tendency to expand programs or cut taxes in good years.

Loans

A small reserve from the fiscal assistance component would be set aside to provide medium term loans to areas that experience an especially sharp, or unexpected fiscal problem. A loan would compel the area to make appropriate fiscal adjustment, whereas a grant would not. Determination of loan eligibility would be made on a case by case basis according to rules set by those administering the fund.

OTHER STABILIZATION POLICIES

The stabilization fund, and the expenditures described in the preceding sections, are the core of a state based countercyclical strategy. But other measures can be taken to reduce local cyclical volatility. These include:

■ *Long run economic development.* By diversifying the local base, cyclical amplitude can be reduced. A major part of such development is to establish an effective local capital market for both debt and equity financing and improve the quality of the local labor force.
■ *Tax reform.* The structure of local taxes can be adjusted to provide a more effective automatic stabilizer. This will involve more volatile revenues, but the stabilization fund protects state-local expenditures from these cycles.
■ *Review of regulations.* Some regulations, particularly usury ceilings, actually exacerbate local cycles. Review and reform of the cyclical impact of these regulations will help.

Long Run Economic Development

A successful long run economic development strategy can help reduce an area's susceptibility to recessions. The diversification of the local economy shifts labor from traditional, cycle-prone, sectors into emerging, less cyclical industries. A tight labor market discourages firms from laying off workers. The tools for such a strategy are discussed in other papers in Studies in State Development Policy, but a few points can be reiterated here.

First, a successful development finance strategy that improves the availability of both debt and equity capital can increase the local birth rate of new firms. Nationwide, the most rapidly growing firms are

198

small young companies, and their growth can provide a counter-cyclical buffer. Also, company birth rates are surprisingly uncyclical—although business failures are cyclical. Developing an attractive birth "matrix" that can be provided by older urban areas is a major step in dampening the downswing.

Second, developing labor skills, as we have argued above, is another way of reducing local cyclical vulnerability. Firms tend to hoard skilled and experienced labor when demand falls, because, if laid-off, such employers may not find employment elsewhere.

Tax Reform

Reforming the state and local tax structure can dampen local cycles. First, highly cyclical revenues act as automatic stabilizers because they ensure that the disposable income of consumers and firms falls by less than the gross income. A progressive income tax is therefore a good economic stabilization device. Those states with regressive tax structures should introduce more progressive schedules both for equity reasons and as a stabilizer. In addition to the personal income tax, other changes that have a similar impact are: 1) reducing the regressivity of the sales tax by exempting food, medical supplies, and other necessities, and including services; and 2) improving the equity of the property tax by replacing home owner exemptions and deductions with circuit-breakers.

These changes are all the more important because another major tax reform—indexing—will actually reduce the cyclical volatility of tax revenues. Indexing is a necessary step toward reducing the inequity and inefficiency induced by inflation. Unless countervailing measures are taken, the effectiveness of the tax structure as an automatic countercyclical tool will be impaired.

There are other steps that can also be taken. The way unemployment insurance premiums for employers are calculated implicitly subsidizes high-turnover firms. They do not pay premiums at a rate high enough to cover the volume of benefits paid their employees. By abolishing the maximum rate and redesigning the premium calculation formula, firms could be encouraged to hoard, rather than layoff, labor.

Regulatory Reform

Regulations can inadvertently contribute to cyclical economic behavior. They may also raise the cost of doing business and slow secular growth. This is not to say that such regulations should be abolished. Regulations provide different levels of government with means to attain a variety of social objectives—from orderly residential development to reduced air pollution. But state governments should be aware that regulations may have undesirable economic impacts that can be mitigated or avoided altogether. The list is potentially endless, but we have focused on a few regulations to illustrate how a review of regulatory activity *199* may help local government.

Usury Ceilings. To reduce the cost of owning a home, several states[5] have imposed usury ceilings—upper limits on the mortgage rate that banks can charge on home mortgages. While the market mortgage rate is below the usury ceiling, there is no effect on the housing market. When inflation pushes up interest rates above the usury rate, financial institutions, to cover their increased cost of funds, must seek assets with a higher yield. Therefore, they drastically reduce their volume of mortgage loans—usually rationing the few they do make by raising the down payment, offering them only to favored customers, and raising the points charged. This effectively excludes those with limited assets from home buying. The ceiling does reduce borrowing costs, but only for those favored few who get mortgages. For many more, the usury ceiling delays homeownership until the market rate falls. The demand for housing is slashed and construction employment falls. The last three recessions—1970, 1974, and 1979—have also been the years of peak interest rates when low state usury ceilings have contributed to the depth of the local recession. This is illustrated in Table 21. It shows the usury ceiling in New York State, the national average mortgage rate, and the ratio of housing permits in New York to housing permits in the nation. When the national rate exceeds the New York ceiling, the ratio falls.

Housing Regulations. States should review their building codes to determine whether laws governing seasonal construction, housing starts, and other aspects of construction may be contributing to the volatility of that industry. Canada has experimented successfully with cash bonuses to encourage winter construction—winterizing construction costs only a few hundred dollars, and if home buyers can be encouraged to buy in the winter, builders can smooth out the seasonal shifts (Vernez and Vaughan, 1978). This would have the added benefit of reducing the labor cost of construction, for workers would no longer demand wages high enough to compensate for the seasonal nature of their work and would draw less unemployment insurance.

The principal could be extended to cover cyclical fluctuations. If impediments to securing mortgages were removed, states could offer cash bonuses to those buying or rehabilitating homes. The bonuses could be tied to the prevailing unemployment rate in the construction sector. Since we have little evidence on the efficacy of such a policy, states should proceed cautiously. The bonus should only be used countercyclically, and sparingly at that, since it is regressive—providing assistance to those rich enough to be able to afford to purchase a home.

Table 21
Single Family Housing Construction and the Usury Gap

	Interest Rates		Usury Gap (N.Y.S. Ceiling- U.S. Rate)	Housing		
Year	N.Y.S. Ceiling	U.S. Average		N.Y.S. Permits	U.S. Starts	N.Y.S. Permits/ U.S. Starts
1960	6.00	6.23	-.23	50,388	994.7	.051
1961	6.00	5.98	+.02	41,424	974.3	.043
1962	6.00	5.93	+.07	39,584	991.4	.040
1963	6.00	5.81	+.19	42,223	1,012.4	.042
1964	6.00	5.80	+.20	44,112	970.5	.045
1965	6.00	5.83	+.17	46,236	963.7	.048
1966	6.00	6.40	-.40	37,800	778.6	.049
1967	6.00[1]	6.53	-.53	36,180	843.9	.043
1968	6.65[2]	7.12	-.47	36,168	899.4	.040
1969	7.42	7.99	-.57	31,596	810.6	.039
1970	7.50	8.52	-1.02	26,988	812.9	.033
1971	7.50	7.75	-.25	34,836	1,151.0	.030
1972	7.50	7.64	-.14	39,012	1,309.2	.030
1973	7.94[3]	8.30	-.36	36,948	1,132.0	.033
1974	8.50	9.13	-.63	27,504	888.1	.031
1975	8.50	9.10	-.60	24,080	892.2	.027
1976	8.50	8.99	-.49	23,058	1,162.8	.020

1. Usury ceiling changed on July 1, 1968 to 7.25%.
2. Usury ceiling changed on February 16, 1969 to 7.50%.
3. Usury ceiling changed on August 15, 1973 to 8.0% and on October 11, 1973 to 8.50%.

SOURCE: Derived by the author from data supplied by the New York State Banking Department, the Board of Governors of the Federal Reserve System, and the New York State Department of Commerce.

Footnotes to Chapter 6

1. The concept of a stabilization fund is not original. In 1977, Michigan took the highly innovative step of creating a "rainy day" fund (PA 76). The enabling legislation is presented in Appendix B. The fund was recommended by a blue-ribbon commission, the Michigan Economic Advisory Council, headed by Michael Blumenthal, later to become Secretary of the Treasury. Thereafter, the legislature took the lead. An excellent discussion of this policy is contained in the Council of State Governments publication, "Innovations: Michigan's Budget and Economic Stabilization Fund," Lexington, Kentucky, 1979. Those interested in obtaining further information should contact the Council of State Governments, the Michigan State Fiscal Agency, or the Michigan Department of Management and Budget.

2. For example, for a state that closely paralleled the nation, full scale expenditure should have commenced in the second quarter of 1970 (allowing for some lag in recognition), been cut back in the second quarter of 1971 (four quarters), and reduced until the second quarter of 1974 (twelve quarters). Full scale expenditures would have been undertaken until the first quarter of 1976 (six quarters), and would have been reduced until the fourth quarter of 1979 (fifteen quarters).

3. The data in the table indicate that Michigan should accumulate approximately $1 billion against a relatively severe recession, which is the statutory limit on the present fund. Actual accumulations by the end of FY 1979 would be $235 million unless there are draw-downs triggered by rising unemployment during 1979. (This is, of course, in the absence of federal or local contributions.)

4. It allows the first $30 plus one third of the remaining earnings to be disregarded when computing welfare eligibility.

5. The lowest ceilings are in Arkansas, Georgia, Iowa, New York, North Dakota, and West Virginia.

GLOSSARY OF TERMS

ACIR	Advisory Commission on Intergovernmental Relations
AFDC	Aid to Families with Dependent Children
APW	Accelerated Public Works Program
ARA	Area Redevelopment Administration
ARFA	Antirecessionary Fiscal Assistance Program
BEA	Bureau of Economic Analysis
CETA	Comprehensive Employment and Training Act
CPI	Consumer Price Index
CWA	Federal Civil Works Administration
EDA	Economic Development Administration
EWRP	Emergency Work Relief Program
FIRE	Finance, Insurance and Real Estate
GAO	General Accounting Office
LPW	Local Public Works Program
PEP	Public Employment Program
PWA	Emergency Administration of Public Works
PWIP	Public Works Impact Program
UI	Unemployment Insurance
WPA	Works Progress Administration

APPENDIX A
STATE-LOCAL VARIATIONS
IN CYCLICAL BEHAVIOR

Analyzing state-local cyclical behavior is limited by the availability of data. Most analyses have been limited to examining cycles in total employment. In view of the importance of job creation for countercyclical policy, this is the single most important economic indicator anyway. The first part of this appendix analyzes how the employment growth rates of states and labor market areas (geographically similar to Standard Metropolitan Statistical Areas) respond to changes in the growth rate of national employment. This not only establishes the variation among areas but also provides local officials with some guidelines as to how their area is likely to respond during an anticipated national recession. The second section of the appendix analyzes why areas respond differently to fluctuations in the national economy.

The analysis in this appendix is about how local areas *tend* to respond to changes in the national economy—that is, their average response over the period 1960 to 1975. During any single cycle, an area may respond uncharacteristically; that is, it may experience an especially sharp recession although it normally is unresponsive to national changes, or it may lead at a particular downturn although its pattern of growth is typically coincident. In another analysis, cycle by cycle, of state and local areas, Vernez et al. (1977) found no strong pattern in the timing of turning points in local cycles in relation to national cycles. Only six states and 24 LMAs have consistently led the nation in the post-1960 recessions. Even fewer states and LMAs have consistently led the nation in recovery. Using an area's past performance at turning points to determine its turning points in an anticipated national cycle would result in incorrect predictions in more than half of the cases.

Further research directed at identifying a leading indicator or the determinants of variations in the timing of local cycles across areas and over time might improve predictions of the timing of turning points in area cycles. Until such research is done, however, public works investments in specific areas of the country must be guided by monitoring monthly total and sectoral employment time-series data. Experience in dating post-1960 cyclical turning points by visual observations of seasonally adjusted time-series data indicates this task is fairly simple and low cost.

Early detection of the timing of initial downturns in states and LMAs in relation to the national downturn provides some indication of the expected duration and severity of local cycles. Areas that lead the nation in recession typically take a long time to return to their initial peak, and experience severe cycles. The reverse tends to be true of areas lagging the nation at downturns.

Areas experiencing the largest cycle amplitudes are generally the same from cycle to cycle. Although large areas tend to have the largest cycle amplitudes, they do not necessarily experience the severest rate of cyclical unemployment. The severest cycles are more often found in areas of the Northeast and Northwest Central census divisions and are characterized by slow employment growth. Even these areas exhibit little consistency from cycle to cycle.

HOW AREAS RESPOND TO NATIONAL FLUCTUATIONS[1]   Four aspects of the relationships between local and national changes in employment growth rates have implications for the design of a countercyclical strategy.

■ *Leads and Lags.* Although an area may not show a consistent pattern of leads and lags with respect to cycle turning points, it may do so with respect to monthly changes in employment growth rate. To the extent that countercyclical programs are timed in relation to the national cycle, the volume and duration of projects should be less in areas that lead the nation than in areas that lag behind.

■ *Conformity.* The degree of conformity measures the extent to which the pattern of local employment growth matches that of the nation as a whole. If a national recession is expected, then high conformity areas should experience a recession, albeit with a lead or lag. Projects should be focused in these areas. Conversely, if during a period of slow growth, an expansion were expected, high conformity areas should recover, and projects should be located in low conformity areas.

■ *Responsiveness.* The magnitude of the change in an area's growth rate in response to a change in the nation's growth rate is a useful indicator. If a national slowdown is expected, a large volume of short run projects should be started in highly responsive areas to moderate the rapid decline in employment the area would experience. Conversely, if, during a recession, the national economy were expected to begin a period of expansion, then efforts should be concentrated in areas of low responsiveness, because they will not recover as rapidly as others.

■ *Relative Secular Growth Rate.* Areas that exhibit a negative growth rate relative to that of the nation are likely to experience considerable unemployment during periods of slow growth nationally. Projects should be initiated in these areas to provide employment opportunities.

To identify the long-term relationship between national and local employment growth, the local monthly employment growth rate was regressed against the national monthly employment growth rate. The   *205* basic formulation of the model is:

$$e_i^t = \alpha_i + \beta_i e_n^{t+j} + \mu;$$

$$t = \text{July 1960}, \ldots \text{December 1974};$$

$$j = -6, -3, -2, -1, 0, 1, 2, 3, 6;$$

where e_i^t is the growth rate of employment in area i in month t, α_i is a constant term, β_i is the estimated coefficient relating national and local employment growth rates in area i, e_n^{t+j} is the monthly employment growth in the nation in month t+j, and μ is a random disturbance term. The monthly employment growth rate was computed as a three-month moving average to smooth out stochastic changes attributable to employment estimating procedures and to such events as strikes and natural disasters. This model was used to identify the lead or lag in local employment growth, the degree of conformity, the responsiveness, and the growth rate of areas in relation to national growth rate.

First, to identify how much an area led or lagged the nation with respect to monthly employment growth rate changes, the model was estimated separately with alternative values of j in e_n^{t+j}, which led or lagged behind e_i^t by 6, 3, 2, and 1 month, as well with j = 0 (area and nation coincident). For each area, the predominant lead or lag relationship with the nation was determined by the regression equation yielding the highest R^2. For example, a region exhibiting the highest R^2 for j = -3 would be most closely linked to the nation through a three-month lag. Its rate of change in employment in this month is most closely affected by the national rate of change three months previously.

Second, from the "best" equation, the conformity, responsiveness, and growth rate were indicated by the estimated values of R^2, β_i, and α_i.

The value of R^2 in the "best" regression indicates how much the area conforms to the national pattern of employment change, whether with a lead or a lag. A high R^2 indicates that a large share of the month-to-month variations in the rate of change of area employment is related to variations in the national rate. A low R^2 has the opposite interpretation.

The responsiveness of ei to changes in e_n^{t+j} growth is indicated by the estimated value of the coefficent β_i. A value of one for this coefficient implies that a one percent change in the employment growth rate at the national level results in a one percent change in the employment growth rate *in the same direction*. A value of between zero and one indicates that a one-percentage point change at the national level leads to a *less* than one-percentage point change at the local level, but also in the same direction. Thus, the area would be said to exhibit a *low* responsiveness to national changes. Finally, a value of more than one indicates a *high* local responsiveness.

The value of the constant term α_i, indicates the area's employment growth rate in the absence of any national growth. A positive constant indicates that, in the absence of any national increase, local employment will continue to grow. For example, the estimated value of .0027 for the constant in the state of Arizona implies that employment in this state would have grown at .27 percent per month even though there might have been no growth in employment at the national level. A negative constant term has the opposite implication. The regression results for states and LMAs are displayed in Tables A.1 and A.2 at the end of this appendix.

Distinct regional patterns appear in the cyclical response of both states and LMAs with respect to all four indicators. This is not unexpected, because the relationship covers a 15 year period. Caution should be used in applying these results: although a state or LMA may exhibit a certain pattern of response over a long period, for any single cycle turning point, or during any one cycle, it may behave "out of character."

First, there is a considerable range in the relationship between state and LMA employment growth rates and changes in the national employment growth rate. For example, Bakersfield, California, led the nation by six months while Stamford, Connecticut, lagged by six months. Only 4 percent of the variations in monthly growth rates in Tuscaloosa could be explained by variations in national rates, whereas 50 percent of the variations in Los Angeles were linked to national changes; a one percentage point increase in national growth would lead to a five percentage point increase in Flint, Michigan but only a 0.24 percentage point increase in Sioux Falls, South Dakota. In the absence of any growth at the national level, Tucson, Arizona, would grow at 0.33 percent per month while Bay City, Michigan, would experience a monthly decline of employment of 0.48 percent.

Second, with respect to all four characteristics, there is a distinct regional pattern in both state and LMA responses. Areas in the Northeast tend to lag behind the nation and are in fairly close conformity, are of average responsiveness, and experience low growth. In the South, areas tend to be coincident with the nation and of low conformity, average responsiveness, and low growth. In the West, areas tend to lead the nation and exhibit low conformity, average responsiveness, and high growth.

Third, large LMAs behave differently from all LMAs taken together; they tend to be coincident with the nation, exhibit high conformity, and have fairly high responsiveness. The tendency for the *207* large LMAs to respond in a similar way to the nation as a whole is probably attributable to their diverse economic structure, which resembles that of the nation as a whole.

Leads and Lags

In the majority of states, fluctuations in the rate of change of employment coincide with those of the nation. Only Arkansas, Iowa, Massachusetts, Minnesota, Nebraska, and Wyoming tend to lag behind the nation. With the exception of Massachusetts, these are primarily agricultural states. Colorado, Idaho, Louisiana, Nevada, New Mexico, Oregon, South Dakota, and Washington tend to lead the nation. Leads and lags are distributed fairly evenly across LMAs about a zero mean. Of the largest LMAs, none differs from the nation by more than one month, and most are coincident with the nation.

Conformity

States that conform most closely to the national employment growth rate are Indiana, Ohio, and Pennsylvania. All three are large states with a large manufacturing labor force. Those that conform least are Colorado, Idaho, Montana, and Wyoming. Low conformity states are clustered in the Mountain, West-North Central, and South-Central regions; high conformity states are clustered in the Middle Atlantic, East-North Central, South Atlantic, and East-South Central regions.

LMAs with high conformity are concentrated in the Middle Atlantic, East-North Central, and South Atlantic regions. LMAs with very low conformity are concentrated in the Mountain and West-North Central regions. However, the regional pattern of conformity is not as clearly defined as the pattern of timing, perhaps because of the importance of LMA size as well as regional location in determining the degree of conformity. The regional pattern of LMAs differs in some ways from the regional pattern by states. Although states in the South Atlantic and West-South Central divisions show a fairly high conformity, a number of LMAs in those areas show low conformity. Large LMAs show a high degree of conformity. The industrial composition of these areas tends to correspond closely to that of the nation. The four large areas with low conformity were Anaheim, San Diego, Denver and Houston.

Responsiveness

The average value for states of the estimated coefficient β_i, which measures responsiveness to changes in the national monthly growth rate, is 0.88. The fact that β_i is below one indicates a tendency for small states to exhibit low responsiveness, because the average, weighted by employment levels, must be one. States with the highest responsiveness are Delaware (1.2), Indiana (1.6), Michigan (2.3), Ohio (1.4), and Washington (1.3). States with very low responsiveness include

Arkansas (0.42), Montana (0.46), Nebraska (0.46), Nevada (0.45), South Dakota (0.41), Utah (0.40), and Wyoming (0.35). These are all small agricultural states. Responsive states are located in the East-North Central, East-South Central, and South Atlantic regions, and in the Pacific Northwest; unresponsive states are located in the Mountain and West-North Central regions.

LMAs in the East-North Central region and in the eastern part of the West-North Central region (the old manufacturing belt), the East-South Central region, and the Pacific Northwest exhibit high responsiveness. Those in the Mountain region exhibit very low responsiveness, as do a cluster of LMAs around New York City. The responsiveness of large LMAs tends to be closer to unity than the coefficients for all LMAs, showing a tendency of large areas to respond in a way that more closely conforms to the nation.

Secular Growth Rates The average value for states of the constant term α_i, which measures the local growth rate that would occur in the absence of growth at the national level, is close to zero (.0002). States with a high value of the constant include Arizona (.0027), Arkansas (.0021), Colorado (.0025), Florida (.0020), Nevada (.0044), and Utah (.0022). These states have a low proportion of their labor force in manufacturing and a high proportion in agriculture, and they tend to be fairly unresponsive to changes in the national employment growth rates; they also tend to lead the nation. States with low coefficients tend to be large manufacturing states that are highly responsive to national changes, lag behind the nation, and conform closely to the national growth pattern.

States with very high values are concentrated in the Southwest and Mountain regions. States with very low secular growth are concentrated in the East-North Central, New England, the Middle Atlantic regions, and the Pacific Northwest. The regional pattern for LMAs is similar to that of states. The New England, Middle Atlantic, East-North Central, and East-South Central regions and the Pacific Northwest exhibit very low values. The southern part of the West, the Mountain, and the West-South Central regions all exhibit high values.

WHY AREAS RESPOND DIFFERENTLY[2]

A number of reasons for variations in economic cycles among the states have been identified in the empirical research. They include: the secular growth rate; the local industrial composition; and local labor market characteristics.

Secular Growth Rate The overall secular population, or employment growth rate, of a region is a major determinant of responses to the growth cycle. Although the mechanism through which secular trends affect cyclical behavior has been neither clearly stated nor empirically tested, a number of possible explanations suggest themselves.

First, the average unemployment rate is strongly and negatively related to the population growth rate (Tideman, 1973). Growth areas, therefore, will typically have relatively tight labor markets, which might encourage firms to minimize employment cycles by hoarding labor. Second, employment in growth areas might also be relatively concentrated in industries meeting local demands (constructing homes, roads, and other longer term projects) and, therefore, be less susceptible to the transmission of a national recession. Firms in growth areas may be new and reflect modern technology and, therefore, be the last to shut down during a recession. Lastly, businessmen in growth regions might be more optimistic than those elsewhere and might not reduce employment as much as their more cautious colleagues.

Borts (1960) concluded that "on the average, the strongly growing states have weak decline rates relative to expansion rates, while the weakly growing states have strong decline rates relative to expansion rates" (p. 193) over the economic cycle.

Industrial Composition   Employment by sector is not evenly distributed through all regions. Industries tend to be concentrated in regions where the productive factors that they use most intensely are available at low cost. Therefore, to the extent that different industries respond differently during cycles, some differences in cyclical behavior among regions is to be expected. The industrial composition hypothesis was described by Isard (1957):

> Differences in the intensity and timing of regional cycles are explained in terms of differences in the sensitivity and responsiveness of particular industries. Cycles of a regional economy are simply composites of the cyclical movement of the economy's industries appropriately weighted (p. 31).

Distinguishing between regional differences in cyclical behavior that are attributable to differences in industrial mix and regional differences that are attributable to other local economic characteristics may be important for the formulation of a countercyclical program. In the first instance, the program might have to be targeted at specific industries, while in the second instance, the program might be oriented toward the individual region.

In order to assess the importance of industrial composition, Borts estimated a hypothetical regional cyclical amplitude—the amplitude the region would have experienced if all its industries had behaved in the same way as they performed at the national level. The hypothetical amplitude was compared with the actual amplitude for two cycles in 33 states. There was a strong relationship between the actual and the hypothetical state cycles in the 1929 to 1937 period, which indicates that differences in industrial composition were an important determinant of differences among states. This relationship was much weaker in the 1948 to 1953 period, indicating that "the postwar cycle was characterized by sharper intra-industry-interstate differences in cyclical behavior than previously" (p. 201).

However, two indices of industrial composition—the share of state employment in manufacturing and mining and the share of state employment in durable-goods manufacturing—were positively correlated with the speed of decline during the cyclical downturn, and were negatively related to the speed of expansion and not strongly correlated with the average annual amplitude (Engerman, 1968). These findings are reinforced by the work of Tideman (1973), who found that the average unemployment in labor-market areas in the United States was significantly and positively related to the share of local employment in the durable-goods sector. This variable was also significantly and positively related to the speed with which the local unemployment rate responded to changes in the national unemployment rate.

The shrinking importance of industrial composition in explaining local variations probably results from: first, the shift of economic activity away from areas of traditional concentration so that differences in local economic structures have narrowed; and, second, from the increased role of multi-branch, national firms that tend to respond to demand reductions by closing older branches, increasing intra-industry variations among areas.[3]

Local Labor Market Characteristics

The amplitude of a region's cycle is affected by the availability of labor. A ready supply of labor, either through immigration or population increase, reduces a firm's need to hoard labor and, therefore, increases cyclical amplitude. Where the local unemployment rate is high, a firm is able to rehire labor during upswing relatively easily from the stock of unemployed. In low unemployment areas, rehiring is less easy, with consequently higher search costs for the firm. In addition, labor in above-average unemployment areas might lack the resources or the skills to be mobile enough to change locations or jobs during cyclical downturns. The result is that cycles in "tight" labor markets are less violent than those in "slack" labor markets, all other factors being equal. The size of the labor market also affects labor mobility: "other things being equal, as size of SMSA increases, alternative employment opportunities increase for any occupation" (Hellman, 1973, p. 62). Therefore, a large area is less prone to extreme cyclical fluctuations. Labor hoarding will   *211* be encouraged because of the repetitive proximity of competitive employers.

The size and density of the labor market may also affect the level of cyclical unemployment in a region. The larger and more dense a labor market, the greater the rewards of searching for jobs and, therefore, the less time a worker spends between jobs, all other things being equal. Tideman (1973) found that the average unemployment rate in a labor market area was strongly and negatively related to the size of the area and the presence of a large urban area.

Footnotes to Appendix A

1. This section is adapted from research conducted by the author while at The Rand Corporation and reported in Section III of *Regional Cycles and Employment Effects of Public Works Investments*, Georges Vernez, Roger Vaughan, Burke Burright and Sinclair Coleman, R-2052-EDA, The Rand Corporation, January 1977.

2. This section is adapted from *Public Works as a Countercyclical Device: A Review of the Issues*, by Roger Vaughan, R-1990-EDA, The Rand Corporation, July 1976, p. 36ff.

3. Thus, instead of all establishments experiencing a decline in employment, some will be closed and some remain at near full capacity.

Table A.1
Results of Regressions of Monthly Rates of Change in State Employment on Monthly Rates of Change in National Employment, 1960-1975[a]

STATES[b]	COEFFICIENT LEAD (-) OR LAG (=)[c]	β_i	CONSTANT α_i	R^2
Alabama	0	.9704	.0003	.56
Arizona	0	.8798	.0027	.19
Arkansas	=1	.4157	.0021	.30
California	0	.8296	.0010	.48
Colorado	-2	.5277	.0025	.10
Connecticut	0	.9987	-.0003	.50
Delaware	0	1.219	-.0002	.27
Florida	0	1.132	.0020	.41
Georgia	0	1.041	.0009	.59
Idaho	-6	.6028	.0017	.11
Illinois	0	.8892	-.0006	.54
Indiana	0	1.601	-.0014	.72
Iowa	=3	.7806	.0006	.37
Kansas	0	.9141	.0001	.36
Kentucky	0	.9302	.0009	.35
Louisiana	-1	.8666	.0006	.31
Maine	0	.8832	.0004	.35
Maryland	0	.7788	.0011	.50
Massachusetts	=1	.6783	.0002	.48
Michigan	0	2.314	-.0030	.45
Minnesota	=1	.9716	.0005	.48
Mississippi	0	.9859	.0010	.44
Missouri	0	.9314	.0004	.52
Montana	0	.4607	.0011	.07
Nebraska	=1	.4589	.0012	.16
Nevada	-1	.4534	.0044	.03
New Hampshire	0	1.138	.0000	.45
New Jersey	0	.7889	.0001	.55
New Mexico	-1	.4767	.0015	.12
New York	0	.7572	.0008	.55
North Carolina	0	1.048	.0008	.65
Ohio	0	1.418	-.0014	.77
Oklahoma	0	.6869	-.0010	.39
Oregon	-2	1.058	.0006	.36
Pennsylvania	0	.9989	-.0010	.74
Rhode Island	0	.9797	-.0008	.36
South Carolina	0	1.067	.0009	.54
South Dakota	-3	.4091	.0014	.07
Tennessee	0	1.016	.0009	.56
Texas	0	.9700	.0012	.34
Utah	0	.3983	.0022	.06
Virginia	0	.6402	.0019	.26
Washington	-1	1.333	-.0005	.40
West Virginia	0	.6484	-.0001	.18
Wisconsin	0	.9182	.0002	.46
Wyoming	=2	.3505	.0014	.02
Average	-	.8829	.0002	—

SOURCE: Georges Vernez et al., *Regional Cycles and Employment Effects of Public Works Investments*, R-2052-EDA, The Rand Corporation, January 1977, p. 295.

a Monthly rate of change is computed on a three-month moving average. Employment in month t, $\bar{E}_t$, is defined as $\bar{E}_t = (E_{t-1} + E_t + E_{t+1})/3$. The rate of change, e_t, is defined as $e_t = (\bar{E}_t - E_{t-1})/\bar{E}_t$.

b Because of lack of data and analysis problems, North Dakota and Vermont are omitted from this table.

c Lead or lag was computed by running 9 separate regressions for each state in which the local employment series was lagged 6, 3, 2, and 1 months, advanced 6, 3, 2, and 1 months, and finally with no lead or lag. The estimated equation with the highest coefficient of determination (R^2) was selected and is shown in this table.

Table A.2
Results of Regressions of Monthly Rates of Change in Labor Market Area Employment on Monthly Rates of Change in National Employment, 1960-1975[a]

LABOR MARKET AREA	LEAD (−) OR LAG (=)b	COEFFICIENT	CONSTANT	R^2
Alabama				
Birmingham	0	1.610	-.0011	.08
Huntsville	-1	1.572	.0014	.03
Mobile	-3	.6266	-.0002	.07
Montgomery	-1	1.016	.0004	.09
Tuscaloosa	-1	.7956	.0016	.04
Arizona				
Phoenix	0	1.107	.0028	.26
Tucson	=1	.3728	.0033	.05
Arkansas				
Fayetteville	-1	1.056	.0030	.06
Little Rock	=1	.4547	.0022	.13
Pine Bluff	0	1.072	.0001	.18
California				
Anaheim	-1	.8265	.0054	.11
Bakersfield	-6	.5842	.0007	.08
Fresno	-2	.6729	.0016	.10
Los Angeles	0	.9835	-.0010	.50
Modesto	-1	.7345	.0024	.04
Oxnard	0	.8305	.0032	.11
Riverside	0	.6552	.0020	.18
Sacramento	-2	.3647	.0019	.05
Salinas	=1	.8405	.0019	.11
San Diego	0	.9011	.0015	.19
San Francisco	0	.7885	.0002	.39
San Jose	0	1.127	.0028	.27
Santa Barbara	-2	.5075	.0029	.04
Stockton	-1	1.143	.0004	.15
Vallejo	=1	.4797	.0020	.05
Colorado				
Denver	-1	.4051	.0027	.06
Connecticut				
Bridgeport	0	.9889	-.0010	.27
New Britain	0	1.465	-.0022	.12
New Haven	0	.6195	.0003	.13
Stamford	=6	.7158	.0005	.17
Waterbury	0	1.155	-.0010	.31
Delaware				
Wilmington	0	1.171	-.0002	.22
Florida				
Ft. Lauderdale	0	2.039	.0016	.31
Jacksonville	=2	.7829	.0012	.14
Miami	0	1.064	.0017	.29
Orlando	0	.8498	.0037	.07
Pensacola	0	.5331	.0015	.09
Tampa	0	1.281	.0015	.30
Georgia				
Atlanta	0	1.032	.0018	.40
Augusta	-1	.9700	.0001	.25
Macon	0	.9402	-.0002	.21
Savannah	=3	1.300	-.0011	.15
Idaho				
Boise	-6	.3131	.0041	.03

Illinois				
Chicago	0	.9374	-.0009	.56
Davenport	=3	.8871	.0000	.19
Peoria	=1	1.004	-.0001	.04
Rockford	0	1.809	-.0017	.28
Indiana				
Evansville	=1	1.506	-.0010	.11
Fort Wayne	0	1.242	.0001	.31
Gary-Hammond	=1	.9750	-.0004	.12
Muncie	0	1.498	-.0016	.16
South Bend	0	1.685	-.0025	.20
Terre Haute	0	1.001	-.0007	.21
Iowa				
Cedar Rapids	=2	1.555	-.0012	.36
Des Moines	0	.6326	.0010	.13
Dubuque	=3	.7788	.0012	.05
Sioux City	-1	1.022	-.0001	.08
Waterloo	=6	1.779	-.0020	.16
Kansas				
Topeka	=6	.5295	.0010	.06
Kentucky				
Lexington	0	1.306	.0019	.19
Louisville	0	1.172	-.0002	.25
Louisiana				
Baton Rouge	-1	.8549	.0020	.06
Lake Charles	-1	1.231	-.0004	.10
Monroe	-3	.9360	-.0003	.10
Shreveport	-3	.9086	.0005	.23
Maine				
Lewiston	=3	1.117	-.0020	.19
Portland	-1	.4977	.0005	.10
Maryland				
Baltimore	0	.7747	.0001	.42
Michigan				
Ann Arbor	0	2.449	-.0021	.17
Bay City	0	3.020	-.0048	.19
Detroit	0	2.506	-.0036	.45
Flint	0	4.983	-.0061	.07
Grand Rapids	0	1.728	-.0013	.41
Jackson	=1	1.673	.0018	.28
Kalamazoo	0	1.436	-.0008	.24
Lansing	0	2.028	-.0011	.10
Muskegon	=1	1.474	-.0020	.20
Saginaw	0	1.851	-.0016	.13
Minnesota				
Minneapolis	0	1.149	.0002	.51
Mississippi				
Jackson	0	.7965	.0016	.27
Missouri				
Springfield	-3	.7046	.0009	.07
Montana				
Billings	0	.5589	.0014	.05
Great Falls	-2	.1490	.0014	.01
Nebraska				
Lincoln	0	.3388	.0012	.04
Omaha	=1	.6093	.0009	.15
Nevada				
Las Vegas	=2	.7661	.0019	.07
Reno	0	-.2840	.0054	.01

New Jersey				
Atlantic City	=1	.6888	.0002	.07
Hackensack	=1	.7923	.0013	.20
Jersey City	=3	.7645	-.0020	.12
Newark	0	.8352	-.0001	.46
Paterson	0	.7638	-.0004	.23
Trenton	0	.8099	.0003	.20
New Mexico				
Albuquerque	-3	.5336	.0021	.08
New York				
Albany	=1	.6820	.0000	.12
Binghamton	0	.8340	-.0011	.27
Buffalo	0	1.758	-.0031	.45
Elmira	0	1.049	-.0013	.10
Nassau-Suffolk	0	.8143	.0017	.22
New York City	0	.5419	-.0013	.21
Rochester	0	1.023	.0000	.48
Rockland County	-2	.6126	.0030	.10
Syracuse	0	.9887	-.0004	.33
Utica	0	.9038	-.0014	.22
Westchester County	0	1.022	-.0006	.25
North Dakota				
Fargo	=1	-.1436	.0075	.04
Ohio				
Youngstown	0	2.045	-.0027	.19
Oklahoma				
Oklahoma City	0	.4101	.0023	.12
Tulsa	0	.9585	.0006	.33
Oregon				
Eugene	-2	.9207	.0016	.09
Portland	-1	1.205	.0004	.47
Salem	-2	.6748	.0023	.05
Pennsylvania				
Allentown	0	.9279	-.0004	.29
Altoona	0	1.140	-.0013	.20
Erie	0	1.167	-.0002	.16
Harrisburg	0	.7735	.0003	.23
Johnstown	=1	1.284	-.0017	.20
Lancaster	0	.8422	.0004	.25
Philadelphia	=1	.8917	.0007	.48
Pittsburgh	0	.9583	-.0011	.30
Reading	0	.9842	-.0005	.35
Scranton	-2	.8942	-.0012	.29
Wilkes-Barre	0	1.100	-.0010	.14
York	0	1.036	-.0002	.33
Rhode Island				
Providence	0	1.081	-.0009	.38
South Carolina				
Columbia	0	.6506	.0028	.13
South Dakota				
Sioux Falls	0	.2373	.0023	.01
Tennessee				
Chattanooga	-3	1.079	.0002	.21
Knoxville	0	.8594	.0007	.20
Texas				
Dallas	=1	1.066	.0013	.42
Houston	=1	.6776	.0029	.19
Vermont				
Burlington	0	1.337	.0012	.16
Springfield	=2	1.797	-.0030	.18
Virginia				
Lynchburg	=3	.9704	-.0001	.27
Roanoke	0	.7303	.0014	.21

Washington				
Seattle	-1	1.959	-.0017	.33
Spokane	0	.8795	.0000	.12
Tacoma	0	1.175	-.0003	.29
Virginia				
Charleston	=3	.7602	-.0005	.10
Wheeling	0	.7446	-.0004	.07
Wisconsin				
Green Bay	=1	.7424	.0020	.24
Kenosha	=2	1.229	.0000	.01
La Crosse	=6	1.048	.0004	.07
Madison	=1	.6543	.0021	.19
Racine	=1	1.145	.0002	.17
Wyoming				
Caspar	-3	.4657	.0006	.02
Cheyenne	=1	.8302	-.0010	.02
Average	—	1.011	.004	—

SOURCE: Georges Verne7 et al., *Regional Cycles and Employment Effects of Public Works Investments,* R-2052-EDA, The Rand Corporation, January 1977, pp. 296ff.

aMonthly rates of change are computed on a three-month moving average. The employment in month, t, $\overline{E}_t$, is defined as $(E_{t-1} + E_t + E_{t+1})/3$. The monthly rate of change, e_t, is defined as $(\overline{E}_t - \overline{E}_{t-1})/\overline{E}_t$.

bLead or lag was computed by running 9 separate regressions for each LMA in which the local employment change series was lagged 6, 3, 2, and 1 months, advanced 6, 3, 2, and 1 months, and finally left with no lead or lag. The estimated equation with the highest coefficient of determination (R^2) was selected and is shown in this table.

APPENDIX B
THE MICHIGAN
STABILIZATION FUND

Below is the enabling legislation setting up the State of Michigan Stabilization Fund (Public Acts 1977, No. 76):

AN ACT to create a counter-cyclical budget and economic stabilization fund; to provide for transfers into and out of the fund; to provide for the maintenance and administration of the fund; to relate the operation of the fund to the budget process of this state; and to prescribe the powers and duties of certain state officers.

The People of the State of Michigan enact:

21.401 Definitions [M.S.A. 3.116(51)]
Sec. 1. As used in this act:

(a) "Adjusted personal income" means the total personal income of this state, less transfer payments, adjusted for inflation. The adjustment for inflation shall be determined by reducing the total personal income of this state less transfer payments for a given calendar year by the average of the Detroit consumer price index for the 12 months ending 6 months before the given calendar year ends.

(b) "Annual growth rate" means the percentage change in adjusted personal income for the current calendar year as compared to adjusted personal income for the calendar year immediately preceding the current calendar year. The annual growth rate shall be rounded off to the nearest 0.1%.

(c) "Current calendar year" means the year that ends on December 31 in which the determination of the transfer into or out of the fund is being made.

(d) "Detroit consumer price index" means the most comprehensive index of consumer prices available for the Detroit area from the bureau of labor statistics of the United States department of labor.

(e) "Fund" means the counter-cyclical budget and economic stabilization fund created by this act.

(f) "General fund revenue" means all general purpose tax revenue and other unrestricted general purpose revenue of the state that is credited to the general fund and from which appropriations may be made.

(g) "Personal income" is as defined by the bureau of economic analysis, U.S. department of commerce.

(h) "Transfer payments" are as defined by the bureau of economic analysis, U.S. department of commerce.

21.406 General appropriation bill to contain final estimate of transfer into or out of fund. [M.S.A. 3.116(56)]
Sec. 6. The legislature shall include a final estimate of the transfer into or out of the fund required by section 3 of this act in the general appropriations

bill which contains the revenue estimate required by section 31 of article 4 of the state constitution of 1963.

21.407 Adjustment of transfer into or out of fund; adjustment of appropriation from fund. [M.S.A. 3.116(57)]

Sec. 7. (1) The transfer into or out of the fund as provided in section 3 of this act, for each fiscal year beginning after September 30, 1978, shall be adjusted in light of revision in the annual growth rate for the calendar year upon which that transfer was made. The adjustment shall be directly proportional to an increase or decrease in the annual growth rate, but the adjustment shall not be in excess of 1% multiplied by the total general fund revenue of the fiscal year upon which the transfer was based. The basis for an adjustment shall be a change in the personal income level for that calendar year as determined by the bureau of economic analysis of the United States department of commerce in the last report it makes prior to April 30 of the fiscal year in which that calendar year ended.

(2) An appropriation from the fund as provided in section 4 shall be adjusted for a change in the unemployment rate statistics for the 4 quarters immediately preceding the quarter in which the appropriation is to be made, as long as an adjustment has not already been made in an appropriation from the fund because of a prior change in the unemployment rate statistics for 1 or more of those 4 quarters. A change in the unemployment rate statistics shall not be made until that change is certified by the director of the Michigan employment security commission.

(3) An adjustment made pursuant to subsection (2) shall not be made unless the change in the unemployment rate statistics would have provided for a different percent of the fund to be appropriated under section 4. If the adjustment creates a general fund liability, that liability shall be offset against future appropriations which would have been made under section 4.

21.408 Rebating excess balance in fund. [M.S.A. 3.116(58)]

Sec. 8. If the balance in the fund at the end of a fiscal year exceeds 25% of the actual state general fund revenue for that fiscal year, the excess shall be rebated on the individual income tax returns filed following the close of that fiscal year according to a schedule to be established by law.

21.409 Appropriation from fund to raise general fund revenue to level originally anticipated. [M.S.A. 3.116 (59)]

Sec. 9. In each fiscal year in which a transfer to the fund takes place, if the general fund revenue falls short of the level upon which a balanced general fund budget was adopted for that year and the shortfall cannot be attributed to a change by public act in the tax rate, the tax base, fee schedules, or any other change in the revenue sources by which the general fund estimate was made, an amount not to exceed the amount deposited into the fund for that fiscal year, may, by majority vote of the members elected to and serving in each house, be appropriated from the fund to raise general fund revenue to the level originally anticipated.

21.402 Counter-cyclical budget and economic stabilization fund; creation; administration; purpose. [M.S.A. 3.116(52)]

Sec. 2. A counter-cyclical budget and economic stabilization fund is created and shall be administered by the state treasurer to assist in stabilizing revenue and employment during periods of economic recession and high unemployment.

21.403 Annual growth rate; transfers into and out of fund; formula. [M.S.A. 3.116(53)]

Sec. 3 (1) When the annual growth rate is more than 2% except as provided in section 12, the percentage excess over 2% shall be multiplied by the total general fund revenue for the fiscal year ending in the current calendar year to determine the amount to be transferred to the fund from the general fund in the fiscal year beginning in the current calendar year.

(2) When the annual growth rate is less than zero, the percentage deficiency under zero shall be multiplied by the total general fund revenue for the fiscal year ending in the current calendar year to determine the eligible amount to be transferred to the general fund from the fund in the current fiscal year. When the formula calls for a larger transfer from the fund than is necessary to balance the current fiscal year general purpose budget, the excess shall remain in the fund.

21.404 Appropriation from fund where state unemployment rate is 8% or more; purposes; table. [M.S.A. 3.116(54)]

Sec. 4. (1) In a calendar quarter following a calendar quarter in which the state unemployment rate as certified by the director of the Michigan employment security commission is 8% or more, an amount may be appropriated from the fund by the legislature for the purposes listed in this section in accordance with the following table:

Percent of unemployment in the calendar quarter preceding the calendar quarter in which an amount may be appropriated	Percent of fund available for economic stabilization during the calendar quarter following a calendar quarter of high unemployment
8.0 - 11.9%	2.5% of fund balance as of first day of calendar quarter.
12.0% and over	8.0% of fund balance as of first day of calendar quarter.

(2) The legislature may appropriate by law money from the fund in the amounts as provided in this section to assist in the following counter-cyclical economic stabilization purposes:

(a) Capital outlay.

(b) Public works and public service jobs.

(c) Refundable investment or employment tax credits against state business taxes for new outlays and hiring in this state.

(c) Refundable investment or employment tax credits against state business taxes for new outlays and hiring in this state.

(d) Any other purpose the legislature may provide by law which provides
220 employment opportunities counter to the state's economic cycle.

21.405 Executive budget to contain estimate of transfer into or out of fund. [M.S.A. 3.116 (55)]

Sec. 5. The executive budget for each fiscal year beginning after September 30, 1978, shall contain an estimate of the transfer into or out of the fund required by section 3 of this act.

21.410 Emergency appropriation; conditions; additional transfer from fund to be made for current fiscal year only. [M.S.A. 3.116(60)]

Sec. 10. (1) The legislature may make an emergency appropriation subject to all of the following conditions:

(a) The maximum appropriation from the fund for budget stabilization as provided in section 3(2) has already been made for the current fiscal year.

(b) The legislature has approved the emergency appropriations bill by a 2/3 majority vote of the members elected to and serving in each House.

(c) The emergency appropriations bill becomes law.

(2) The additional transfer from the fund may be made only for the current fiscal year.

21.411 Combining amounts in fund; accrual of earnings from investment of fund; separate accounting; crediting transfer to fund. [M.S.A. 3.116(51)]

Sec. 11. Amounts in the fund may be combined by the state treasurer with other amounts in the state treasury for purposes of cash management. The earnings from investment of the fund shall accrue to the fund. The fund shall be accounted for separately from other funds of the state. A transfer to the fund shall be credited toward the fund balance at the start of the fiscal year in which the transfer takes place subject to later revision according to section 7 in the same fiscal year.

21.412 Transfer when annual growth rate is more than 4%. [M.S.A. 3.116(62)]

Sec. 12. For the fiscal year beginning October 1, 1977, a transfer shall be made only when the annual growth rate is more than 4%. The percentage excess over 4% shall be multiplied by the total general fund revenue for the fiscal year beginning October 1, 1976, to determine the amount to be transferred to the fund from the general fund.

This act is ordered to take immediate effect.

Approved August 2, 1977.

APPENDIX C
JOBS CREATED BY
COUNTERCYCLICAL PUBLIC
WORKS AND PUBLIC
EMPLOYMENT PROGRAMS[1]

Since a major objective of the public works and public employment and training components of a countercyclical strategy is to provide jobs for those left underemployed or unemployed by a recession, a major task in planning a state stabilization strategy is determining how many jobs—and jobs for whom—are created, and also what type of workers and households will typically benefit. The following analysis, of necessity, rests on past experience with federal programs, but the results can provide some estimates and lessons for state officials as they design their own stabilization strategies.

THE NUMBER OF JOBS CREATED Gross short run employment generated by a program is the sum of three types of impacts:[2]

■ *Direct employment* created by the expenditure of public funds in the form of wages to on site labor for public works and to public employees for public service employment.
■ *Indirect employment* created in industries supplying the program with materials, supplies, and services.
■ *Induced employment* resulting from the consumption expenditures by those workers directly and indirectly employed by the projects and the major supplying industries.

This distinction is important. First, each type of job is created at different speeds. Direct jobs will be first, and their speed can be controlled by program administrators. Induced jobs will follow after a lag and are difficult to control. Second, the geographical distribution of the jobs differs. Direct jobs are more likely to be filled by local labor. Indirect and induced jobs will be generated where supplying industries are located. Third, only the eligibility for direct jobs can be influenced by hiring guidelines. Other types of jobs are less amenable to selective hiring. Fourth, by identifying induced jobs, potential supply bottlenecks can be anticipated.

Direct Job Creation   Table C.1 shows estimates of the number of direct jobs created per 1 billion of 1975 dollars by public works projects and public service employment programs. Deflating these data to 1980 dollars yields estimates that new public works generated an average of 1.2 to 2.1 on site jobs per $100,000 of expenditure, while projects involving repair and rehabilitation generated 1.2 and 2.5 jobs. Public service employment programs generated between 12 and 14 jobs per $100,000—four to seven times more than public works projects. The difference is largely attributable to two factors: 90 percent of public service employment funds were for direct wages, and only 10 percent for materials and equipment; for public works, however, between 20 and 40 percent of the expenditure is spent on wages for on site labor. Second, a maximum annual wage ceiling of $10,000 to $12,000 was imposed on public service employment, while on site labor salaries are those prevailing in the construction industry.

The number of on site jobs created by public works varies by type of project. On site labor requirements differ depending on whether private contractors (bid projects) or local government agencies (force account projects) build the projects (Sulvetta and Thompson, 1975). Among PWIP projects, the average force account project generated nearly twice as many on site jobs (3.2 per $100,000) as the average bid project (1.8 per $100,000).

The number of persons that will work under a program will be larger than the number of man-years shown in Table C.1 because the average worker usually holds a job for less than a year—a man-year could provide jobs for 12 persons working one month each. Under the PWIP program of 1972-1973, the average duration of employment was one month. Because of the nature of public works jobs, 58 percent of the workers on the projects sampled held jobs for no more than 80 hours (Sulvetta and Thompson, 1975). High labor turnover on public works projects reduces their ability to assure income or skill maintenance during an economic slowdown. In contrast, public service jobs have been of much higher duration—13.4 months under the PEP program—with only small variations around this mean among different socioeconomic groups (Westat, 1975).

Indirect Job Creation   Estimates of the number of jobs created in major supplying industries, presented in Table C.1 are available only for new public works construction. The national input-output table was used to convert on site demands into final demands for labor using industry-specific marginal ratios of output to employment. The average project generates an estimated 0.7 indirect man-years in supplying industries per $100,000 expended. Indirect job creation varies from 0.6 to 1.6 man-years per $100,000, depending on the project. About one third of this employment is   *223*

TABLE C.1
Estimated Gross Direct and Indirect Employment Effects Per $1 Billion of 1975 Dollars on PW or PSE Programs, by Type of Projects (in man-years)

	Estimated Direct Employment by Selected Studies (man-year)[a]					Indirect Employm
	Vernez et al. (1977)	Sulvetta & Thompson (1975)	National Council for UED (1975)	Westat (1975)	CBO (1975)	Vernez e (1977)
PUBLIC WORKS, NEW CONSTRUCTION						
Building Construction						
Private one-family housing	19,076					9,02
Public housing	31,947					8,64
Schools	26,987	18,970				10,93
Medical buildings	30,062	24,372				10,17
Nursing homes	29,573					10,40
College housing	33,547					10,56
Federal office buildings		18,600				
Municipal office buildings		18,600				
Multi-purpose municipal buildings		13,754				
Jails and police stations		11,220				
Fire, ambulance or rescue vehicle stations		19,633				
Municipal airport buildings and passenger terminals		25,736				
Heavy Construction						
Highways or roads	20,089	18,595				10,48
Water and sewer lines		21,372				
Water lines		14,080				
Sewer lines	27,295	16,079				10,61
Water/sewer system		27,098				
Sewer plants	29,404					47
Civil works						
Large earth-fill dams	38,578					8,67
Small earth-fill dams	39,271					10,37
Local flood protection	45,396					9,80
Pile dikes	36,987					13,37
Levees	43,991					4,52

	Estimated Direct Employment by Selected Studies (man-year)[a]					Indirect[b] Employment
	Vernez et al. (1977)	Sulvetta & Thompson (1975)	National Council for UED (1975)	Westat (1975)	CBO (1975)	Vernez et al. (1977)
Revetments	17,120				24,941	
Powerhouse construction	26,444				13,665	
Medium concrete dams	43,227					8,442
Lock and concrete dams	32,773					14,621
Large multiple purpose projects	49,351					9,174
Dredging	45,484					6,642
Miscellaneous	34,836					10,240
Others						
Recreational facilities		16,207				
Conservation, beautification		19,992				
Industrial site or parks		14,787				
Sample Average	33,387	18,278	28,150[c]			10,725
PUBLIC WORKS, REPAIRS AND ADDITIONS						
Building additions		15,861				
Building renovations, remodeling and restorations		17,360	39,050[c]			
PUBLIC SERVICE EMPLOYMENT				133,000[d]	125,000[e]	

NOTES: All estimates are of gross employment accounting for no employment substitution due to either the mode of financing or the displacement of state and local expenditures by federal expenditures. Blank means not available.

a Direct employment is defined as number of jobs created on-site for public works and public service employment.

b Indirect employment is defined as number of jobs created in major supplying industries of materials for public works construction. Estimates shown are estimates of jobs increase over present levels (marginal) rather than increase of jobs in average.

c From survey of 46 public works projects proposed by eight cities under the Public Works Impact Program.

d Average annual cost per job under the public employment program was estimated at about $7500 including administrative costs and fringe benefits.

e CBO assumed a cost of $8000 per job which is approximately equal to the average cost per job under Title VI of CETA, including fringe benefits and administrative costs.

SOURCE: Vernez and Vaughan, September 1978, p. 31.

created in the manufacturing sector, one third in the transportation sector, and one third in the wholesale and retail trade sector. Indirect job creation by public service employment programs has been negligible since most expenditures were for participant wages. These estimates are, at best, rough approximations.

Total Job Creation   On site and indirect employment represents between one third and one half of the total gross jobs generated by increased public works investments and up to 85 percent for a public service employment program (Tables C.1 and C.2). The remaining jobs result from consumption expenditures of participants and investment expenditures of businesses in response to increased demands among sectors and regions, but concentrated on non-durable goods, as are jobs resulting from a personal income tax cut.

Table C.2 presents estimates of the total number of jobs created per $1 billion expended in public service employment, public works, and three alternative programs—government purchases, personal tax cuts, and revenue-sharing. Also shown in the table is the timing of job creation following initiation of outlays; the initial impact shown is spread over three to six months. For each of these programs there are two, sometimes three, estimates that were made using different models and assumptions. Because of the different models employed, the estimates presented in Table C.2 are order of magnitude rather than precise measures of total job impact. Comparing programs, a public service employment program that includes provisions for a wage ceiling and a requirement for funds to be spent mostly on participants' wages creates the most jobs, particularly during the first year. However, if displacement of local by federal funds is high, reflected in the lower figure in the range, public service employment has no clear advantage over the other programs. Tax cuts create the fewest jobs, although at least one estimate places a personal tax cut on a equal footing with revenue-sharing, government purchases, and public works. There is no strong evidence that the three latter programs create significantly different numbers of jobs.

Displacement makes it difficult to accurately estimate the number of jobs created, not only by public service employment but also by any fiscal program that channels funds through state and local governments such as public works and antirecessionary revenue-sharing.

WHO BENEFITS?   The discussion in Chapter 4 showed that there are wide sectoral, occupational, and regional variations in the impacts of national business cycles. This section examines how the jobs created by countercyclical public works and public service employment programs match these variations.

Table C.2
Alternative Estimates of Total Employment Generated
by Selected Countercyclical Programs
(in man-years)

Type of Program	Source	Increase in jobs per $1 billion		
		Initial effect	*12 months*	*24 months*
Public Works				
Corps of Engineers				65,000
Highway				81,000
Railroad and mass transit	Bezdek and Hannon (1974)	NA	NA	84,000
Educational facilities				85,000
Water and waste treatment				82,000
Sewer plant			90,600	108,000
Flood protection	Vernez et al., (1977)		127,000	183,000
Federal office building			42,300	131,000
Accelerated public works[a]	CBO (1975)	16-46,000	56,70,000	64-80,000
Public Service Employment[b]	CBO (1975)	80-125,000	90-145,000	90,150,000
	Johnson and Tomola (1975)	17-111,000	31-126,000	77-162,000
Government Purchases	CBO (1975)	20-50,000	40-70,000	60-80,000
	Johnson and Tomola (1975)	6,000	54,000	99,000
Tax Cut[c]	Bezdek and Hannon (1974)	NA	NA	87,000
	CBO (1975)	12-22,000	39-52,000	45-60,000
	Johnson and Tomola (1975)	200	15,000	51,000
Revenue-sharing to state and local governments	CBO (1975)	40-77,000	70-97,000	72-100,000

NOTE: NA means not available.

a The range shown reflects alternative assumptions on the mix of public works projects that might be implemented.

b The range shown reflects alternative assumptions on displacement of state and local funds by federal funds. The higher figure reflects no displacement, while the lower figures reflect moderate displacement (CBO) or large displacement (Johnson and Tomola).

c In all estimates the tax cut is assumed to be entirely on personal taxes. If the tax cut were to be one-third corporate and two-thirds personal, job creation would be about 50 percent smaller (CBO, 1975).

SOURCE: Roger H. Bezdek and Bruce Hannon, "Energy, Manpower and The Highway Trust Fund," *Science,* Vol. 185, No. 4152, August 1974, pp. 669-675; Congressional Budget Office, *Temporary Measures to Stimulate Employment,* Congress of the United States, U.S. Government Printing Office, Washington, D.C., September 1975; George E. Johnson and James D. Tomola, *The Efficacy of Public Service Employment Programs,* Office of Evaluation, U.S. Department of Labor, Technical Analysis Paper No. 17A, June 1975; Georges Vernez et al., *Regional Cycles and Employment Effects of Public Works Investments,* The Rand Corporation, R-2052-EDA, January 1977.

Sectors and Industries   Public works target effectively on the industries most affected by national recessions—construction and durable goods. Estimates presented above indicate that approximately one third of the amount spent on public works projects goes for on site labor in the construction sector, and about one job in four created by a public works program is in the construction sector. This is compatible with the relatively large cyclical amplitude of this sector. Forty percent to sixty percent of the cost of a public works project is for supplies of material, although the amount varies considerably among projects. Table C.3 shows the dollar demands per $1000 expended for the output of selected industries by the project making the heaviest demand on that industry. Public works projects make relatively heavy demands on the lumber and wood products industry (SIC 24) and the primary metals industry (SIC 33). Both industries experience high cyclical amplitude. Some heavy construction projects make intensive demands on the transportation equipment industry (SIC 37), which also exhibits high cyclical amplitude. On the other hand, heavy construction projects also draw upon the output of the mining sector (SIC 14), which exhibits low cyclical amplitude, raising the possibility of supply constraints in mining.

For public service employment programs, most expenditures go for salaries and thus are directed toward creating jobs in the public sector, which does not exhibit strong cyclical patterns. The success of the program, therefore, depends on the mobility of the labor force between local public and private sectors.

The pattern of demand for supplies and services arising from a marginal increase in public service employment expenditures has not been investigated. From the pattern of demands for supplies of materials and services arising from the average pattern of state and local expenditures shown in Table C.3 the following observations can be made. The local public sector places considerable demands upon the construction sector, particularly for maintenance and repair works, about half as much as actual construction projects per $1000 of

228

expenditure. Public services also demand supplies from the chemicals industry (SIC 28) and the petroleum and related products industry (SIC 29), two industries that exhibit low cyclical amplitude. Since countercyclical public employment funds are designated for personnel rather than service delivery, however, there will be less demand for materials and services than is suggested by these average data.

Both public works and public service employment programs may also create jobs because of the increased consumption spending by those benefiting from direct and indirect jobs. It is difficult to estimate the distribution of these jobs among sectors. Increased consumer expenditures will be spent predominantly on housing and food. Among the industries identified in Table C.3 private consumption and expenditures are concentrated on petroleum products (SIC 29)—a low amplitude industry—electrical equipment (SIC 36), and transportation equipment (SIC 37)—a high amplitude industry.

Occupations

Over half of those employed in the public sector are in professional and technical occupations and service, while the construction sector employs a heavy concentration of craft and related workers and unskilled laborers. In general, the public sector draws upon occupations that are not heavily affected by national cyclical downturns, while the construction sector is composed of occupations that exhibit high cyclical amplitude.

The distribution of occupations differs by level of government. Professional and technical workers compose a much higher percentage of workers at the state government level than at the local level. Conversely, local governments employ a higher concentration of laborers and service workers than state governments. Neither level of government employs a high percentage of craftsmen and operatives. Therefore, the demand for different occupations will depend upon the allocation of public service employment funds between state and local governments.

It is difficult from these average data to determine the extent to which a public service employment program could utilize skilled or unskilled labor. The results of two studies are conflicting with respect to the share of new jobs that could be filled by unskilled labor. The National Civil Service League conducted interviews with Chicago City Personnel Administrators in 1970 and 1971, and reported that 70 percent of the new jobs needed immediately were suitable for unskilled labor. These jobs included attendants, assistants, and custodial workers. Levy and Wiseman (1975) investigated needed positions in San Francisco and Oakland, limiting their search to existing government slots in the central municipal and educational branches of public service. To assure conservative estimates of demand, they included only those positions that were truly accessible to low-skilled

Table C.3
Dollar Requirements for Selected Supplies of Materials Resulting from Expenditure of $1000 on Local Public Services, Selected Public Works Projects,[a] and Private Consumption

SIC Number	Supplying Industries[b] Description	State and Local Public Services Amount	Selected Public Works Projects[c] Project Type	Selected Public Works Projects[c] Amount	Private Consumption Expenditures
14[d]	Mining	—	Revetments	219	NA
15,17[e]	Construction	192	College Housing	—	—
24[e]	Lumber and Wood Products	17	One-family Housing	165	8
27	Printing and Publishing	25		—	1
28[d]	Chemicals	23	One-family Housing	23	21
29[d]	Petroleum and Related Products	—	Highway Construction	70	—
32	Stone, Clay and Glass Products	—	Sewer Lines	141	—
33	Primary Metal Products	15	Lock and Concrete Dams	157	—
34	Fabricated Metal Products	11	Local Flood Protection	119	—
35	Nonelectrical Machinery (excluding Construction Machinery)	—		—	1
36	Electrical Equipment	—	Powerhouses	297	17
37[e]	Transportation Equipment	—	Powerhouses	217	32
49	Electric, Gas, Water, and Sanitary Service	155	Dredging	117	
[f]	Transportation and Warehousing	34	NA	—	NA
[g]	Wholesale and Retail Trade	39	Revetments	300	NA
[h,d]	Finance and Insurance	30	Federal Office Buildings	302	NA
65,66[d]	Real Estate and Rental	35	NA	—	NA
73,76[d]	Business Services	59	NA	—	NA

NOTES: A dashed line means that dollar requirements are negligible. NA means not available.

a Requirements include some induced demands since inter-industry purchases are included.

b These are identified initially through input-output sectors. Where there is a simple, corresponding SIC code definition, it is provided.

c Project with the highest dollar requirement per $1000 is listed. For a full list of dollar requirements for 22 types of projects, see Vernez et al., Tables 4.2 and 4.3.

d Low cyclical amplitude industry.

e High cyclical amplitude industry.

f Includes SICs 40-48.

g Includes SICs 50-59.

h Includes SICs 60-63.

SOURCE: Georges Vernez et al., *Regional Cycles and Employment Effects of Public Works Investments*, The Rand Corporation, R-2052-EDA, January 1977; Bureau of Economic Analysis, *Survey of Current Business*, Vol. 54, No. 2, 1974, U.S. Department of Commerce, Washington, D.C., 1974.

labor.[4] It was found that 21 percent of 3971 jobs available in Oakland and 6 percent of 24,034 jobs available in San Francisco could use low-skilled workers. Further research from a much broader sample of cities is needed to determine the types of jobs that might be created by a countercyclical public service employment program. The demand for supplies of materials by public works projects generates manufacturing jobs, a sector that contains a high concentration of operatives and craft workers, two occupational groups typically experiencing a high rate of cyclical unemployment.

Socioeconomic Groups

Table C.4 compares the socioeconomic characteristics of participants in a number of past service employment programs (PEP and CETA Titles II and VI), the Public Works Impact Program, and Manpower programs directed predominantly at structural unemployment, and the characteristics of program participants with those of the unemployed and the labor force. Public works and public service employment programs have uneven benefits for the groups in the labor force most affected by the recession.

Countercyclical public service employment programs reach proportionately more males than the manpower programs directed at structural unemployment. The concentration on male employment remains above the share of males in total unemployment, but this is compatible with the fact that males are more affected by *cyclical* unemployment than females. Countercyclical public works programs probably target almost exclusively on male labor, which constitutes 95 percent of the work force in the construction industry and 80 percent in the durable goods industry.

The low targeting of countercyclical public service employment and public works programs on the young (aged 21 or less) is not consistent with the relatively high concentration of youth in both total and cyclical unemployment. About one fifth of public service employment program jobs go to the young, but they represent more than one third of all those unemployed during recessions. Less than 10 percent of the jobs in public works projects are expected to go to youth. Targeting on youth requires an expansion of manpower programs that provide training and other services. Youth is heavily represented in past and present manpower programs (Table C.4).

Workers with a high school education or more are overrepresented in countercyclical public service employment programs. During the second quarter of FY 1976, nearly 80 percent of new entrants to public service employment under the CETA program were well educated, a result of the fact that the average education of state and local employees is above that of workers in general. Public service employment programs have provided little or no money for training or supplies, which has encouraged the hiring of those that need the fewest support services. Providing productive jobs for at least half the cyclically unemployed may require the inclusion of a training component in countercyclical public service employment programs or an expansion of manpower programs during recessionary years.

Both countercyclical public works and public service employment programs have provided a large share of jobs for minorities, although to a lesser extent than manpower programs. The purpose of countercyclical programs is to provide jobs for the unemployed. Yet up to 30 percent of public service employment participants and 60 percent of PWIP participants were reported as having been employed on the day prior to program entry, despite the public service employment program provisions that required from one to four weeks of unemployment for program eligibility; PWIP had no eligibility requirement.

Another important conclusion derived from Table C.4 is that countercyclical programs draw a number of participants who were not in the labor force on the day prior to program entry. There is, however, no information to indicate whether these enrollees are new entrants or re-entrants—perhaps discouraged workers—to the labor force.

A secondary goal of PSE programs is to reduce dependence on public assistance by providing a productive alternative to welfare. Table C.4 indicates that up to 15 percent of public service employment participants continued to receive some form of public assistance—including Aid to Families with Dependent Children, public housing, or food stamps—whlie enrolled in the program. Reduced welfare costs are a benefit, but not as extensive as one would expect.

Footnotes to Appendix C

1. This appendix is adapted from *Assessment of Countercyclical Public Works and Public Employment Programs,* by Georges Vernez and Roger Vaughan, R-2214-EDA, The Rand Corporation, September 1978, Sections III and IV.

2. In addition to short-run job creation, public works, public service employment, and other fiscal programs may lead to the creation of jobs for maintenance and operation and may attract new firms to the area. These effects result from induced structural changes that stimulate local economic development. Studies of long-run employment effects are not reviewed in this report. For a review of the long-run employment effects of public works, see Vaughan (1976, pp. 62-69). Net job creation will differ from gross job creation because of displacement and substitution (Chapter II).

3. These estimates are derived from studies of input requirements or from program evaluation studies. See Vernez and Vaughan (1978, Appendix H) and Vernez et al. (1977). The 1975 estimates reported in these studies have been converted into 1980 dollars using the Department of Commerce composite index of construction costs, and an estimate of a 12 percent cost increase 1979-1980. This leads to a deflation of earlier job creation estimates per dollar of 0.65. Public service employment estimates have been deflated by the CPI, a 0.60 deflation.

4. If public employment funds were used to fill regular civil service jobs, the number of jobs would decline by 30 or 40 percent.

Table C.4
Comparison of Participant Characteristics Among Manpower, Public Service, and Public Works Programs, and the General Labor Force
(percent)

Participant Characteristics	Manpower Programs		Public Service Employment Programs				Public Works Program	Labor Force	
	Pre-CETA Categorical Program[a] (FY 1974)	CETA Title I (FY 1975)	PEP[b] (FY 1971-72)	CETA Title II (FY 1975)	CETA Title VI (FY 1975)	CETA All Titles 2nd Q (1976)	PWIP[c] (FY 1972-73)	Unemployed Population (FY 1975)	Labor Force
Sex									
Men	57.7	54.4	72.0	65.8	70.2	64.0	NA	54.9	60.1
Women	42.3	45.6	28.0	34.2	29.8	36.0	NA	45.1	39.9
Age									
Under 22 years	63.1	61.7	19.0	23.7	21.4	20.0	NA	34.8	24.0
22 to 44 years	30.5	32.1	66.0	62.9	64.8	67.0		46.0	42.0
45 years and over	6.2	6.1	14.0	13.4	13.8	13.0		19.1	33.7
Education									
8 years and under	15.1	13.3	26.0	9.4	8.4	8.0	NA	15.1	11.7
9-11 years	15.1	47.6		18.3	18.2	15.0		28.9	17.5
12 years and over	33.6	39.1	74.0	72.3	73.3	77.0		56.0	70.8
Race									
White	54.9	54.6	60.0	65.1	71.1	69.0	67.0	81.1	88.6
Nonwhite	45.1	45.4	40.0	34.9	28.9	31.0	33.0	18.9	11.4

Labor Force Status Prior to Program								
Employed	NA	23.0	23.0	30.0[f]	30.0[f]	27.0	65.0	56.0
Unemployed	NA	49.0	51.9	51.0[f]	53.0[f]	53.0	27.0	5.2
Underemployed	NA	NA	7.8	17.0[f]	17.0[f]	20.0	8.0	NA
Not in labor force	NA	28.0	17.3[d]	NA	NA	14.0	NA	38.8
Public Assistance Recipient[e]	NA	NA					NA	
AFDC	NA	15.5	12.0	6.6	5.6	5.0	NA	
Other	NA	11.3	NA	9.2	8.1	17.0	NA	

NOTES: NA means not available. Blank means not applicable.

a Programs funded under the Economic Opportunity Act and the Manpower Development and Training Act.

b Funded under the Emergency Employment Act of 1971.

c Public Works Impact Program from sample survey of 226 projects.

d Reflects labor force status one month prior to program entrance.

e Includes Aid to Families with Dependent Children, food stamps, public housing, Supplemental Security Income program, and other public assistance programs. Because some enrollees may receive benefits from more than one program, figures for AFDC and others may add to more than total for public assistance.

f These figures are for the CETA Title II and VI programs combined. Separate figures are not available.

SOURCE: *Employment and Training Report of the President*, 1976; Westat, Inc., *Longitudinal Evaluation of the Public Employment Program and Validation of the PEP Data Bank*, prepared for the Office of Policy, Evaluation, and Research, U.S. Department of Labor, April 1975; Westat Inc., *Continuous Longitudinal Manpower Survey, Report No. 4*, prepared for the Office of Policy, Evaluation, and Research, U.S. Department of Labor, November 1976; Anthony J. Sulvetta and Norman L. Thompson, *An Evaluation of the Public Works Impact Program (PWIP), Final Report*, Economic Development Administration, U.S. Department of Commerce, April 1975.

BIBLIOGRAPHY

Abramovitz, Moses, "The Nature and Significance of Kuznet's Cycles," *Economic Development and Cultural Change,* Vol. IX, April 1961.

Adams, Earl W., and Michael H. Spiro, "The Timing of the Response of Employment to Construction Authorization," *Applied Economics,* No. 4, 1972, pp. 125-133.

Advisory Commission on Intergovernmental Relations, *State-Local Finances in Recession and Inflation,* A-70, Washington, D.C., May 1979a.

_____. *Significant Features of Fiscal Federalism, 1978-79* Edition, M-115, Washington, D.C., May 1979b.

_____. *Countercyclical Aid and Economic Stabilization,* A-69, Washington, D.C., December 1978.

_____. *Federal Stabilization Policy: The Role of State and Local Governments,* Washington, D.C., July 1978.

_____. *Federal Grants: Their Effects on State-Local Expenditures, Employment Levels and Wage Rates,* A-61, Washington, D.C., February 1977.

_____. *Measuring the Fiscal "Blood Pressure" of the States, 1964-1975,* M-111, Washington, D.C., February 1977.

American Economic Association, *Readings in Business Cycles,* Robert A. Gordon and Lawrence R. Klein (eds.), Irwin, Inc., Homewood, Illinois, 1965.

Anderson, L.C., and J. Jordan, "Monetary and Fiscal Actions: A Test of Their Relative Importance in Economic Stabilization," *Federal Reserve Bank of St. Louis Review,* November 1968.

Anderson, Wayne F., and John Shannon, "Slumpflation—Its Effect on Local Finances," *Public Management,* Vol. 57, No. 3, Washington, D.C., 1975.

Ando, Albert, and E. Cary Brown, "Lags in Fiscal Policy," *Stabilization Policies: A Series of Research Studies Prepared for the Commission on Money and Credit,* Prentice-Hall, Englewood Cliffs, New Jersey 1963.

Arles, J.P., "Emergency Employment Schemes," *International Labor Review,* January 1974, pp. 69-88.

Bahl, Roy W., "Recession, Inflation and the State/Local Fisc," *Public Management,* Vol. 57, No. 3, March 1975.

Bailey, Martin J., *National Income and the Price Level: A Study in Macro-Economic Theory,* McGraw-Hill, New York, 1962.

_____. "The Welfare Cost of Inflationary Finance," *Journal of Political Economy,* April 1956, pp. 93-110.

Baily, Martin Neil, "Stabilization Policy and Private Economic Behavior," *Brookings Papers on Economic Activity,* No. 1, 1978, pp. 11-61.

Baily, Martin Neil, and James Tobin, "Inflation, Unemployment, and Direct Job Creation," presented at Brookings Conference on Direct Job Creation, Washington, D.C., April, 1977.

Bakke, Wight E., "Manpower Policy During a Recession," in Ivar Berg (ed.), *Human Resources and Economic Welfare, Essays in Honor of Eil Ginsberg,* pp. 89-127.

Ball, Claiborne M., "Employment Effects of Construction Expenditures," *Monthly Labor Review*, February 1965.

Barrows, R.L., and D.W. Bromley, "Employment Impacts of the Economic Development Administration's Public Works Program," *American Journal of Agricultural Economics*, Vol. 57, February 1975, pp. 46-54.

Bassett, Keith, and Peter Haggett, "Towards Short-term Forecasting for Cyclic Behavior in a Regional System of Cities," *Regional Forecasting*, edited by Michael Chisholm, Allen E. Frey, and Peter Haggett, Butterworths, London, 1971, pp. 389-413.

Baumol, W.J., "Macroeconomics of Unbalanced Growth: The Anatomy of Urban Crisis, " *The American Economic Review*, 1967.

Bednarzik, Robert W., "The Plunge of Employment During the Recent Recession," *Monthly Labor Review*, Vol. 98, No. 12, pp. 3-10, December 1975a.

――――. "Involuntary Part-Time Work: A Cyclical Analysis," *Monthly Labor Review*, Vol. 98, No. 9, September 1975b, pp. 12-18.

Bednarzik, Robert W., and Stephen M. St. Marie, "Employment and Unemployment in 1976," *Monthly Labor Review*, Vol. 100, No. 2, February 1977, pp. 3-13.

Berney, Robert E., "Income Elasticities for Tax Revenues: Techniques of Estimation and Their Usefulness for Forecasting," paper presented at Western Economic Association Conference, 1971.

Bezdek, Roger H., "Occupational Employment Sensitivity to Shifting Patterns of Federal Expenditure," *Socio-Economic Planning Science*, Vol. 8, 1974, pp. 95-100.

――――. "The Employment Effects of Counterbudget," *Journal of Economic Issues*, 1972, pp. 171-186.

Bishop, Wallace B., et al., *A Methodology for Evaluation of the Economic Development Administration's Public Works Program*, U.S. Department of Commerce, Economic Development Administration, Washington, D.C., 1969.

Blackburn, J.O., "An Optimal Unemployment Rate: Comment," *Quarterly Journal of Economics*, August 1969, pp. 518-521.

Blinder, Alan S., and Robert M. Solow, "The Analytic Foundations of Fiscal Policy," *The Economics of Public Finance*, The Brookings Institution, Washington, D.C., 1975.

Bluestone, Barry and Bennett Harrison, "Economic Development, the Public Sector, and Full Employment: An Outline for a Plan," in Raskin, Ed., 1978.

Bolton, Roger E., *Defense Purchases and Regional Growth*, The Brookings Institution, Washington, D.C., 1966.

Borts, G.H., "Regional Cycles of Manufacturing Employment in the United States, 1914-1953," *Journal of American Statistical Association*, Vol. 55, 1960, pp. 151-211.

Bosworth, Barry, "Capacity Creation in Basic-Materials Industries," Brookings Papers on Economic Activity, No. 2, 1976, pp. 297-350.

Boulding, Kenneth E., and Martin Pfaff, eds., *Redistribution to the Rich and Poor: The Grants Economics of Income Distribution*, Wadsworth Publishing Co., Belmont, California, 1972.

Bradshaw, Thomas F., and Janet L. Scholl, "Workers on Layoff: A Comparison of Two Data Series," *Monthly Labor Review,* November 1976, pp. 29-33.

Brechling, F., "Trends and Cycles in British Regional Unemployment," *Oxford Economic Papers,* Vol. 19, 1967, pp. 1-21.

Brenner, M. Harvey, *Estimating the Social Costs of National Economic Policy,* U.S. Congress, Joint Economic Committee, Washington, D.C., 1976.

_____. *Mental Illness and the Economy,* Harvard University Press, Cambridge, Massachusetts, 1973.

Briscoe, Alden T., "Public Service Employment in the 1930s: The WPA," in Harold L. Sheppard et al. (eds.), *The Political Economy of Public Service Employment,* D.C. Heath and Company, Lexington, Massachusetts, 1972.

Brown, E.C., "Fiscal Policy in the Thirties: A Reappraisal," *American Economic Review,* December 1956, pp. 857-879.

Brunner, Karl, "Our Perenial Issue: Monetary Policy and Inflation," University of Rochester, Graduate School of Management, September 1979.

Bureau of the Census, *Value of New Construction Put in Place,* 1947-1974 C 30, 745, U.S. Department of Commerce, Washington, D.C., 1975.

Bureau of the Census, Census of Population, *1970 Occupations by Industry,* Final Report PC (2)-7C, U.S. Department of Commerce, Washington, D.C., 1972.

Bureau of Economic Analysis, "The Input-Output Structure of the U.S. Economy: 1967," *Survey of Current Business,* U.S. Department of Commerce, Washington, D.C., February 1974.

Bureau of Labor Statistics, *Characteristics of Construction Agreements,* 1972-1973, Bulletin 1819, U.S. Department of Labor, Washington, D.C., 1974.

_____. *Selected Earnings and Demographic Characteristics of Union Members,* Report No. 417, U.S. Department of Labor, Washington, D.C., 1972.

_____. *Seasonality and Manpower in Construction,* Bulletin 1642, U.S. Department of Labor, Washington, D.C., 1970.

_____. *Labor and Material Requirements for Public Housing Construction,* Bulletin 1821, U.S. Department of Labor, Washington, D.C., June 1968.

_____. *Labor and Material Requirements for School Construction,* Bulletin 1586, U.S. Department of Labor, Washington, D.C., 1968.

Burgess, Paul L., and Jerry L. Kingston, "The Impact of Unemployment Insurance Benefits on Reemployment Success," *Industrial and Labor Relations Review,* Vol. 30, No. 1, October 1976, pp. 25-31.

Burns, A.F., and W.C. Mitchell, *Measuring Business Cycles,* National Bureau of Economic Research, New York, 1946.

Casetti, E., L. King, and D. Jeffrey, "Structural Imbalance in the U.S. Urban-Economic System, 1960-1965," *Geographic Analysis,* Vol. 3, 1971, pp. 239-255.

Clark, G. Scott, "Labor Hoarding in the Durable Goods Industries," *American Economic Review,* Vol. 63, No. 5, December 1973, pp. 811-824.

Cohen, Malcolm S., and William H. Gruber, "Variability by Cyclical Unemployment," *Monthly Labor Review,* August 1967, pp. 8-11.

Congressional Budget Office, *The Fiscal Policy Response to Inflation,* Washington, D.C., January 1979.

————. *Countercyclical Uses of Federal Grant Programs*, Washington, D.C., November 1978.

————. *Inflation and Growth: The Economic Policy Dilemma*, Washington, D.C., July 1978.

————. *Phasing Down the Antirecession Programs*, Washington, D.C., June, 1978.

————. *Short Run Measures to Stimulate the Economy*, Washington, D.C., March 1977.

————. *Temporary Measures to Stimulate Employment*, Congress of the United States, U.S. Government Printing Office, Washington, D.C., September 1975.

Conroy, Michael E., *The Challenge of Urban Economic Development: An Evaluation of Policy-Related Research on Alternative Goals*, University of Texas at Austin, July 1974.

CONSAD Research Corporation, *A Study of the Effects of Public Investment*, prepared for the Office of Economic Research, Economic Development Administration, U.S. Department of Commerce (PB184084), Washington, D.C., May 1969.

Cook, Philip J., and Robert H. Frank, *The Inflationary Effects of Public Service Employment*, prepared for U.S. Department of Labor, Manpower Administration, Washington, D.C., June 1971.

Council of State Governments, *Inflation: States Act to Restrain Costs and Prices*, Lexington, Kentucky, 1979.

————. *Innovations: Michigan's Budget and Economic Stabilization Fund*, Lexington, Kentucky, 1979.

Crider, Robert, "The Impact of Inflation on State and Local Governments," Urban and Regional Development Series, No. 5, Academy for Contemporary Problems, Columbus, Ohio, 1978.

————. "The Impact of Recession on State and Local Governments," Urban and Regional Development Series, No. 6, Academy for Contemporary Problems, Columbus, Ohio 1978.

Crocker, C.R., "Advances in Winter Construction Methods Extend Building Season," *The Constructor*, January 1966.

Curtiss C. Harris Associates, Inc., *Regional Analysis of Federal Expenditures*, prepared for the Economic Development Administration, U.S. Department of Commerce, Washington, D.C., July 1969.

Davis, Karen, *The Impact of Inflation and Unemployment on Health Care of Low Income Families*, Reprint Series 328, The Brookings Institution, Washington, D.C., 1978.

Dillon, Conley H., "Channeling Government Contracts into Depressed Areas," *Western Political Quarterly*, Vol. 16, 1963, pp. 279-293.

Economic Development Administration, *Local Public Works Program: Status Report*, U.S. Department of Commerce, Washington, D.C., 1978.

Ehrenberg, Ronald G., and Ronald L. Oaxaca, "Unemployment Insurance, Duration of Unemployment, and Subsequent Wage Gain," *The American Economic Review*, December 1976, pp. 754-766.

Eisner, Robert, "Fiscal and Monetary Policy Reconsidered," *American Economic Review*, Vol. 59, December 1969, pp. 897-905.

_____. "A Permanent Income Theory for Investment," *American Economic Review*, Vol. 57, June 1967, pp. 363-387.

Employment and Training Report of the President, U.S. Government Printing Office, Washington, D.C., 1976.

Engerman, S., "Regional Aspects of Stabilization Policy," in L. Needlemen (ed.), *Regional Analysis*, Penguin Books, London, 1968, pp. 277-334.

Fechter, Alan, "Public Employment Programs: An Evaluation Study," *Studies in Public Welfare*, U.S. Government Printing Office, Washington, D.C., December 30, 1974.

Federal Reserve Bank of Minneapolis, *Eliminating Policy Surprises: An Inexpensive Way to Beat Inflation*, 1978 Annual Report, Minneapolis, 1978.

Feldstein, Martin S., *The Effect of Unemployment Insurance on Temporary Layoff Unemployment*, Discussion Paper No. 20, Harvard Institute of Economic Research, November 1976a.

_____. "Temporary Layoffs in the Theory of Unemployment," *Journal of Political Economy*, Vol. 84, No. 5, October 1976b, pp. 937-958.

First National City Bank, *Monthly Economic Letter*, June 1975, pp. 8-10.

Flaim, Paul O., "Discouraged Workers and Changes in Unemployment," *Monthly Labor Review*, March 1973, pp. 8-30.

Friedman, Milton, "Nobel Lecture: Inflation and Unemployment," *Journal of Political Economy*, Vol. 85, No. 3, 1977, pp. 451-472.

_____. "The Role of Monetary Policy," *American Economic Review*, March 1968, pp. 1-17.

Friedman, Milton, and Anna Schwartz, *A Monetary History of the United States, 1867-1960*, prepared for the National Bureau of Economic Research, Princeton University Press, Princeton, New Jersey, 1963.

Gallaway, Lowell E., "Labor Mobility, Resource Allocation, and Structural Unemployment," *American Economic Review*, Vol. 53, 1963, pp. 694-716.

Gartner, Alan, Russell A. Nixon, and Frank Riessman, *Public Service Employment: An Analysis of Its History, Problems and Prospects*, Praeger, New York, 1973.

Gramlich, Edward M., "Stimulating the Macro Economy Through State and Local Governments," *American Economic Review*, Vol. 69, No. 2, 1979, pp. 180-185.

U.S. General Accounting Office, *Report to the Congress: Impact of Antirecession Assistance on 52 Governments*, Washington, D.C., May 1978.

_____. *Impact of Antirecession Assistance on 15 State Governments*, Washington, D.C., February 1978.

_____. *Impact of Antirecession Assistance on 16 County Governments*, Washington, D.C., February 1978.

U.S. General Accounting Office, *Impact of Antirecession Assistance on 21 City Governments*, Washington, D.C., February 1978.

_____. *Antirecession Assistance—An Evaluation*, Washington, D.C., November, 1977.

_____. *Antirecession Assistance is Helping But Distribution Formula Needs Reassessment*, Washington, D.C., July 1977.

————. *Observations Concerning the Local Public Works Program,* Report of the Comptroller General of the United States, Washington, D.C., February 1977a.

————. *More Benefits to Jobless Can Be Attained in Public Service Employment,* Report of the Comptroller General of the United States, CEd-77-48, Washington, D.C., February 1977b.

Gilroy, Curtis L., and Robert J. McIntire, "Job Losers, Leavers, and Entrants: A Cyclical Analysis," *Monthly Labor Review,* November 1974, pp. 35-39.

Goldstein, Jon H., *The Effectiveness of Manpower Training Program: A Review of Research on the Impact on the Poor,* Studies in Public Welfare, Subcommittee on Fiscal Policy of the Joint Economic Committee, Congress of the United States, Washington, D.C., November 20, 1972.

Gordon, Robert J., "Can the Inflation of the 1970s Be Explained?" *Brookings Papers on Economic Activity,* No. 1, 1977, pp. 253-277.

————. "The Impact of Aggregate Demand on Prices," *Brookings Papers on Economic Activity,* No. 3, 1975, pp. 213-270.

Gramlich, Edward M., "Stimulating the Macro Economy Through State and Local Governments," *American Economic Review,* Vol. 69, No. 2, 1979, pp. 180-185.

————. "State and Local Budgets the Day After It Rained: Why Is the Surplus So High?" *Brookings Papers on Economic Activity,* No. 1, 1978, pp. 191-214.

————. "Impacts of Minimum Wages on Other Wages, Employment, and Family Incomes," *Brookings Papers on Economic Activity,* No. 2, 1976, pp. 409-461.

Gramlich, Edward M., and Harvey Galper, "State and Local Fiscal Behavior and Federal Grant Policy," *Brookings Papers on Economic Activity,* No. 1, 1973, pp. 15-58.

Greer, Douglas F., and Stephen A. Rhoades, "A Test of the Reserve Labour Hypothesis," *The Economic Journal,* Vol. 87, 1977, pp. 290-299.

Greytak, David, and Bernard Jump, *The Effect of Inflation on State and Local Government Finances 1967-74,* Occasional Paper No. 25, Maxwell School of Citizenship and Public Affairs, Syracuse University, New York, 1975.

Greytak, David, and A. Dale Tussing, "Revenue-Stabilizing Grants: A Proposal," *Proceedings of the Sixty-Fourth Annual Conference on Taxation,* Kansas City, Missouri, September 1971.

Hall, Robert E., "The Role of Public Service Employment in Federal Unemployment Policy," *Proceedings of a Conference on Public Service Employment,* National Commission for Manpower Policy, May 1975, pp. 19-97.

————. "Turnover in the Labor Force," *Brookings Papers on Economic Activity,* No. 3, 1972, pp. 709-764.

————. "Prospects for Shifting the Phillips Curve Through Manpower Policy," *Brookings Papers on Economic Activity,* No. 3, 1971, pp. 659-722.

Hannon, Bruce, and Roger H. Bezdek, "Job Impact of Alternatives to Corps of Engineers Projects," *Engineering Issues,* October 1973, pp. 521-531.

Harris, C.P., and A.P. Thirlwall, *Interregional Variations in Cyclical Sensitivity to Unemployment in the United Kingdom,* 1949-1964, Oxford University Institute of Economics and Statistics, Vol. 30, 1968, pp. 55-66.

Haveman, Robert H., and John V. Krutilla, *Unemployment, Idle Capacity, and the Evaluation of Public Expenditures,* prepared for Resources for the Future, Inc., Johns Hopkins University Press, Baltimore, 1968.

Hellman, Daryl A., "The Spatial Distribution of Unemployment by Occupation—A Further Note," *Journal of Regional Science*, Vol. 13, No. 3, 1973.

Hendershott, Patrick H., "The Impact of a Tax Cut on Interest Rates and Investment: Crowding Out, Pulling In and All That," presented at the Conference on Tax Reform, Office of Tax Analysis, U.S. Department of the Treasury, Washington, D.C., July 17, 1975.

Hoeber, Johannes U., "Some Characteristics of Accelerated Public Works Projects," *Redevelopment*, September 1964, pp. 3-4.

Hollister, Robinson C., and John L. Palmer, "The Impact of Inflation on the Poor," in Boulding and Pfaff eds., 1972.

Hosek, James R., *Unemployment Patterns Among Individuals*, The Rand Corporation, R-1775-EDA, August 1975.

Hurd, Rick, "The Myth of the Unemployment-Inflation Tradeoff," in Raskin, ed., 1978.

Isard, Walter, "The Value of the Regional Approach in Economic Analysis," *Regional Income: Studies in Income and Wealth*, Vol. 21, Princeton University Press, Princeton, New Jersey, 1957.

Jerome, Harry, *Migration and Business Cycles*, National Bureau of Economic Research, New York, 1926.

Johnson, George E., and James D. Tomola, "The Fiscal Substitution Effect of Alternative Approaches to Public Service Employment Policy," Technical Analysis Paper No. 41, U.S. Department of Labor, Office of Research and Evaluation, Office of the Assistant Secretary for Policy, Evaluation and Research, Washington, D.C., September 1976.

————. *The Efficiency of Public Service Employment Programs*, Office of Evaluation, U.S. Department of Labor, Washington, D.C., Technical Analysis Paper, No. 17A, June 1975.

Katona, George, and Eva Mueller, *Consumer Response to Income Increase*, The Brookings Institution, Washington, D.C., 1968.

Keran, M., "Monetary and Fiscal Influences on Economic Activity—The Historical Evidence," *Federal Reserve Bank of St. Louis Review*, November 1969, pp. 5-23.

Kesselman, Jonathan, *Displacement and Productivity of Work Relief: Lessons of the Great Depression*, Brookings Conference on Direct Job Creation, Preliminary Draft, March 1977.

Keynes, J.M., *The General Theory of Employment, Interest and Money*, MacMillan, London, 1936.

King, L., E. Casetti, and D. Jeffrey, "Cyclical Fluctuations in Unemployment Levels in U.S. Metropolitan Areas," *Tijdschrift Voor Econ. En Soc. Geografie*, September-October 1972.

————. "Economic Impulses in a Regional System of Cities: A Study of Spatial Interaction," *Regional Studies*, Vol. 3, 1969, pp. 213-218.

Kosters, M., and Finis Welch, "The Effects of Minimum Wage on the Distribution of Changes in Aggregate Employment," *American Economic Review*, Vol. 62, No. 3, June 1972.

Laidler, David, and Michael Parkin, "Inflation: A Survey," *Economic Journal*, December 1975, pp. 741-809.

Leontief, Wassily, *The Structure of American Economy, 1919-1951*, Oxford University Press, New York, 1951.

Lewis, Wilfred, Jr., *Federal Fiscal Policy in the Postwar Recessions*, The Brookings Institution, Washington, D.C., 1962.

Levin, David J., "Receipts and Expenditures of State and Local Governments, 1959-1976," *Survey of Current Business*, Vol. 58, No. 5, May 1978, pp. 16-17.

Levitan, Sar A., *Federal Aid to Depressed Areas: An Evaluation of the Area Redevelopment Administration*, Johns Hopkins University Press, Baltimore, Maryland, 1964.

Levitan, Sar A., and Robert Taggart (eds.), *Emergency Employment Act: The PEP Generation*, Olympus, Salt Lake City, 1974.

Levy, Frank, and Michael Wiseman, "An Expanded Public Service Employment Program: Some Demand and Supply Considerations," *Public Policy*, Vol. 23, No. 1, Winter 1975, pp. 105-134.

Lucas, R.E., and L.A. Rapping, "Real Wages, Employment and Inflation," *Journal of Political Economy*, September 1969, pp. 721-754.

Manchester, Alden, and Linda Brown, "Do the Poor Pay More?," *National Food Situation*, Washington, D.C., June 1977.

McGuire, M.C., "Notes on Grants-in-Aid and Economic Interactions Among Governments," *Canadian Journal of Economics*, May 1973.

Matthews, R.C.O., *The Trade Cycle*, Cambridge University Press, Cambridge, 1959.

Manpower Administration, *Training and Entry into Union Construction*, Research Monograph No. 39, U.S. Department of Labor, Washington, D.C., 1975.

Manpower Report of the President, U.S. Government Printing Office, Washington, D.C., 1975.

Marston, Stephen T., "Employment Instability and High Unemployment Rates," *Brookings Papers on Economic Activity*, No. 1, 1976, pp. 169-210.

Miller, Roger Leroy, "The Reserve Labor Hypothesis: Some Tests of Its Implications," *The Economic Journal*, Vol. 81, No. 321, March 1971, pp 17-35.

Miller, E., "The Economics of Matching Grants: The ABC Highway Program," *National Tax Journal*, June 1974.

Mills, D. Quinn, *Industrial Relations and Manpower in Construction*, MIT Press, Cambridge, Massachusetts, 1972.

Mintz, Ilse, "Dating United States Growth Cycles," *Explorations in Economic Research*, Vol. 1, No. 1, Summer 1974.

Mirengoff, William, and Lester Rindler, *The Comprehensive Employment and Training Act: Impact on People, Places, Programs, An Interim Report*, National Academy of Sciences, Washington, D.C., 1976.

Mirer, Thad W., *The Distributional Impact of Inflation and Anti-Inflation Policy*, Discussion Paper 231-74, Institute for Research on Poverty, Madison, Wisconsin, 1974.

Modigliani, Franco, and Charles Stendel, "Is a Tax Rebate an Effective Tool for Economic Stabilization?," *Brookings Papers on Economic Activity*, No. 1, 1977, pp. 175-209.

243

Moore, B., and J. Rhodes, "Evaluating the Effects of British Regional Economic Policy," *The Economic Journal,* Vol. 83, No. 329, 1973, pp. 87-110.

Moore, Geoffrey H., "Tested Knowledge of Business Cycles," *Forty-Second Annual Report of the National Bureau of Economic Research,* New York, 1962.

Nathan, Richard P., "Public Service Employment—Compared to What? *Proceedings of a Conference on Public Service Employment,* National Commission for Manpower Policy, Washington, D.C., May 1975, pp. 99-121.

Nathan, Richard P., Robert F. Cook, Janet M. Galchik, Richard W. Long, and Associates, *Monitoring the Public Service Employment Program,* Preliminary Report on the Brookings Institution Monitoring Study of the Public Service Employment Programs for the National Commission for Manpower Policy, The Brookings Institution, Washington, D.C., 1978.

Nathan, Richard P., and Charles F. Abrams, *Revenue Sharing: The Second Round,* The Brookings Institution, Washington, D.C., 1977.

Nathan, Richard P., Allen D. Manvel, and Susannah E. Calkins, *Monitoring Revenue Sharing,* The Brookings Institution, Washington, D.C., 1975.

National Advisory Council on Economic Opportunity, *Eleventh Report,* Washington, D.C., June 1979.

National Commission for Manpower Policy, *Job Creation Through Public Service Employment,* Report No. 6, Vol. II, Washington, D.C., March 1978.

National Planning Association, *An Evaluation of the Economic Impact Project of the Public Employment Program,* Final Report, Vol. 1, May 22, 1974.

Neff, P., and A. Weifenbach, *Business Cycles in Selected Industrial Areas,* University of California Press, Berkeley, 1949.

Nulty, Leslie, *Understanding the New Inflation: The Importance of the Basic Necessities,* The Exploratory Project for Economic Alternatives, Washington, D.C., 1977.

Olson, John C., "Decline Noted in Hours Required to Erect Federal Office Buildings," *Monthly Labor Review,* October 1976, pp. 18-22.

Palmer, John L., and Michael C. Barth, *The Impacts of Inflation and Higher Unemployment: With Special Emphasis on the Low Income Population,* Technical Analysis Paper No. 2, Office of Income Security, U.S. Department of Health, Education and Welfare, October 1974.

Palmer, John L., John E. Todd, and Howard P. Tuckman, *The Distributional Impact of Higher Energy Prices: How Should the Federal Government Respond?,* Reprint 331, The Brookings Institution, Washington, D.C., 1978.

Perry, Charles R., Richard L. Rowan, Bernard E. Anderson, and Herbert R. Northrup, *The Impact of Government Manpower Programs: In General, and on Minorities and Women,* Manpower and Human Resources Studies, No. 4, Industrial Research Unit, The Wharton School, University of Pennsylvania, 1975.

Perry, George L., "Slowing the Wage-Price Spiral: The Macroeconomic View," *Brookings Papers on Economic Activity,* No. 2, 1978, pp. 259-301.

————. "Unemployment Flow in the U.S. Labor Market," *Brookings Papers on Economic Activity,* No. 2, 1972, pp. 245-292.

Phelps, E.S. (ed.), *Microeconomic Foundations of Employment and Inflation Theory,* Norton, New York, 1970.

Phelps, E.S., "Phillips Curves, Expectations of Inflation and Optimal Unemployment Over Time," *Economics*, August 1967, pp. 254-281.

_____. "Anticipated Inflation and Economic Welfare," *Journal of Political Economy*, February 1965, pp. 1-17.

Phillips, A.W., "The Relation Between Unemployment and the Rate of Change of Money Wages in the U.K., 1862-1957," *Economics*, November 1958, pp. 283-299.

Phillips, Bruce D., "A Note on the Spatial Distribution of Unemployment by Occupation in 1968," *Journal of Regional Science*, Vol. 12, No. 2, 1972. Polenske, Karen R., *Shifts in the Regional and Industrial Impact of Federal Government Spending*, U.S. Department of Commerce, Economic Development Administration, Washington, D.C., 1969.

Portney, Paul R., "Congressional Delays in U.S. Fiscal Policymaking," *Journal of Public Economics*, No. 5, 1976, pp. 237-247.

President Jimmy Carter, "The Federal, State and Local Anti-Inflation Program: An Intergovernmental Partnership," Washington, D.C., 1978.

Rafuse, Robert W., "Cyclical Behavior of State-Local Finances," in R.A. Musgrave, ed., *Essays in Fiscal Federalism*, The Brookings Institution, Washington, D.C., 1965.

Raskin, Ira E., "A Conceptual Framework for Research on the Cost-Effective Allocation of Federal Resources," *Socio-Economic Planning Science*, Vol. 9, 1975, pp. 1-10.

Raskin, Marcus, Editor, *The Federal Budget and Social Reconstruction*, Institute for Policy Studies, Washington, D.C., 1978.

Roberts, R. Blaine, and Henry Fishkind, "The Role of Monetary Forces in Regional Economic Activity: An Econometric Simulation Analysis," *Journal of Regional Science*, Vol. 19, No. 1, 1979, pp. 15-29.

Robertson, D.H., *Growth, Wages, Money*, Cambridge University Press, London, 1961.

Roos, Lawrence K., "Monetary Targets—Their Contribution to Policy Formation," *Federal Reserve Bank of St. Louis*, May 1979, pp. 12-15.

Ross, Arthur M., "Guideline Policy—Where We Are and How We Got There," in George P. Shultz and Robert Z. Aliber (eds.), *Guidelines, Informed Controls, and the Market Place*, University of Chicago Press, Chicago, 1966.

Rossana, Robert J., "Unemployment Insurance Programs: A New Look for the Eighties," *Federal Reserve Bank of Philadelphia Business Review*, August 1979, pp. 19-25.

Smith, Ralph E., Jean E. Vanski, and Charles C. Holt, "Recession and the Employment of Demographic Groups," *Brookings Papers on Economic Activity*, No. 3, 1974, pp. 737-760.

Stanley, David T., "Running Short, Cutting Down: Five Cities in Financial Distress," unpublished, The Brookings Institution, Washington, D.C., March 1976.

Straszheim, Mahlon, *An Introduction and Overview of Regional Money Capital Markets*, U.S. Department of Commerce, Economic Development Administration, Washington, D.C., April 1970.

Structural Clay Products Institute, *Cold Weather Construction Techniques*, Washington, D.C., 1967.

Sulvetta, Anthony J., and Norman Thompson, *An Evaluation of the Public Works Impact Program (PWIP)*, U.S. Department of Commerce, Economic Development Administration, Washington, D.C., April 1975.

Sum, Andrew M., and Thomas P. Rush, "The Geographic Structure of Unemployment Rates," *Monthly Labor Review*, March 1975, pp. 3-9.

Tanner, J.H., "Lags in the Effects of Monetary Policy: A Statistical Investigation," *American Economic Review*, December 1969, pp. 794-805.

Teeters, Nancy H., "Built-In Flexibility of Federal Expenditures," *Brookings Papers on Economic Activity*, Vol. 3, 1971.

Teigen, Ronald L., "The Effectiveness of Public Works as a Stabilization Device," in W.O. Smith and R.O. Teigen (eds.), *Readings in Money, National Income, and Stabilization Policy*, Irwin Dorsey, Homewood, Illinois, 1970.

Thirlwall, A.P., "Regional Unemployment as a Cyclical Phenomenon," *Scottish Journal of Political Economy*, Vol. 13, 1966, pp. 205-219.

Tideman, T. Nicolaus, "Defining Area Distress in Unemployment," *Public Policy*, Vol. 21, No. 4, Fall 1973, pp. 441-492.

Tobin, William J., *Public Works and Unemployment: A History of Federally Funded Programs*, Economic Development Administration, U.S. Department of Commerce, Washington, D.C., April 1975.

U.S. Congress, Joint Economic Committee, *The Current Fiscal Condition of Cities: A Survey of 67 of the 75 Largest Cities*, Washington, D.C., July 1977.

———. *The Current Fiscal Position of State and Local Governments*, Washington, D.C., December 1975.

U.S. House of Representatives, *A National Public Works Investment Policy*, prepared for the Committee on Public Works, U.S. House of Representatives, 93rd Congress, 2nd Session, November 1974.

U.S. National Resources Planning Board, *Security, Work and Relief Policies*, Washington, D.C., 1942.

Varhelyi, Miklos A., and Edward F. Pearson, "Studies in Inflation Accounting: A Taxonomization Approach," *Quarterly Review of Economics and Business*, Vol. 19, No. 1, 1979, pp. 9-27.

Vaughan, Roger J., *State Taxation and Economic Development*, Council of State Planning Agencies, Washington, D.C., 1979.

———. "Jobs for the Urban Unemployed," in Herrington Bryce, Ed., *Revitalizing Cities*, Lexington Books, Lexington, Massachusetts, 1979.

———. "The Use of Federal Grants for Countercyclical Job Creation," in *Fiscal Federalism and Grants in Aid*, Committee on Urban Public Economics, The Urban Institute, No. 1, 1979.

———. *Public Works as a Countercyclical Device: A Review of the Issues*, The Rand Corporation, R-1990-EDA, July 1976.

Vernez, Georges, and Roger Vaughan, "Countercyclical Public Works Programs," in L. Kenneth Hubbell, (ed.), *Fiscal Crisis in American Cities: The Federal Response*, Ballinger, Cambridge, Massachusetts, 1979.

———. *Assessment of Countercyclical Public Works and Public Employment Programs*, R-2214-EDA, The Rand Corporation, September 1978.

Vernez, Georges, et al., *Regional Cycles and Employment Effects of Public Works Investments*, The Rand Corporation, R-2052-EDA, January 1977.

Vogel, Robert C., "The Responsiveness of State and Local Receipts to Changes in Economic Activity: Extending the Concept of the Full Employment Budget," in Joint Economic Committee, *Studies in Price Stability and Economic Growth*, 94th Congress, Washington, D.C., June 30, 1975.

Wachtel, Howard and Peter Adelsheim, "Inflation or Unemployment or 'Which Came First, the Chicken or . . . '", in Raskin, Ed., 1978.

Warren, Ronald S., Jr., "Measuring Flow and Duration as Jobless Rate Components," *Monthly Labor Review*, Vol. 100, No. 3, March 1977, pp. 71-72.

Weber, Arnold, *In Pursuit of Price Stability*, The Brookings Institution, Washington, D.C., 1973.

Westat, Inc., *Characteristics of Enrollees Who Entered CETA Programs During Calendar Year 1975*, Employment and Training Administration, U.S. Department of Labor, Washington, D.C., November 1976.

————. *Longitudinal Evaluation of the Public Employment Program and Validation of the PEP Data Bank: Final Report*, Manpower Administration, U.S. Department of Labor, Washington, D.C., April 1975.

Willes, Mark H., "Eliminating Policy Surprises: An Inexpensive Way to Beat Inflation," Federal Reserve Bank of Minneapolis, Annual Report, 1978.

————. "The Scope of Countercyclical Monetary Policy," *Journal of Money Credit and Banking*, August 1971, pp. 630-648.

Wiseman, Michael, "Public Employment as Fiscal Policy," *Brookings Papers on Economic Activity*, No. 1, 1976, pp. 67-114.

————. "On Giving a Job: The Implementation and Allocation of Public Service Employment," in *Achieving the Goals of the Employment Act of 1946—Thirtieth Anniversary Review, Vol. 1, Employment*, prepared for the Subcommittee on Economic Growth of the Joint Economic Committee, 94th Congress, U.S. Government Printing Office, Washington, D.C., 1975.

INDEX

249

stabilization of, 142–43, 198–200

"Poor jobs": accident rates in, 16; as factor in crime, 21

Poverty, standards of, 57, 97

Procurement, 122

Productivity, 30–31, 33

Public works, 143–44, 149, 159, 191–92; allocation of, 166–67; eligibility for, 154

Rates, interest, 115

Recession, 95, 125, 157; causes of, 128; impacts of, 129

Revenues, state tax, 185–86

Rigidities: price, 104–5; structural, 26, 49, 81

Satisfaction, job, 22

Segments, 35, 49

Skills, worker, 28, 30, 33, 80–82

South, the, 8–9, 44

Stability, price, 108, 114–15

Stabilization: economic, 174; interest rate, 113; price, 95, 100

"Stagflation," 96

Stagnation, economic, 48–49

Structure, labor market, 35–40

Subsidies: tax, 49, 61, 66, 82–83; wage, 83, 196

Substitution, 160

Suburbs, satellite, 43

Sunbelt, 8–9, 11, 16, 18, 25, 42, 44, 47, 57, 111. *See also* South, the

Sunset laws, 121

Supply-and-demand, 24–26, 28, 98

Supply, money, 114, 116

"Supply side," 115

Taft-Hartley Act, 18, 44

Targeting, 172

Tax: corporate income, 154; personal income, 119, 154; property, 120; sales, 119

Technology, production, 73

Triggering, 158–59, 179, 183, 197

Underemployment, 10, 13

Unemployment, 10, 46, 111; cyclical, 131, 165, 173; definition of, 10; frictional, 129; institutional, 130–31, 145; structural, 129–30

Unions, 17, 44, 51, 69; decline of, 18–19, 46; worker preference for, 18

Utilities, 122–23

Wages, 11, 25, 51

Welfare, 21

World War II, 36, 44, 49

CONTRIBUTORS

Michael Barker is Executive Director of the Gallatin Institute, an economic policy research group based in Washington, D.C., and Editor of *Politics & Markets*, a monthly newsletter. He was formerly Director of Policy Studies at The National Governors' Association's Council of State Planning Agencies, where he was responsible for advising the nation's governors on the development of alternative economic policies. From 1975 to 1978 he was an aide to Massachusetts Governor Michael Dukakis. Mr. Barker is Editor of the twelve-volume *Studies in State Development Policy*, published by The National Governors' Association. He has written widely on industrial policy, financial regulation, business finance, and economic and community development. He has also been an economic policy adviser to The National Urban Coalition, The Democratic National Committee, and numerous federal and state officials.

David M. Gordon is Chairman of the Department of Economics at The New School for Social Research, and director of the New York-based Institute for Labor Education and Research, a not-for-profit group providing economic research and educational support to labor unions. He is the author of *Theories of Poverty and Underemployment*, the principal author of *What's Wrong with the U.S. Economy?*, the Editor of *Problems in Political Economics: An Urban Perspective*, and, most recently, the co-author of *Segmented Work, Divided Workers: The Historical Transformation of Labor in the United States*. Dr. Gordon writes frequently for both academic and popular journals. He received a B.A. from Harvard College and a Ph.D. in economics from Harvard University.

Roger J. Vaughan is a Senior Fellow at The Gallatin Institute in Washington, D.C., and Senior Editor of the monthly newsletter, *Politics & Markets*. He has been an aide to former New York Governor Hugh Carey, an assistant vice-president in Citibank's economics department, and an urban economist at the Rand Corporation. He is a frequent economic policy adviser to Members of Congress, and has been a consultant to the Democratic National Committee. A graduate of Oxford University, Dr. Vaughan received a Ph.D. in economics from the University of Chicago. He writes regularly on industrial policy, employment training, federal tax policy, and infrastructure finance. Under the sponsorship of The Twentieth Century Fund, Dr. Vaughan is currently completing a study of the impact of public policy on innovation and entrepreneurship in the U.S. economy.

About the Council of State Planning Agencies: The Council, formed in 1965 as an affiliate of the National Governors' Association, is a   **251** membership organization comprised of the policy and planning staff of the nation's governors. Through its Washington office, the Council provides technical assistance to governors' offices and state officials on a wide spectrum of policy issues. From time to time, the Council also performs both policy and technical research on state and national policy.